ANTHOLOGY OF HUMAN RELATIONS, RACISM, AND OTHER FORMS OF OPPRESSION IN THE UNITED STATES OF AMERICA

ANTHOLOGY OF HUMAN RELATIONS, RACISM, AND OTHER FORMS OF OPPRESSION IN THE UNITED STATES OF AMERICA

First Edition

EDITED BY

Lynn Davis

St. Cloud State University

cognella® | ACADEMIC PUBLISHING

Bassim Hamadeh, CEO and Publisher
Janny Li, Acquisitions Editor
Tony Paese, Project Editor / Associate Editor
Christian Berk, Associate Production Editor
Jackie Bignotti, Production Artist
Danielle Gradisher, Licensing Associate
Natalie Piccotti, Director of Marketing
Kassie Graves, Vice President of Editorial
Jamie Giganti, Director of Academic Publishing

Cover: Copyright © 2015 Depositphotos/Nito103.

Printed in the United States of America.

ISBN: 978-1-5165-4409-7 (pbk) / 978-1-5165-4410-3 (br)

cognella® | ACADEMIC PUBLISHING

CONTENTS

INTRODUCTION

Race defines every aspect of social life in America. It is historical, social and cultural. Race has been socially constructed to understand the basic differences in human relations over centuries ago. It still survives as the bedrock in shaping human lives to this day. These readings help develop and analyze the basic understanding of the concept of race and the realities of racism and white supremacy as cornerstones of the institutions in America. It documents historical and contemporary racial oppressions manifested in the world around us. The readings examine structures like education, media, and government, highlighting their similarities and differences in the mechanisms of racism. A closer look at racism against minority groups like American Indians/Native American, Chican@s and Latin@s, African Americans, Asian Americans and Biracial and Multi-Racial exemplifies the workings of racism. The interconnectedness of racial oppression framework and other forms of oppression like religious intolerance, sexism, ableism and ageism have been used to regulate racism. Above all, the readings advance the ideas of social change and the need to build skills and techniques to develop anti-racist consciousness.

PART I

DECONSTRUCTING RACISM AND WHITE PRIVILEGE

Introduction

The study of race is nothing new to America. "Racial formation as a sociohistorical process by which racial categories are created, lived out, transformed and destroyed". "It is a matter of social structure and cultural representation" (Omi and Winant, 2015). Race affects every aspect of American life. Racial hierarchy implies the existence of a group at the top, middle, and bottom of the social ladder. But racial formation today is no longer a virtual monolith as it was in years past. Historically, immigrants were encouraged to assimilate into "American" society and thus granted access to privileges and benefits that came with being white. Many groups now designated as "white" were not originally considered as such. Through "collective social mobility" some groups became stronger, changing class status over time. Other groups embraced pluralism by accepting the dominant "American" culture without giving up their native culture.

The term "social structures" refers to the larger social systems that are bounded together or to the influential patterns of social relationships. These network of relationships often called "social Systems" are organized by varied institutions like government, community, and the media. And there are three main levels in which race functions within such social structures: micro, meso, and macro. Due to significant inequalities in such social systems, people of color are generally placed on unequal lines that are influenced by race. Owing to such inequalities, these relationships within the communities are now forced to think about ways to reduce inequalities and eliminate injustices. As such, the umbrella term "affirmative action" was introduced. This term has been heavily stigmatized due to its misrepresentation. However, there are still legitimate concerns as to how it affects both whites and other minority group members.

This is evident in the historical understanding of Christopher Columbus, whose fables of finding the Americas are no longer held sacred in modern day history. As such, the indigenous perspective on Christopher Columbus is necessary for ethically viewing the past. Educators are required as by their titles to provide authentic representation of cultural groups and sociopolitical issues, while avoiding stereotypes. Their task is to guide the minds of the next generation, circumventing the discrepancies of the past, thus creating a platform for the future. And this is what this section hopes to achieve.

CHAPTER 1

Racial Formation & Racism

Racial Formation

Understanding Race and Racism in the Post-Civil Rights Era

Michael Omi and Howard Winant

In 1982–83, Susie Guillory Phipps unsuccessfully sued the Louisiana Bureau of Vital Records to change her racial classification from black to white. The descendent of an 18th century white planter and a black slave, Phipps was designated "black" in her birth certificate in accordance with a 1970 state law which declared anyone with at least 1/32nd "Negro blood" to be black.

The Phipps case raised intriguing questions about the concept of race, its meaning in contemporary society, and its use (and abuse) in public policy. Assistant Attorney General Ron Davis defended the law by pointing out that some type of racial classification was necessary to comply with federal record-keeping requirements and to facilitate programs for the prevention of genetic diseases. Phipps's attorney, Brian Begue, argued that the assignment of racial categories on birth certificates was unconstitutional and that the 1/32nd designation was inaccurate. He called on a retired Tulane University professor who cited research indicating that most Louisiana whites have at least 1/20th "Negro" ancestry.

In the end, Phipps lost. The court upheld the state's right to classify and quantify racial identity.[1]

Phipps's problematic racial identity, and her effort to resolve it through state action, is in many ways a parable of America's unsolved racial dilemma. It illustrates the difficulties of defining race and assigning individuals or groups to racial categories. It shows how the racial legacies of the past—slavery and bigotry—continue to shape the present. It reveals both the deep involvement of the state in the organization and interpretation of race, and the inadequacy of state institutions to carry out these functions. It demonstrates how deeply Americans both as individuals and as a civilization are shaped, and indeed haunted, by race.

Having lived her whole life thinking that she was white, Phipps suddenly discovers that by legal definition she is not. In U.S. society, such an event is indeed catastrophic.[2] But if she is not white, of what race is she? The state claims that she is black, based on its rules of classification,[3] and another state agency, the court, upholds this judgment. Despite the classificatory standards that have imposed an either-or logic on racial identity, Phipps will not in fact "change color." Unlike what would have happened during slavery times if one's claim to whiteness was success-fully challenged, we can assume that despite the outcome of her legal challenge, Phipps will remain in most of the social relationships she had occupied before the trial. Her socialization, her familial and friendship networks, her cultural orientation, will not change. She will simply have to wrestle with her newly acquired "hybridized" condition. She will have to confront the "other" within.

The designation of racial categories and the assignment of race is no simple task. For cen-turies, this question has precipitated intense debates and conflicts, particularly in the U.S.—dis-putes over natural and legal rights, over the distribution of resources, and indeed, over who shall live and who shall die.

A crucial dimension of the Phipps case is that it illustrates the inadequacy of claims that race is a mere matter of variations in human physiognomy, that it is simply a matter of skin "color." But if race cannot be understood in this manner, how can it be understood? We cannot fully hope to address this topic—no less than the meaning of race, its role in society, and the forces that shape it—in one chapter, nor indeed in one book. Our goal in this chapter, however, is far from modest: we wish to offer at least the outlines of a theory of race and racism.

What Is Race?

There is a continuous temptation to think of race as an essence, as something fixed, concrete and objective. And there is also an opposite temptation: to imagine race as a mere illusion, a purely ideological construct that some ideal non-racist social order would eliminate. It is nec-essary to challenge both these positions, to disrupt and reframe the rigid and bipolar manner in which they are posed and debated, and to transcend the presumably irreconcilable relationship between them.

The effort must be made to understand race as an unstable and "decentered" complex of social meanings constantly being transformed by political struggle. With this in mind, let us propose a definition: race is a concept that signifies and symbolizes social conflicts and in-terests by referring to different types of human bodies. Although the concept of race invokes biologically-based human characteristics (so-called "phenotypes"), selection of these particu-lar human features for purposes of racial signification is always and necessarily a social and historical process. In contrast to the other major distinction of this type, that of gender, there is no biological basis for distinguishing among human groups along the lines of race.[4] Indeed, the categories employed to differentiate among human groups along racial lines reveal themselves, upon serious examination, to be at best imprecise, and at worst completely arbitrary.

If the concept of race is so nebulous, can we not dispense with it? Can we not "do without" race, at least in the "enlightened" present? This question has been posed often, and with greater frequency in recent years.[5] An affirmative answer would of course present obvious practical difficulties: it is rather difficult to jettison widely held beliefs, beliefs which moreover are central to everyone's identity and understanding of the social world. So the attempt to banish the concept as an archaism is at best counterintuitive. But a deeper difficulty, we believe, is inherent in the very formulation of this schema, in its way of posing race as a problem, a misconception left over from the past, and suitable now only for the dustbin of history.

A more effective starting point is the recognition that despite its uncertainties and contradictions, the concept of race continues to play a fundamental role in structuring and representing the social world. The task for theory is to explain this situation. It is to avoid both the utopian framework that sees race as an illusion we can somehow "get beyond," and also the essentialist formulation that sees race as something objective and fixed, a biological datum.[6] Thus we should think of race as an element of social structure rather than as an irregularity within it; we should see race as a dimension of human representation rather than an illusion. These perspectives inform the theoretical approach we call racial formation.

Racial Formation

We define racial formation as <u>the sociohistorical process by which racial categories are created, lived out, transformed, and destroyed.</u> Our attempt to elaborate a theory of racial formation will proceed in two steps. First, we argue that racial formation is a process of historically situated projects in which human bodies and social structures are represented and organized. Next we link racial formation to the evolution of hegemony, the way in which society is organized and ruled. Such an approach, we believe, can facilitate understanding of a whole range of contemporary controversies and dilemmas involving race, including the nature of racism, the relationship of race to other forms of differences, inequalities, and oppression such as sexism and nationalism, and the dilemmas of racial identity today.

From a racial formation perspective, race is a matter of both social structure and cultural representation. Too often, the attempt is made to understand race simply or primarily in terms of only one of these two analytical dimensions.[7] For example, efforts to explain racial inequality as a purely social structural phenomenon are unable to account for the origins, patterning, and transformation of racial difference. Conversely, many examinations of racial difference—understood as a matter of cultural attributes a la ethnicity theory, or as a society-wide signification system, a la some poststructuralist accounts—cannot comprehend such structural phenomena as racial stratification in the labor market or patterns of residential segregation.

An alternative approach is to think of racial formation processes as occurring through a linkage between structure and representation. Racial projects do the ideological "work" of making these links. A racial project is simultaneously an interpretation, representation, or explanation of racial dynamics, and an effort to reorganize and redistribute resources along particular racial lines. Racial projects connect what race means in a particular discursive practice and the ways in which both social structures and everyday experiences are racially organized, based upon that meaning. Let us consider this proposition, first in terms of large-scale or macro-level social processes, and then in terms of other dimensions of the racial formation process.

Racial Formation as a Macro-Level Social Process

To interpret the meaning of race is to frame it social structurally. Consider for example, this statement by Charles Murray on welfare reform:

> My proposal for dealing with the racial issue in social welfare is to repeal every bit of legislation and reverse every court decision that in any way requires, recommends, or awards differential treatment according to race, and thereby put us back onto the track that we left in 1965. We may argue about the appropriate limits of government intervention in trying to enforce the ideal, but at least it should be possible to identify the ideal: Race is not a morally admissible reason for treating one person differently from another. Period.[8]

Here there is a partial but significant analysis of the meaning of race: it is not a morally valid basis upon which to treat people "differently from one another." We may notice someone's race, but we cannot act upon that awareness. We must act in a "color-blind" fashion. This analysis of the meaning of race is immediately linked to a specific conception of the role of race in the social structure: it can play no part in government action, save in "the enforcement of the ideal." No state policy can legitimately require, recommend, or award different status according to race. This example can be classified as a particular type of racial project in the present-day U.S.—a "neoconservative" one.

Conversely, to recognize the racial dimension in social structure is to interpret the meaning of race. Consider the following statement by the late Supreme Court Justice Thurgood Marshall on minority "set-aside" programs:

> A profound difference separates governmental actions that themselves are racist, and governmental actions that seek to remedy the effects of prior racism or to prevent neutral government activity from perpetuating the effects of such racism.[9]

Here the focus is on the racial dimensions of social structure—in this case of state activity and policy. The argument is that state actions in the past and present have treated people in very different ways according to their race, and thus the government cannot retreat from its policy responsibilities in this area. It cannot suddenly declare itself "color-blind" without in fact perpetuating the same type of differential, racist treatment.[10] Thus, race continues to signify difference and structure inequality. Here, racialized social structure is immediately linked to an interpretation of the meaning of race. This example too can be classified as a particular type of racial project in the present-day U.S.—a "liberal" one.

These two examples of contemporary racial projects are drawn from mainstream political debate; they may be characterized as center-right and center-left expressions of contemporary racial politics.[11] We can, however, expand the discussion of racial formation processes far beyond these familiar examples. In fact, we can identify racial projects in at least three other analytical dimensions: first, the political spectrum can be broadened to include radical projects, on both the left and right, as well as along other political axes. Second, analysis of racial projects can take place not only at the macro-level of racial policy-making, state activity, and collective action, but also at the level of everyday experience. Third, the concept of racial projects can be applied across historical time, to identify racial formation dynamics in the past. We shall now offer examples of each of these types of racial projects.

The Political Spectrum of Racial Formation

We have encountered examples of a neoconservative racial project, in which the significance of race is denied, leading to a "color-blind" racial politics and "hands off" policy orientation; and of a "liberal" racial project, in which the significance of race is affirmed, leading to an egalitarian and "activist" state policy. But these by no means exhaust the political possibilities. Other racial projects can be readily identified on the contemporary U.S. scene. For example, "far right" projects, which uphold biologistic and racist views of difference, explicitly argue for white supremacist policies. "New right" projects overtly claim to hold "color-blind" views, but covertly manipulate racial fears in order to achieve political gains.[12] On the left, "radical democratic" projects invoke notions of racial "difference" in combination with egalitarian politics and policy.

Further variations can also be noted. For example, "nationalist" projects, both conservative and radical, stress the incompatibility of racially-defined group identity with the legacy of white supremacy, and therefore advocate a social structural solution of separation, either complete or partial.[13] As we saw in Chapter 3, nationalist currents represent a profound legacy of the centuries of racial absolutism that initially defined the meaning of race in the U.S. Nationalist concerns continue to influence racial debate in the form of Afrocentrism and other expressions of identity politics.

Taking the range of politically organized racial projects as a whole, we can "map" the current pattern of racial formation at the level of the public sphere, the "macro-level" in which public debate and mobilization takes place.[14] But important as this is, the terrain on which racial formation occurs is broader yet.

Racial Formation as Everyday Experience

Here too racial projects link signification and structure, not so much as efforts to shape policy or define large-scale meaning, but as the applications of "common sense." To see racial projects operating at the level of everyday life, we have only to examine the many ways in which, often unconsciously, we "notice" race.

One of the first things we notice about people when we meet them (along with their sex) is their race. We utilize race to provide clues about who a person is. This fact is made painfully obvious when we encounter someone whom we cannot conveniently racially categorize—someone who is, for example, racially "mixed" or of an ethnic/racial group we are not familiar with. Such an encounter becomes a source of discomfort and momentarily a crisis of racial meaning.

Our ability to interpret racial meanings depends on preconceived notions of a racialized social structure. Comments such as, "Funny, you don't look black," betray an underlying image of what black should be. We expect people to act out their apparent racial identities; indeed we become disoriented when they do not. The black banker harassed by police while walking in casual clothes through his own well-off neighborhood, the Latino or white kid rapping in perfect Afro patois, the unending faux pas committed by whites who assume that the nonwhites they encounter are servants or tradespeople, the belief that nonwhite colleagues are less qualified persons hired to fulfill affirmative action guidelines, indeed the whole gamut of racial stereotypes—that "white men can't jump," that Asians can't dance, etc. etc.—all testify to the way a racialized social structure shapes racial experience and conditions meaning. Analysis of such stereotypes reveals the always present, already active link between our view of the social structure—its demography, its laws, its customs, its threats—and our conception of what race means.

Conversely, our ongoing interpretation of our experience in racial terms shapes our relations to the institutions and organizations through which we are imbedded in social structure. Thus we expect differences in skin color, or other racially coded characteristics, to explain social differences. Temperament, sexuality, intelligence, athletic ability, aesthetic preferences, and so on are presumed to be fixed and discernible from the palpable mark of race. Such diverse questions as our confidence and trust in others (for example, clerks or salespeople, media figures, neighbors), our sexual preferences and romantic images, our tastes in music, films, dance, or sports, and our very ways of talking, walking, eating, and dreaming become racially coded simply because we live in a society where racial awareness is so pervasive. Thus in ways too comprehensive even to monitor consciously, and despite periodic calls—neoconservative and otherwise—for us to ignore race and adopt "color-blind" racial attitudes, skin color "differences" continue to rationalize distinct treatment of racially-identified individuals and groups.

To summarize the argument so far: the theory of racial formation suggests that society is suffused with racial projects, large and small, to which all are subjected. This racial "subjection" is quintessentially ideological. Everybody learns some combination, some version, of the rules of racial classification, and of her own racial identity, often without obvious teaching or conscious inculcation. Thus are we inserted in a comprehensively racialized social structure. Race becomes "common sense"—a way of comprehending, explaining, and acting in the world. A vast web of racial projects mediates between the discursive or representational means in which race is identified and signified on the one hand, and the institutional and organizational forms in which it is routinized and standardized on the other. These projects are the heart of the racial formation process.

Under such circumstances, it is not possible to represent race discursively without simultaneously locating it, explicitly or implicitly, in a social structural (and historical) context. Nor is it possible to organize, maintain, or transform social structures without simultaneously engaging, once more either explicitly or implicitly, in racial signification. Racial formation, therefore, is a kind of synthesis, an outcome, of the interaction of racial projects on a society-wide level. These projects are, of course, vastly different in scope and effect. They include large-scale public action, state activities, and interpretations of racial conditions in artistic, journalistic, or academic fora,[15] as well as the seemingly infinite number of racial judgments and practices we carry out at the level of individual experience.

Since racial formation is always historically situated, our understanding of the significance of race, and of the way race structures society, has changed enormously over time. The processes of racial formation we encounter today, the racial projects large and small which structure U.S. society in so many ways, are merely the present-day outcomes of a complex historical evolution. The contemporary racial order remains transient. By knowing something of how it evolved, we can perhaps better discern where it is heading. We therefore turn next to a historical survey of the racial formation process, and the conflicts and debates it has engendered.

The Evolution of Modern Racial Awareness

The identification of distinctive human groups, and their association with differences in physical appearance, goes back to prehistory, and can be found in the earliest documents—in the Bible, for example, or in Herodotus. But the emergence of a modern conception of race does not occur until the rise of Europe and the arrival of Europeans in the Americas. Even the hostility and suspicion with which Christian Europe viewed its two significant non-Christian "others"—the Muslims and the Jews—cannot be viewed as more than a rehearsal for racial formation, since these antagonisms, for all their bloodletting and chauvinism, were always and everywhere religiously interpreted.[16]

It was only when European explorers reached the Western Hemisphere, when the oceanic seal separating the "old" and the "new" worlds was breached, that the distinctions and categorizations fundamental to a racialized social structure, and to a discourse of race, began to appear. The European explorers were the advance guard of merchant capitalism, which sought new openings for trade. What they found exceeded their wildest dreams, for never before and never again in human history has an opportunity for the appropriation of wealth remotely approached that presented by the "discovery."[17]

But the Europeans also "discovered" people, people who looked and acted differently. These "natives" challenged their "discoverers'" preexisting conceptions of the origins and possibilities of the human species.[18] The representation and interpretation of the meaning of the indigenous peoples' existence became a crucial matter, one which would affect the outcome of the enterprise of conquest. For the "discovery" raised disturbing questions as to whether all could be considered part of the same "family of man," and more practically, the extent to which native peoples could be exploited and enslaved. Thus religious debates flared over the attempt to reconcile the various Christian metaphysics with the existence of peoples who were more "different" than any whom Europe had previously known.[19]

In practice, of course, the seizure of territories and goods, the introduction of slavery through the encomienda and other forms of coerced native labor, and then through the organization of the African slave trade—not to mention the practice of outright extermination—all presupposed a worldview which distinguished Europeans, as children of God, full-fledged human beings, etc., from "others." Given the dimensions and the ineluctability of the European onslaught, given the conquerors' determination to appropriate both labor and goods, and given the presence of an axiomatic and unquestioned Christianity among them, the ferocious division of society into Europeans and "others" soon coalesced. This was true despite the famous 16th-century theological and philosophical debates about the identity of indigenous peoples.[20]

Indeed debates about the nature of the "others" reached their practical limits with a certain dispatch. Plainly they would never touch the essential: nothing, after all, would induce the Europeans to pack up and go home. We cannot examine here the early controversies over the status of American souls. We simply wish to emphasize that the "discovery" signaled a break from the previous proto-racial awareness by which Europe contemplated its "others" in a relatively disorganized fashion. In other words, we argue that the "conquest of America" was not simply an epochal historical event—however unparalleled in its importance. It was also the advent of a consolidated social structure of exploitation, appropriation, domination. Its representation, first in religious terms, but soon enough in scientific and political ones, initiated modern racial awareness.

The conquest, therefore, was the first—and given the dramatic nature of the case, perhaps the greatest—racial formation project. Its significance was by no means limited to the Western Hemisphere, for it began the work of constituting Europe as the metropole, the center, of a series of empires which could take, as Marx would later write, "the globe for a theater."[21] It represented this new imperial structure as a struggle between civilization and barbarism, and implicated in this representation all the great European philosophies, literary traditions, and social theories of the modern age.[22] In short, just as the noise of the "big bang" still resonates through the universe, so the overdetermined construction of world "civilization" as a product of the rise of Europe and the subjugation of the rest of us, still defines the race concept.

[...]

Race, Racism, and Hegemony

Parallel to the debates on the concept of race, recent academic and political controversies about the nature of racism have centered on whether it is primarily an ideological or structural phenomenon. Proponents of the former position argue that racism is first and foremost a matter of beliefs and attitudes, doctrines and discourse, which only then give rise to unequal and unjust practices and structures.[23] Advocates of the latter view see racism as primarily a matter of economic stratification, residential segregation, and other institutionalized forms of inequality that then give rise to ideologies of privilege.[24]

From the standpoint of racial formation, these debates are fundamentally misguided. They discuss the problem of racism in a rigid "either-or" manner. We believe it is crucial to disrupt the fixity of these positions by simultaneously arguing that ideological beliefs have structural consequences, and that social structures give rise to beliefs. Racial ideology and social structure, therefore, mutually shape the nature of racism in a complex, dialectical, and overdetermined manner.

Even those racist projects that at first glance appear chiefly ideological turn out upon closer examination to have significant institutional and social structural dimensions. For example, what we have called "far right" projects appear at first glance to be centrally ideological. They are rooted in biologistic doctrine, after all. The same seems to hold for certain conservative black nationalist projects that have deep commitments to biologism.[44] But the unending stream of racist assaults initiated by the far right, the apparently increasing presence of skinheads in high schools, the proliferation of neo-Nazi websites on the Internet, and the appearance of racist talk shows on cable access channels, all suggest that the organizational manifestations of the far right racial projects exist and will endure.[25]

By contrast, even those racisms that at first glance appear to be chiefly structural upon closer examination reveal a deeply ideological component. For example, since the racial right abandoned its explicit advocacy of segregation, it has not seemed to uphold—in the main—an ideologically racist project, but more primarily a structurally racist one. Yet this very transformation required tremendous efforts of ideological production. It demanded the rearticulation of civil rights doctrines of equality in suitably conservative form, and indeed the defense of continuing large-scale racial inequality as an outcome preferable to (what its advocates have seen as) the threat to democracy that affirmative action, busing, and large-scale "race-specific" social spending would entail.[26] Even more tellingly, this project took shape through a deeply manipulative coding of subtextual appeals to white racism, notably in a series of political campaigns for high office that have occurred over recent decades. The retreat of social policy from any practical commitment to racial justice, and the relentless reproduction and divulgation of this theme at the level of everyday life—where whites are now "fed up" with all the "special treatment" received by nonwhites, etc.—constitutes the hegemonic racial project at this time. It therefore exhibits an unabashed structural racism all the more brazen because on the ideological or signification level it adheres to a principle to "treat everyone alike."

In summary, the racism of today is no longer a virtual monolith, as was the racism of yore. Today, racial hegemony is "messy." The complexity of the present situation is the product of a vast historical legacy of structural inequality and invidious racial representation, which has been confronted during the post-World War II period with an opposition more serious and effective than any it had faced before. The result is a deeply ambiguous and contradictory spectrum of racial projects, unremittingly conflictual racial politics, and confused and ambivalent racial identities of all sorts.

Notes

1 *San Francisco Chronicle*, September 14, 1982, May 19, 1983. Ironically, the 1970 Louisiana law was enacted to supersede an old Jim Crow statute which relied on the idea of "common report" in determining an infant's race. Following Phipps' unsuccessful attempt to change her classification and have the law declared unconstitutional, a legislative effort arose which culminated in the repeal of the law. See *San Francisco Chronicle*, June 23, 1983.

2 Compare the Phipps case to Andrew Hacker's well-known "parable" in which a white person is informed by a mysterious official that "the organization he represents has made a mistake" and that "... [a]ccording to their records ... , you were to have been born black: to another set of parents, far from where you were raised." How much compensation, Hacker's official asks, would "you" require to undo the damage of this unfortunate error? See Hacker, *Two Nations: Black and White, Separate, Hostile, Unequal* (New York: Charles Scribner's Sons, 1992), pp. 31–32.

3 On the evolution of Louisiana's racial classification system, see Virginia Dominguez, *White By Definition: Social Classification in Creole Louisiana* (New Brunswick: Rutgers University Press, 1986).

4 This is not to suggest that gender is a biological category while race is not. Gender, like race, is a social construct. However, the biological division of humans into sexes—two at least, and possibly intermediate ones as well—is not in dispute. This provides a basis for argument over gender divisions—how natural?" etc.—which does not exist with regard to race. To ground an argument for the "natural" existence of race, one must resort to philosophical anthropology.

5 "The truth is that there are no races; there is nothing in the world that can do all we ask race to do for us. ... The evil that is done is done by the concept, and by easy—yet impossible—assumptions as to its application." (Kwame Anthony Appiah, *In My Father's House: Africa in the Philosophy of Culture* (New York: Oxford University Press, 1992.) Appiah's eloquent and learned book fails, in our view, to dispense with the race concept, despite its anguished attempt to do so; this indeed is the source of its author's anguish. We agree with him as to the non-objective character of race, but fail to see how this recognition justifies its abandonment. This argument is developed below.

6 We understand essentialism as *belief in real, true human essences, existing outside or impervious to social and historical context.* We draw this definition, with some small modifications, from Diana Fuss, *Essentially Speaking: Feminism, Nature, & Difference* (New York: Routledge, 1989), p. xi.

7 Michael Omi and Howard Winant, "On the Theoretical Status of the Concept of Race," in Warren Crichlow and Cameron McCarthy, eds., *Race, Identity, and Representation in Education* (New York: Routledge, 1993).

8 Charles Murray, *Losing Ground: American Social Policy, 1950–1980* (New York: Basic Books, 1984), p. 223.

9 Justice Thurgood Marshall, dissenting in *City of Richmond v. J.A. Croson Co.*, 488 U.S. 469 (1989).

10 See, for example, Derrick Bell, "Remembrances of Racism Past: Getting Past the Civil Rights Decline," in Herbert Hill and James E. Jones, Jr., eds., *Race in America: The Struggle for Equality* (Madison: The University of Wisconsin Press, 1993), pp. 75–76; Gertrude Ezorsky, *Racism and Justice: The Case for Affirmative Action* (Ithaca: Cornell University Press, 1991), pp. 109–111; David Kairys, *With Liberty and Justice for Some: A Critique of the Conservative Supreme Court* (New York: The New Press, 1993), pp. 138–41.

11 Howard Winant has developed a tentative "map" of the system of racial hegemony in the U.S. circa 1990, which focuses on the spectrum of racial projects running from the political right to the political left. See Winant, "Where Culture Meets Structure: Race in the 1990s," in idem, *Racial Conditions: Theories, Politics, Comparisons* (Minneapolis: University of Minnesota Press, 1994).

12 A familiar example is use of racial "code words." Recall George Bush's manipulations of racial fear in the 1988 "Willie Horton" ads, or Jesse Helms's use of the coded term "quota" in his 1990 campaign against Harvey Gantt.

13 From this perspective, far right racial projects can also be interpreted as "nationalist." See Ronald Walters, "White Racial Nationalism in the United States," *Without Prejudice* I, 1 (Fall, 1987).

14 Howard Winant has offered such a "map" in "Race: Theory, Culture, and Politics in the United States Today," in Marcy Darnovsky et al., eds., *Contemporary Social Movements and Cultural Politics* (Philadelphia: Temple University Press, 1994).

15 We are not unaware, for example, that publishing this work is in itself a racial project.

16 Although the Inquisition pioneered racial anti-semitism with its doctrine of "limpieza de sangre" (the claim that Jews could not be accepted as converts because their blood was "unclean"), anti-semitism only began to be seriously racialized in the 18th century, as George L. Mosse shows in *Toward the Final Solution: A History of European Racism* (New York: Howard Fertig, 1978).

17 As Marx put it:

> The discovery of gold and silver in America, the extirpation, enslavement, and entombment in mines of the aboriginal population, the beginning of the conquest and looting of the East Indies, the turning of Africa into a warren for the commercial hunting of blackskins, signalized the rosy dawn of the era of capitalist production. These idyllic proceedings are the chief momenta of primitive accumulation. (Karl Marx, *Capital*, Vol. I (New York: International Publishers, 1967), p. 751.)

David E. Stannard argues that the wholesale slaughter perpetrated upon the native peoples of the Western hemisphere is unequalled in history, even in our own bloody century. See his *American Holocaust: Columbus and the Conquest of the New World* (New York: Oxford University Press, 1992).

18 Winthrop Jordan provides a detailed account of the sources of European attitudes about color and race in *White Over Black: American Attitudes Toward the Negro, 1550–1812* (New York: Norton, 1977 [1968]), pp. 3–43.

19 In a famous instance, a 1550 debate in Valladolid pitted the philosopher and translator of Aristotle, Gines de Sepulveda, against the Dominican Bishop of the Mexican state of Chiapas, Bartolome de Las Casas. Discussing the native peoples, Sepulveda argued that

> In wisdom, skill, virtue and humanity, these people are as inferior to the Spaniards as children are to adults and women to men; there is as great a difference between them as there is between savagery and forbearance, between violence and moderation, almost—I am inclined to say, as between monkeys and men (Sepulveda, "Democrates Alter," quoted in Tsvetan Todorov, *The Conquest of America: The Question of the Other* (New York: Harper and Row, 1984), p. 153).

In contrast, Las Casas defended the humanity and equality of the native peoples, both in terms of their way of life—which he idealized as one of innocence, gentleness, and generosity—and in terms of their readiness for conversion to Catholicism, which for him as for Sepulveda was the true and universal religion (Las Casas, "Letter to the Council of the Indies," quoted ibid, p. 163). William E. Connolly interrogates the linkages proposed by Todorov between early Spanish colonialism and contemporary conceptions of identity and difference in *Identity/Difference: Democratic Negotiations of Political Paradox* (Ithaca: Cornell University Press, 1991), pp. 40–48).

20 In Virginia, for example, it took about two decades after the establishment of European colonies to extirpate the indigenous people of the greater vicinity; 50 years after the establishment of the first colonies, the elaboration of slave codes establishing race as prima facie evidence for enslaved status was well under way. See Jordan, *White Over Black*.

21 *Capital*, P. 751.

22 Edward W. Said, *Culture and Imperialism* (New York: Alfred A. Knopf, 1993).

23 See Miles, *Racism*, p. 77. Much of the current debate over the advisability and legality of banning racist hate speech seems to us to adopt the dubious position that racism is primarily an ideological phenomenon. See Mari J. Matsuda et al, *Words That Wound: Critical Race Theory, Assaultive Speech, and the First Amendment* (Boulder, CO: Westview Press, 1993).

24 Or ideologies which mask privilege by falsely claiming that inequality and injustice have been eliminated. See Wellman, *Portraits of White Racism*.

25 Racial teachings of the Nation of Islam, for example, maintain that whites are the product of a failed experiment by a mad scientist.

26 Elinor Langer, "The American Neo-Nazi Movement Today," *The Nation*, July 16/23, 1990.

27 Such arguments can be found in Nathan Glazer, *Affirmative Discrimination*, Charles Murray, *Losing Ground*, and Arthur M. Schlesinger, Jr., *The Disuniting of America*, among others.

Discussion Questions

1   What is race?

2   How did race become an integral part of America's history?

3   Can race be used as a political tool to create difference and social inequities?

4   Can an individual's race provide clues about the person?

5   Is society immersed with projects that represent race to which all are subject? If yes, why so? If no, why not?

CHAPTER 2

White Privilege

White Privilege

The Other Side of Racism

Kathleen Fitzgerald

In this chapter, the focus is on race privilege, the idea that if some racial/ethnic groups experience disadvantages, there is a group that is advantaged by this very same system. Studying whiteness forces us to acknowledge that all of us have a place in the relations of race. As obvious as this may seem, this is a concept many people are unfamiliar with and it is also a relatively new focus in the social sciences. Prior to the late twentieth century, sociologists were guilty of either ignoring race or focusing on racial/ethnic "others" in their analysis of the "race problem." Scientists avoided analyzing and interrogating the role of whites in American race relations as did the average white American. For people of color, the advantages whites receive due to their racial group membership are more than obvious. As mentioned in Chapter 1, such differences in perspective are at least partially the result of people's standpoint; where one exists in the social structure influences how one views the world. Examples of whiteness as a social construction and white privilege follow:

- Hispanics are being described as the "new Italians," emphasizing their assimilation into whiteness (Leonhardt 2013).
- A Delavan-Darien, Wisconsin, high school "American Diversity" class came under fire for teaching white privilege. A parent's complaint that the subject matter was indoctrinating students into white guilt received national attention ("'White Privilege' lesson ..." 2013).
- White privilege plays out in the restaurant industry, as front-of-the-house, tipped employees are overwhelmingly white, while back-of-the-house, hourly wage employees are overwhelmingly black or Latino.

- White privilege provides its recipients with protection from suspicion; thus, whites are unlikely to face the kind of situation Trayvon Martin faced in February 2012, when a neighborhood watchman decided he looked suspicious and eventually shot the unarmed seventeen-year-old to death.
- European soccer is seen by some fans as the privileged domain of whites, as black players are taunted with racist chants from fans, causing at least one of the black players and his teammates on AC Milan to walk off the field during a match ("AC Milan Players ..." 2013).

The Social Construction of Whiteness

We introduced the idea of the social construction of race in the previous chapter; to say race is socially constructed is to recognize that racial groups are socially designated categories rather than biological ones; thus, racial categories change across time and place. Whiteness is also a social construction, although recognizing this requires that we first acknowledge that "white" is a race rather than simply the norm. Thus, to say that whiteness is socially constructed is to emphasize which groups have been defined as white has changed across time and place (see Box 2.1 Global Perspectives),

Instead of white being about skin color or one's genetic makeup as we have been socialized to understand it, being designated as white is a social and political process. Many racial/ethnic groups that are considered white today have not always been defined as white. Irish Americans, Italian Americans, Greek Americans, and Jewish Americans have, instead, become white over time. "Becoming white" is a process whereby a formerly racially subordinate group is granted access to whiteness and white privilege, with all the benefits this entails. **White privilege** refers to the rights, benefits, and advantages enjoyed by white persons or the immunity granted to whites that is not granted to nonwhites; white privilege exempts white people from certain liabilities others are burdened with.

Racial Categorization and Power

The privileges associated with being designated white may make it seem like the option of becoming white is in the best interest of racial/ethnic minority groups. However, while racial categorization is fluid and does change over time, racial/ethnic minority groups do not have complete agency in determining whether they become white. During some eras in US history, Mexican Americans demanded they be recognized as white, while at other times they have actively worked to maintain their Mexican heritage (Foley 2008; Rodriguez 2005). This has resulted in Latinos' having a somewhat ambiguous racial status even to this day. Another reason for a group's ambiguous racial status is the power given to official documentation, such as who has been defined as white in legal decisions (Lopez 1996). The US Census, for instance, uses such racial and ethnic categories as "non-Hispanic white" and "Hispanic," which are intended

BOX 2.1

Global Perspectives:

Constructing Whiteness in Brazil

Racial categories change across time and place. Someone that is defined as white in Brazil may not be defined as white in the United States, whereas an African American may be defined as white in Brazil. Much like the United States, Brazil has a multiracial history, with people of indigenous, African, and European ancestry making up its population. Brazil has had a much more pronounced history of interracial relationships, however, that has resulted in an amalgamation of races to a greater extent than in the United States. Due to such amalgamation, Brazil used to be referred to as a racial democracy, a notion that is today considered to be a misrepresentation of Brazilian race relations.

While Brazil never established a system of racial segregation like that in the United States, other strategies were used to privilege whiteness. During the period of massive immigration into Brazil, 1882 to 1934, the Brazilian government openly expressed a preference for white migrants (Pinho 2009). During other periods in Brazilian history, whitening was promoted through encouraging miscegenation, where they were encouraged to marry white to better the race (Telles 2009). During the 1930s, there was an emphasis on "behavioral whitening," which involved rejecting cultural practices associated with African or indigenous cultures and instilling new habits of education, health,

hygiene, and diet that were considered to be closer to white (Pinho 2009).

While Brazilians are less likely to use the term *race* and instead refer to color, due to the discrimination associated with blackness, many Brazilians seek to avoid that designation (Telles 2009). On the 2000 census, 54 percent of Brazilians declared themselves to be *branco* (white) (Bailey 2008). However, racial census categories are rarely used. Instead, Brazilians tend to use terms referring to skin color, of which there are over one hundred, albeit only about six of those terms are used with any consistency: (*branco* (white), *moreno* (brown, although not the census term for brown), *pardo* (the census term for brown), *Moreno claro* (light brown), *preto* (the census term for black) and *negro* (a common term for black not found on the census)) (Telles 2004). To be defined as white in Brazil is about more than skin color. It involves concerns with gradations of skin colors and hair types, as well as social class affiliation (Pinho 2009). While in the United States, gradations of color within racial groups are noted (for instance, the light skin preference found within Latino and African American communities), in Brazil, color differences within the entire population are significant. Being white in Brazil, as in the United States, imparts economic advantages, social prestige, and political power to its recipients.

Figure 2.1   Native American students at the Carlisle Indian School, a government-run boarding school. The primary objective of Native American boarding schools was the forced assimilation of Native American children, as this photo exemplifies by the children's appearance, specifically, their short haircuts and mainstream clothing.

to emphasize the ethnic status of Latinos, but are also about race. Thus, there are **structural** constraints, such as government racial categorizations and legal decisions, to defining a group's racial/ethnic status.

However, there is also **agency**, the extent to which a group of people have the ability to define their own status. People are not simply pawns existing within larger social structures. Individuals and groups act within these structures and, through such actions, can change them.

Since the 1960s, many Mexican Americans have embraced pluralism rather than assimilation. **Pluralism** is when a group embraces and adapts to the mainstream society without giving up their native culture. For instance, Mexican Americans' choosing to keep their language alive by speaking Spanish in their homes while learning English so as to participate in the dominant culture, is an example of pluralism. **Assimilation**, long the preferred model for race relations among the dominant group in American society, is the push toward acceptance of the dominant, Anglo culture, at the expense of one's native culture (see Chapter 5). Groups are expected to become American by dropping any connection to their native culture, such as language, customs, or even a particular spelling of their name.

Historically, immigrants were encouraged to assimilate into "American" society. What this really meant was that they were expected to assimilate to the white norm, known as Anglo-conformity. Thus, "American" culture was synonymous with "white culture." Previous generations of immigrants were pressured to become American by dropping their accents or native language and cultural practices associated with their native country. Today, the assimilationist thrust remains, as the English-Only movement emphasizes. This is a movement that attempts to make English the national language, to get states to pass laws eliminating bilingual education in schools, and to make government materials, such as signs in Social Security offices or Medicaid brochures, for instance, available only in English.

There are both push and pull factors at work, when it comes to whitening: the dominant group may embrace the assimilation of the subordinate group for political reasons and the subordinate group may seek assimilation, and thus embrace whitening, for access to the privileges it accords. This is accomplished by embracing, or at least acquiescing to, the racial hierarchy. As mentioned previously, racial/ethnic groups do have agency, yet they are not always operating under conditions that allow them to exercise their agency. While some groups challenge the assimilationist push, as did many Chicanos (a term Mexican activists embraced during the 1960s), most succumb. They succumb because access to white privilege makes life easier; such as by offering certain children advantages that every parent hopes for. White privilege is a difficult offer to resist—acceptance versus exclusion; benefits versus obstacles.

Becoming White

Many groups of people that are today unquestionably seen as white have not always been so. Irish, Greek, Jewish, and Italian Americans have all experienced a "whitening process" in different historical eras, when their group shifted from being perceived as nonwhite to being seen as white. The process of becoming white varied for each group, but each group becomes white in response to larger social and cultural changes. There are three specific eras in the history of whiteness in the United States (Jacobson 1998). The first is the passage of the first naturalization law in 1790 that declared "free white persons" to be eligible for citizenship. The second era (from the 1840s to 1924) emerged as significant numbers of less desirable European immigrants, such as the Irish, challenged this notion of citizenship and required a redefinition of whiteness and, ultimately, the implementation of a white racial hierarchy. Whiteness was redefined again in 1920 at least partially in response to the rural to urban migration of African Americans, which solidified the previously fractured white racial grouping. Groups such as the Irish and Jews, who had held a "probationary" white statuses in previous generations, were now "granted the scientific stamp of authenticity as the unitary Caucasian race" (Jacobson 1998:8).

Irish Americans

Historian Noel Ignatiev (1995) explored how an oppressed group in their home country, the Catholic Irish, became part of the oppressing racial group in the United States. The whitening process for Irish Americans involved the denigration of blacks. This transformation was even more shocking because Irish Americans were not considered white during the early periods of Irish immigration. In fact, early Irish immigrants lived in the black community, worked with black people, and even intermarried with blacks.

The Irish becoming white, thus increasing their status in the racial hierarchy, has essentially been attributed to a larger political agenda. In this case, the Democratic Party sought the support of the Irish during the antebellum and immediate postbellum eras and was able to attract them primarily due to the party's proimmigrant position at the time. This was a very successful strategy, as Irish voters became the most solid voting bloc in the country by 1844, throwing their support overwhelmingly behind the Democratic Party (Ignatiev 1995).

Although the Democratic Party is recognized today as the party that passed civil rights legislation and generally is supported by the black community, at the time, racial politics looked very different. By the end of the Civil War, southern whites ruled the Democratic Party, and President Lincoln, a Republican, was held responsible for the emancipation of slaves. African American men that could vote during Reconstruction and in the North during Jim Crow tended to support the Republican Party. Most southern whites, on the other hand, overwhelmingly supported the Democratic Party, including their explicitly racist ideologies. Thus, in the mid-nineteenth century, Irish Americans were assimilated into American society through a politics of race: their acceptance as whites hinged on their acceptance and perpetuation of a racist system, particularly, antiblack sentiment (Ignatiev 1995).

Irish Americans intentionally distanced themselves from blacks and even supported Jim Crow and other racist policies that were designed to oppress blacks. An essential truth emerged: in the United States, to be considered white, a person must not be associated with blackness and subordination. Black and white are relational concepts, meaning they only have meaning in relation to each other. We learn to understand who we are partially through an understanding of who we are not. For many groups that are now considered white, distancing themselves from blacks involved accepting the American racial hierarchy and participating in the racism directed at people of color.

Mexican Americans

Racial categorization is not a straightforward process. Some racial/ethnic groups maintain a more fluid racial status. As mentioned previously, Hispanics represent this kind of ambiguity. The term "Hispanic" refers to US residents whose ancestry is Latin American or Spanish, including Mexican Americans, Cuban Americans, Central Americans, and so on. The term "Hispanic" was first used by the US government in the 1970s and first appeared on the US Census in 1980. Thus, all Mexican Americans are considered to be Hispanic, but not all Hispanics are Mexican Americans.

The racial status of Mexican Americans has shifted throughout the nineteenth and twentieth centuries. Mexicans in the newly conquered Southwest at the close of the Mexican-American War in 1848, for instance, were accorded an intermediate racial status: they were not considered to be completely uncivilized, as the indigenous Indians of the region were, due to their European (Spanish) ancestry (Almaguer 1994). They were treated as an ethnic group, similar to European white ethnic immigrants. However, by the 1890s, as whites began to outnumber Mexicans throughout the Southwest, Mexicans became racialized subjects (Rodriguez 2005).

Mexican Americans have been legally defined as white, despite the fact that their social, political, and economic status has been equivalent to that of nonwhites (Foley 2008). According to the 2010 US Census, "Hispanic" is an ethnic group, not a racial group. This was not always how the census categorized Mexicans, however. In 1930, the Census Bureau had created a separate racial category for Mexicans, which for the first time, declared Mexican Americans to be nonwhite. This designation did not end the ambiguity surrounding the racial categorization of Mexicans, however. Census takers at the time were instructed to designate people's racial status as Mexican if they were born in Mexico or if they were "definitely not white," with no real instruction for differentiating how anyone would know which Mexican was "definitely not white." Consequently, due to such ambiguity, the US Census discontinued this designation in subsequent censuses. In 1980, the bureau created two new ethnic categories of whites: "Hispanics" and "non-Hispanic" (Foley 2008). This resulted in many Latinos' choosing "other" for their race, which motivated the Census Bureau to add a question concerning ethnic group membership after the question concerning racial group membership, to try to determine who is Hispanic. The Census Bureau is considering adding "Hispanic" as a racial category on the 2020 census.

While such official maneuverings provided structural constraints on the racial/ ethnic identification choices of Latinos, Latinos also exercised their agency. Many Mexican Americans during the 1930s through 1950s, for instance, demanded to be recognized as white as a way to avoid Jim Crow segregation. Much like the whitening process for Irish Americans, for Mexican Americans, distancing themselves from blacks became the objective rather than challenging the racial hierarchy through an embrace of a nonwhite racial status. Mexican Americans, particularly those in the middle class, often supported the racial segregation of schools and the notion of white supremacy. Today, while some Latinos enjoy a status as white ethnics, many others, primarily Mexicans and recent Latino immigrants, remain excluded from the privileges of whiteness. Often this exclusion has been linked to their social class or skin color, as "a dark-skinned non-English-speaking Mexican immigrant doing lawn and garden work does not share the same class and ethnoracial status as acculturated, educated Hispanics ... Hispanicized Mexican Americans themselves often construct a 'racial' gulf between themselves and 'illegal aliens' and 'wetbacks'" (Foley 2008:62–3).

[...]

White Privilege

While the privileges associated with whiteness are not new, the academic exploration and understanding of white privilege is relatively new. Sociologists that study race have shifted the analysis from a focus solely on people of color to one that includes whites and their role in race relations. This necessary shift focuses on what Paula Rothenberg (2008) refers to as "the other side of racism," white privilege. In the United States, individuals identified and defined as white make up the group with the unearned advantages known as white privilege. Whiteness refers to the multiple ways white people benefit from institutional arrangements that appear to have nothing to do with race (Bush 2011). This analytical shift to an analysis of and an understanding of white privilege requires that we recognize "white" as not only a race but as a social construction.

Racial hierarchies, status hierarchies based upon physical appearance and the assumption of membership in particular categories based upon these physical features, exist in the United States and throughout the world, albeit with much variation. Hierarchies imply that a group exists at the top while others exist somewhere in the middle, and still others on the bottom rungs of the hierarchy. The group at the top is the group that benefits from the racial hierarchy in the form of race privilege. The seminal work on white privilege is the self-reflexive essay by Peggy McIntosh (2008), "White Privilege: Unpacking the Invisible Knapsack." McIntosh defines *white privilege* as "an invisible package of unearned assets which I can count on cashing in each day, but about which I was 'meant' to remain oblivious. White privilege is like an invisible weightless knapsack of special provisions, maps, passports, codebooks, visas, clothes, tools, and blank checks" (2008:123). There are several aspects to this definition that warrant attention: the claims that white privilege is invisible, it is unearned, and that white people are socialized to count on this, while simultaneously not recognizing it as privilege.

Race affects every aspect of our lives: it informs how all of us view the world, our daily experiences, and whether or not opportunities are available due to our membership in particular racial/ethnic groups. While the importance of race has long been recognized for racial/ethnic minorities, until recently, even social scientists have overlooked the significance of race in the daily lives of whites. Part of this problem emerges from a lack of recognition that "white" is a race, rather than merely the norm, the human standard against which all other groups are measured (a perspective

REFLECT AND CONNECT

Do you belong to a racial/ethnic group that has experienced a changing racial status, such as those discussed here, that became white? If so, were you aware of this? If not, why do you think you were unaware of this? Reflect on the significance of this for your life today.

which is itself part of white privilege). Some have called for the development of a **new white consciousness**, "an awareness of our whiteness and its role in race problems" (Terry 1970:17). Social scientists have finally heeded this call and white people are now being asked to recognize how race and privilege operate in their world.

White Privilege as Taboo

The discussion of white privilege will undoubtedly make many students uncomfortable. Recently, a high school in Wisconsin has come under fire for teaching white privilege in an "American Diversity" class. Some parents complained that the subject matter was akin to indoctrination and meant to divide the students and provoke white guilt (*The Huffington Post* 2013).

This is the invisible side of racism—the advantages offered to the dominant group by an unjust system. Why has it taken so long for social scientists to focus on something as seemingly obvious as the "other side of racism"? A racial bias embedded not only in the discipline of sociology but in our culture is part of the explanation. Additionally, whiteness has been normalized to the point of invisibility in both our culture and in science. In addition, privilege is meant to remain invisible. Those benefiting from such societal arrangements, even if these are people that actively oppose racism, have difficulty seeing the advantages they reap from these arrangements.

Interrogating white privilege is not meant to alienate white people or exclude people of color from conversations concerning race. Instead, it is meant to bring everyone to the table to discuss race, racism, racial inequality, and race privilege. Professor Helen Fox provides a strong argument for why it is so essential to engage white people in discussions of race and privilege:

> I am convinced that learning how to reach resistant white students is central to our teaching about race. These are the future power brokers of America, the ones who by virtue of their class, their contacts, and their per-ceived "race" will have a disproportionate share of political and economic clout (2001:83).

For people of color, conversations surrounding race are not new; such conversations have likely been quite common for them. People of color experience explicit **racial socialization**, meaning they are taught in their families, in schools, and through the media that their race mat-ters. White people, on the other hand, may have difficulties with the topic of race and privilege for the simple fact that such conversations have likely been uncommon in their lives.

White people experience racial socialization as well, it is just more subtle. White racial socialization comes in the form of an unspoken entitlement. Whites are socialized to protect their privilege, partially through denial of such privilege. White privilege allows whites the privilege of not having to think about race—not having to think about how race might affect them that day.

Whiteness is understood by whites as a culture void, as lacking culture, as an unmarked cate-gory in direct opposition to the view that minorities have rich and distinct cultures (Frankenberg

1993). People of color are seen to have a recognizable culture (for instance, the presence of BET (Black Entertainment Television), Latin music, Asian food, etc.) that whites are perceived to lack. For example, Frankenberg (1993) found that white women in interracial relationships often viewed themselves as having no culture, often citing envy of racial/ethnic minorities because of their obvious culture and accompanying identity.

There are some problems with viewing white culture as actually cultureless. The first is that it reinforces whiteness as the cultural norm. Whites are everywhere in cultural representations—advertising, film, television, books, museums, public history monuments—yet the claim is made that this is just culture, not white culture. Additionally, by claiming to be cultureless, whites can ignore white history. Thus, the political, economic, and social advantages whites have accumulated historically are easier to overlook when claiming there is no such thing as white culture (Frankenberg 1993).

Seeing Privilege

White privilege—"an elusive and fugitive subject" as Peggy McIntosh described it in 1998—has gone unexamined primarily because it is the societal **norm**. For sociologists, social norms are a significant aspect of culture and they refer to the shared expectations about behavior in a society, whether implicit or explicit. There are several reasons why white privilege is hard for white people to see. The first problem is the intentional invisibility of white privilege. Privilege is maintained through ignoring whiteness. According to McIntosh, "in facing [white privilege], I must give up the myth of meritocracy ... [M]y moral condition is not what I had been led to believe. The appearance of being a good citizen rather than a troublemaker comes in large part from having all sorts of doors open automatically because of my color" (McIntosh 1988). Part of privilege is the assumption that your experience is normal; it does not feel like a privileged existence.

While inequality is easy to see, privilege is more obscure. White people can easily see how racism "makes people of color angry, tired, and upset, but they have little insight into the ways that not having to worry about racism affects their own lives" (Parker and Chambers 2007:17). For people of color, white privilege is not a difficult concept to grasp—it is clear from their standpoint that racial disadvantage has a flip side that amounts to advantages for the dominant group. Despite this, for white people, seeing race is difficult and is the "natural consequence of being in the driver's seat" (Dalton 2008:17).

REFLECT AND CONNECT

Take a moment and think about your childhood, specifically reflecting on when you discovered your race. When did you discover you were white, African American, or Latino, or whatever? For people of color, this is generally not a difficult task. For whites, this might be more difficult.

WITNESS

"And here I am, just another alienated middle-class white girl with no culture to inform my daily life, no people to call my own" (interviewee quoted in Frankenberg 1993).

It is difficult for most white people to discuss ways they benefit from white privilege, and many get offended when asked to think about some advantage they have accrued due to being white. Many students can recognize whether they attended a well-funded public school that adequately prepared them for college. Recognition of privilege does not negate hard work, but it is an acknowledgment that not everyone had the same educational opportunities, particularly individuals that attended poor schools predominantly populated with racial/ethnic minority students.

White privilege is problematic for many white people because it can feel insulting. Americans are taught that we live in a **meritocracy**, where individuals get what they work for, where rewards are based upon effort and talent. This ideology helps us understand poverty along individualized "blame the victim" lines rather than thinking of it as a social problem. In other words, if people are poor, it is presumed to be due to some inadequacy on their part. The opposite of the "blame the victim" ideology is also true. When people succeed in American society their success is often attributed to hard work, motivation, intelligence, or other individualized characteristics that are meant to set the person apart from less successful individuals. The idea of white privilege challenges this. It forces us to recognize that some people, due to their membership in particular racial/ethnic groups, are systematically disadvantaged and face more obstacles in their lives while members of other racial/ethnic groups are systematically advantaged, with more doors opened and more opportunities available to them. It may take their individual talents, motivation and intelligence to take advantage of the open door, but it must be acknowledged that not everyone had the door opened for them in the first place. This is often how privilege manifests itself.

White privilege is uncomfortable for many white students to grasp because the word *privilege* does not appear to describe their life. Poor and working-class white people are often offended by such a notion because they do not see themselves as beneficiaries of the system in any way. They work hard and have very little, relatively speaking. Indeed, many white people are members of the **working poor**, people who work full-time and still fall below the poverty line in the United States. How can they be considered privileged? To be able to understand this, we have to recognize the complexities involved in the multiple status hierarchies that exist in American society. One can lack class privilege, but still have race privilege, for instance.

The idea of white privilege is that all people identified and treated as white benefit from that status, even if they face disadvantages in other arenas, such as social class. To truly understand how race operates in the United States, it is essential that we recognize this. White privilege offers poor whites something: the satisfaction that at least they do not exist on the bottom rungs of the societal hierarchy—that, despite their poverty, they are at least not black. Additionally, despite any other disadvantages a white person may have, when they walk into a job interview, or restaurant, or any situation, the primary characteristic noted is that they are white, which is their passport for entry, as Peggy McIntosh (2008) describes. Race and gender are

BOX 2.2

Race in the Workplace:

White Teachers Making Meaning of Whiteness

Alice McIntyre, teacher and author of *Making Meaning of Whiteness: Exploring Racial Identity with White Teachers* (1997), explains that entering the teaching profession offered her "numerous occasions to 'see' my whiteness and to experience the ways in which race and racism shaped my life, my teaching, my politics, and my understanding of privilege and oppression, especially as they relate to the educational system in the United States" (1997:2). Upon returning to graduate school after twelve years of classroom teaching, she became interested in how white student teachers embrace the cultural understandings of children and how those understandings reinforced white privilege. One of the primary questions motivating her research was, what impact does one's white racial identity have on one's notion of what it means to be a teacher?

McIntyre believes that for white teachers to be more effective in the classroom, they must interrogate their own racial socialization, specifically how they are socialized into a position of privilege and a sense of entitlement. She argues that white teachers have an obligation to reflect on their race and its influence on their teaching. "White student teachers need to be intentional about being self-reformers ... *purposefully thinking through their racial identities as salient aspects of their identities*" (*italics in original,* 1997:5). This cannot be achieved without linking identities to the larger social structure and institutions.

Her goal is to help white student teachers "develop teaching strategies and research methodologies aimed at disrupting and eliminating the oppressive nature of whiteness in education" (1997:7). She is aware of the difficulties surrounding such a task. As she explains, "There is no comfort zone for white people when it comes to discussing white racism" (1997:43).

what sociologists call **master statuses** in our society, statuses that are considered so significant they overshadow all others and influence our lives more than our other statuses.

The combination of the invisibility of white privilege and the fact that all white people are implicated in the racial hierarchy through their privilege also makes it a disturbing concept for many white people. Interrogating white privilege is a particularly difficult task because it is both structural and personal. It forces those who are white to ask questions that concern not only structural advantage (such as, how are schools structured in ways that benefit white people?) but individual privilege as well (in what ways was my educational attainment at least partially a result of racial privilege?). Again, while it is uncomfortable to acknowledge being unfairly advantaged, this is exactly what white privilege is.

Additionally, it is important to recognize in what arenas we may be advantaged (oppressors) and in what arenas we may be disadvantaged (oppressed). As a white person, I have race privilege (see Box 2.2 Race in the Workplace). As a woman, I have disadvantages within a **patriarchy**, a male-dominated society. On a global scale, there are certain advantages, from my odds of survival to the educational and economic opportunities I have had access to, to having been born in a wealthy, First World country versus in an impoverished nation.

White Privilege Versus White Racism

Discussing white privilege makes many whites feel uncomfortable because it implicates them in a racist social structure. Thus, doesn't that make them racist? Is there a difference between white privilege and **white racism**? Feagin and Vera (1995) define white racism as "the socially organized set of attitudes, ideas, and practices that deny African Americans and other people of color the dignity, opportunities, freedoms and rewards that this nation offers white Americans" (p. 7). That is clearly a broad definition of white racism—it certainly goes above and beyond the idea that many whites take comfort in, which is that a racist is someone that is actively involved in a white supremacist organization, participates in hate crimes, or believes in the innate inferiority of nonwhites. However, it is not that clear-cut. As the definition implies, as long as people of color are denied opportunities, it is white racism, and what goes unspoken is that the flip side of this racism is that those become opportunities for white people. In other words, these are two sides of the same coin—without white racism, there is no white privilege. To work actively against racism, whites also have to work against privilege. For instance, if a white employee of a restaurant recognizes racialized patterns, such as people of color working in the kitchen and white staff working the dining room, they can point these out to management. Additionally, there are those who argue that simply living in American society makes one racist—it is the norm in our society, found in the subtle messages we all receive every day. Thus, neutrality is not equated with being nonracist. The only way to be nonracist in American society is to actively work against racism, such as by joining a racial justice organization. Many racial justice organizations are affiliated with religious institutions, for instance, or can be found on university campuses. They can also easily be found online by searching "antiracist activism" or "racial justice activism." Beyond actually joining a racial justice organization, one can simply work to be an ally to people of color in the struggle to end racism. Being an ally involves speaking up when you see racial injustice occurring, assuming racism is everywhere, everyday, and understanding the history of whiteness and racism (Kivel 2011).

Ideologies, Identities, and Institutions

In the previous chapter, we explored the ways race operates in the form of racial ideologies, racial identities, and institutional racism. We expand on that discussion to show the ways race privilege informs racial ideologies and racial identities, as well as fostering institutional privileges.

Racial Ideologies of Color-blindness

Ideologies are not just powerful; they operate in the "service of power" through providing a frame for interpreting the world (Bonilla-Silva 2010; Thompson 1984). It is through cultural belief systems that so many nonwhite groups embrace the racial hierarchy, embrace racism, as a way to obtain white privilege. The current reigning racial ideology is that of color-blindness.

Color-blindness supports white privilege because it encourages a mentality that allows us to say we don't see race, that essentially we are color-blind. Paradoxically, this ideology persists within a society literally obsessed with race. The elections of President Barack Obama and the ongoing racial discourse surrounding both elections are good examples. In 2007, discussions of race surrounded Super Bowl XLI because it was the first time an African American head coach had led their team to the Super Bowl, much less the fact that both teams, the Chicago Bears and the Indianapolis Colts, had black head coaches. People of mixed-race ancestry continually report being asked, "What are you?," which is evidence of the ongoing significance of race rather than a commitment to color-blindness.

Clearly, Americans see color, we see race, and we attach significance to it. The power of the color-blind ideology is threefold:

1 **We ignore racism.** We have a racist society without acknowledging any actual racists (Bonilla-Silva 2006). Racism is alive and well, yet individuals cling to color-blindness, thus, eliminating their personal responsibility for it. Sociologist Eduardo Bonilla-Silva (2010) argues that the color-blind ideology "barricades whites from the United States' racial reality" (p. 47).

2 **We ignore white privilege.** Haney-Lopez (2006) refers to this as "color-blind white dominance." By claiming color-blindness white people can ignore the ways white privilege benefits them and can ignore ongoing racism.

3 **We perceive whiteness as the norm.** Color-blindness fuels perceptions of whiteness as the norm and as synonymous with racial neutrality.

A glaring example of the preceding third item, perceiving whiteness as the norm, was found in media coverage of Hurricane Katrina in 2005. For days, media coverage showed thousands of displaced and desperate people, overwhelmingly black, seeking shelter from the rising flood waters, yet race was never mentioned. When it finally was mentioned, many white people were angered by what they saw as the media "racializing" what they perceived as a race-neutral tragedy; clinging to color-blind ideologies, they insisted that those left behind to face the devastation were simply people, not black people. The fact that they were black was somehow deemed irrelevant or mere coincidence. Yet, this tragedy was clearly "raced" and "classed" as well. It was not simply coincidence that it was predominantly poor black people that were left behind to drown as the levees broke and the city of New Orleans experienced devastating flooding.

New Orleans is an overwhelmingly black city and a very poor city. When the mayor announced a mandatory evacuation due to the impending hurricane, transportation should have been provided because so many poor, black New Orleanians did not own an automobile. As a matter of public policy, when considering a mandatory evacuation, one has to consider not just transportation but where people are going to go. Poor people are not able to simply get a hotel room in another city to wait out the storm as a middle-class person could.

Racial ideologies change over time as culture changes. What is essential is that we recognize how the racial ideologies manifest themselves in different eras, that we gauge the influence of such ideologies, and perhaps most important, recognize how the dominant group benefits from such ideologies.

Figure 2.2   A home damaged by the flooding of New Orleans due to the levee breaches after Hurricane Katrina in 2005. These homes are in New Orleans' Ninth Ward, an overwhelmingly poor and African American community that suffered some of the worst flooding.

White Racial Identity

Social scientists have only recently begun studying white racial identity development (Helms 1990; McDermott and Samson 2005). Much effort has been put into the study of white ethnic identity development (Alba 1990; Rubin 1994; Stein and Hill 1977; Waters 1990), black racial identity development (Burlew and Smith 1991; Helms 1990; Resnicow and Ross-Gaddy 1997), and shifting racial identities (Fitzgerald 2007; Korgen 1998; Rockquemore and Brunsma 2002), while white racial identities went unexamined. When sociologists have focused on white racial identity development, it has generally been in conjunction with white supremacist movements, but of course, all whites have a racial identity not just those belonging to such organizations (Dees and Corcoran 1996; Gallagher 2003). Some research finds that white racial identity development is surprisingly similar for white supremacists as well as for white racial justice activists (Hughey 2010, 2012).

For the most part, people of color have been forced to think about race, not just in the abstract, but as something fundamental to who they are, how they are perceived, and thus, how they see themselves. Whites, however, develop a white racial identity without much conscious thought or discussion. As James Baldwin has said, being white means never having to think about it. Janet Helms (1990) identifies stages of white racial identity development beginning with whites who have had no contact with other races, moving to those who learn about race and privilege, to those who see inequalities as the fault of the other races. For white people progressing through these first three of six stages of racial identity development, the question becomes, how do they get to see themselves as white in a raced world rather than as neutral, nonraced, or the norm?

In the first stage of white racial identity development, whites have had little contact with people of color and thus, have developed a sense of superiority over them based upon social stereotypes and media representations. Whites in stage one have difficulty seeing white privilege and may even resist the idea. Some of these folks are outright racists, while others are not blatant racists but may perceive people of color in stereotypical ways, such as lazy or dangerous. There is nothing inevitable about identity development—most whites are in stage one and many never move beyond the first stage (Helms 1990).

For those whites who progress in their identity development, according to Helms (1990), stage two is characterized by fear and guilt that stems from seeing themselves, perhaps for the first time, as holding racial prejudices. As they learn more about race in American society, it challenges what they thought they knew about the world. They are seeing racism and privilege for the first time. Often, whites respond to this guilt and fear through retrenchment, which is the third stage.

In the retrenchment stage, whites deal with their guilt by blaming the victim, declaring that racial inequality is the fault of minorities. Not all white people move backward at this stage. Instead, some progress through the next stages, eventually developing a healthy white identity that is not based on guilt or a sense of superiority.

Many whites struggle with seeing themselves as white. As mentioned previously, whiteness is viewed by many whites as bland, cultureless, thus, white people are more likely to lack an overt racial identity. In fact, this lack of a sense of white identity is due to the fact that whiteness is generally seen as the norm. By bemoaning their lack of a racial identity, whites help maintain the separate status of racial/ethnic minorities, who are perceived as different, as "other" in American society. What is in operation is white privilege: the privilege to *not* think about race, the privilege to *not* recognize the dominant culture as white culture rather than as racially neutral, and the privilege to overlook the fact that whiteness, rather than being absent, is ever present as the unnamed norm.

Identities are more than personal. They are products of particular sociohistorical eras. Thus white identities, like all racial identities, are social, historical, and political constructions. The fact that white as a racial identity is rarely visible is evidence of the operation of white privilege in our lives today. Identities are political and they are a response to changing social and political contexts. Native American activism during the 1970s resulted in more individuals officially identifying as Native American (Nagel 1996). The racial identity of white Americans often goes unacknowledged, with the exception of historical eras that challenge the taken-for-grantedness of whiteness and white privilege. For instance, during the civil rights movement, white Americans began to explicitly claim their whiteness if for no other reason than they viewed the privileges associated with their whiteness as being challenged. The racial socialization of whites, their sense of entitlement, was being challenged every day. As black civil rights activists demanded equal rights, whites counterattacked with rhetoric concerning the perceived loss of their own rights (Sokol 2006). Today, in a less racially charged atmosphere, most whites are unlikely to see themselves in racial terms. However, white people working toward racial justice do view white as a race and their life experiences as racialized (see Box 2.3 Racial Justice Activism).

Institutional Privilege

Just as sociologists have identified racial discrimination within all of our major social institutions, white privilege can be found in these arenas as well: in banks/lending institutions, educational systems, media, religious institutions, and government, just to name a few. This is the most diffi-cult arena to make race privilege visible. Institutional racism was introduced in the first chapter and refers to everyday business practices and policies that result in disadvantage for some racial groups, intentionally or not. **Institutional privilege** is even more difficult to identify since privi-lege is designed to remain invisible, in its institutionalized form it becomes even more obscure. In addition to the advantages individuals accumulate through white privilege; it also takes the form of customs, norms, traditions, laws, and public policies that benefit whites (Williams 2003). Throughout this text, various societal institutions will be explored exposing not only the racial inequality embedded in them but also the ways white privilege is built into the specific business practices and policies within each institution. In exploring institutional privilege, it is useful to ask, what group benefits from a particular arrangement, policy, or practice?

BOX 2.3
Racial Justice Activism:
Tim Wise on White Identity and Becoming a Racial Justice Activist

Tim Wise has been working as an antiracist activist since he was twenty-one years old. He details his path to antiracist work in his book *White Like Me: Reflections on Race from a Privileged Son* (2005). During his college years at Tulane University in New Orleans, he immersed himself in activist work, primarily working as an anti-apartheid activist and a Central American peace activist.

Wise explains that he was not aware that, even as he worked to eradicate racism across the globe, he was doing absolutely nothing about racism in his own community, thus he was reinforcing his own white privilege despite his activism. This contradiction was pointed out to him by an African American woman and New Orleans native during a question-and-answer period concerning the university's decision to divest in South Africa. She pointedly asked him, in his four years of living in New Orleans, "What one thing have you done to address apartheid in this city, since, after all, you benefit from that apartheid" (2005:114). After his inability to adequately respond to that question and much self-reflection, he explained "I had been blind to the way in which my own privilege and the privilege of whites generally had obscured our understanding of such issues as accountability, the need to link up struggles (like the connection between racism in New Orleans and that in South Africa), and the need to always have leadership of color in any antiracist struggle, however much that requires whites to step back, keep our mouths shut and just listen for a while" (2005:117).

After graduating from college, Wise took that lesson seriously and began his career as an antiracist activist, working as a youth coordinator for the Louisiana Coalition Against Racism and Nazism, which opposed the political candidacy of neo-Nazi Senate candidate David Duke. He moved up the ranks of the organization and eventually became one of the most visible faces associated with the anti-Duke effort (2005:11). Wise now earns a living lecturing and writing about white privilege and antiracist activism.

Wise acknowledges that there is significant resistance to whites' engaging in antiracist activist work because they lack antiracist role models to whom they can look for guidance, they fear alienating family and friends with their views, and "because resistance is difficult ... many whites who care deeply about issues of racism and inequality will find ourselves paralyzed either by uncertainty, fear or both" (2005:62). He emphasizes that despite these obstacles to resistance, "experiences taught me that to be white in this country doesn't have to be a story of accepting unjust social systems. There is not only one way to be in this skin. There are choices we can make, paths we can travel, and when we travel them, we will not be alone" (p. 63).

While engaging in this kind of work has resulted in some death threats, hate mail, and being followed by skinheads on at least one occasion, Wise argues that "I put up with whatever cost I have to put up with, because the cost of not doing the work is greater ... People of color have to do this work as a matter of everyday survival. And so long as they have to, who am I to act as if I have a choice in the matter? Especially when my future and that of my children in large part depends on the eradication of racism? There is no choice" (2005:6).

Figure 2.3   Antiracist activist, author, and speaker Tim Wise.

To help understand what is meant by institutional privilege, we explore several policies and practices that have allowed whites to accumulate wealth and inhibited people of color from wealth accumulation. This includes the policies and practices of banking and lending institutions as well as government policies and practices.

Racial minorities have been systematically excluded from wealth creation with very real, concrete consequences. Slavery is the most obvious example. In addition to the cruelty and inhumanity of this institution, it was also a system that deterred wealth accumulation by the great majority of blacks and supported the massive accumulation of wealth by some whites. For over 240 years, blacks labored in America without being compensated. Clearly that places them in a disadvantaged position in terms of wealth accumulation. While only a small portion of the population owned slaves, it is estimated that about 15 million white Americans today have slave-owning ancestors (Millman 2008). Of our first eighteen presidents, thirteen owned slaves. Two recent presidents, father and son George H. W. and George W. Bush, are descendants of slave owners, contributing, of course, to their great wealth and political power to this day.

Upon emancipation, reparations for former slaves were promised, most in the form of land. The promised "forty acres and a mule," however, never materialized. During the Reconstruction era, the federal government established the Freedmen's Bureau to provide food, education, medical care, and in some cases, land, to newly freed slaves as well as to needy whites (see Chapter 5). Although this agency only lasted one year and was unable to meet the needs of the great majority of newly freed slaves, it is significant that more whites benefited from this government agency than blacks.

Native American Land Loss

The exploitation of Native Americans often involved the taking of land; an estimated 2 billion acres of land was transferred to the United States government from American Indian Tribes through treaties in exchange for tribal sovereignty (Newton 1999). European Americans confiscated land that Native peoples populated, forced their removal, and sometimes engaged in acts of genocide so as to acquire land. This theme of Native land loss at the hands of whites is hardly new; most of us learned of this in grade school. However, we need to reflect more on the significance. Native land loss is always presented as a collective problem, which it was, as tribes lost their lands and livelihoods as they were repeatedly relocated to less valuable lands. What we tend not to realize is that this is a significant loss at the individual level as well. Land is equivalent to wealth in the white mainstream culture (Native peoples, however, generally did not believe people could own the land and they instead saw themselves as stewards of the land). Who benefited when all those Native people were forced off of the lands on which they lived? White people took the land as their own, thus acquiring wealth. Native land loss at the hands of whites goes beyond giant land swindles involving treaties between the federal government and tribal governments. Throughout the country there were smaller, everyday, localized swindles. Additionally, many states established laws that did not allow Native people to own land, thus, limiting their ability to accumulate wealth and simultaneously contributing to the ability of white people to accumulate wealth.

Issues of Wealth Accumulation

These historical examples of the exploitation of racial minorities in terms of wealth accumulation have a flip side: white advantage. Whites historically and currently benefit from the exclusion of other racial/ethnic groups. For instance, laws supported the rights of white Americans to own homes and businesses while banks and lending institutions provided them the necessary capital to do so. This was not a given for people of color. Until the 1960s, laws explicitly excluded people of color from obtaining business loans in many places. White people were subsidized in acquiring their own homes, and thus establishing equity, which eventually became wealth that was passed on to the next generation (Oliver and Shapiro 1995). This is significant if for no other reason than wealth accumulates. Federal Reserve studies confirm that even today, minorities get fewer home loans, even when their economic situations are comparable to whites. "The poorest white applicant, according to this [the Federal Reserve] report, was more likely to get a mortgage loan approved than a black in the highest income bracket" (Oliver and Shapiro 1995:20). The consequences of this are profound since for most Americans home ownership represents their primary and often only source of wealth (see Chapter 8).

Ideologies of white supremacy fuel white identities of entitlement and, thus, the creation of institutions that deny access to anyone but whites are deemed acceptable. Ideologies of

REFLECT AND CONNECT

Think about how much white privilege you may have. If you are white, did your ancestors own slaves? Ask your parents the following questions: Did your parents or grandparents have access to home and/or business loans? Did they own their own homes or land? Did your parents or grandparents own a business? Did your parents or grandparents attend college? Have you received or do you expect to receive an inheritance? Are your parents paying for your college, thus making significant student loan borrowing unnecessary? If you can answer yes to any of these, you have more than likely benefited from white privilege in a very material, concrete way.

color-blindness in our current era fuel a "raceless" identity in whites that allows them to deny ongoing racism, while still enjoying race privilege.

Challenging White Privilege

What can or should be done about white privilege? Is it necessary to challenge white privilege? Is it possible? It is easier to condemn racism than to challenge one's own privilege. Understanding white privilege is essential, yet incomplete, because, as McIntosh notes, "describing white privilege makes one newly accountable" (2008:109). In other words, if we see privilege, do we not have an obligation to work to eradicate it? While white privilege allows whites to ignore their race and avoid confronting the advantages associated with it, many white Americans actively challenge white privilege as part of their commitment to racial justice and as a way to challenge their own sense of entitlement (e.g., Warren 2010; Wise 2005). White civil rights activists were rejecting their own race privilege through their activism on behalf of full civil rights for people of color, for instance (e.g., Murray 2004; Zellner 2008).

Racial justice activists argue that white privilege is the proverbial "elephant in the room" that white people agree to ignore (Parker and Chambers 2007). White theologians have called for an end to the silence surrounding white privilege within religious institutions (Cassidy and Mikulich 2007). Stories of racial justice activism are featured in "Racial Justice Activism" boxes in each chapter. Now, we are going to explore why challenging white privilege is not only necessary, but is actually in the interests of white people.

For many white people, being introduced to the concept of white privilege invokes intense feelings of guilt. They often respond by saying they should not be made to feel guilty for being white, as it was hardly their choice. Or they feel that by focusing on privilege, it takes away from their achievements or the achievements of their parents. This is not the intent. White guilt is a normal reaction to learning about historical and current atrocities inflicted upon racial minorities by whites. When it comes to race, our country has an ugly history that cannot be ignored. Guilt is uncomfortable psychologically, so people tend to work to alleviate the feeling. Thus, such guilt has the potential to motivate change, to get white people to understand how they are racist, how they contribute to racial oppression, and what they can do to end it. It is important to recognize white privilege.

It is necessary for a complete understanding of the role race plays in all of our lives, both at the individual and societal levels. Additionally, opposing the racial inequities associated with whiteness is not the same thing as opposing white people (Williams 2003).

It is important to critically investigate white privilege because while privilege offers advantages, whites are also losers under this system of structural inequality. There are many unrecognized ways whites lose under this system: it is expensive, financially and morally, to ignore white privilege in the workplace because it remains an uncomfortable environment for people of color and thus, their retention is less likely. The only way white people can remain part of this racial hierarchy is to compartmentalize—separate their head from their heart. There are long-term consequences of such compartmentalization, primarily in terms of failing to recognize our common humanity (Kendall 2006). Helms's stages of racial identity development are helpful in understanding our common humanity. Through this model, we can see that racial identity is not fixed. We can change; we can progress in terms of understanding ourselves along racial lines as well as understanding the operation of our societal racial hierarchy.

Tim Wise (2008) argues that white people pay a tremendous price for maintaining white privilege and that it is actually in the interest of whites to dismantle the racial hierarchy. Wise offers the following bit of advice to whites interested in working for racial justice: "The first thing a white person must do to effectively fight racism is to learn to listen, and more than that, to believe what people of color say about their lives ... One of the biggest problems with white America is its collective unwillingness to believe that racism is still a real problem for nonwhite peoples, despite their repeated protestations that it is" (2005:67).

One of the reasons offered by whites fighting for racial justice is the moral one: that this is an unjust system and, thus, it should be dismantled. Ignoring both inequality and privilege dehumanizes all of us. Racial justice activists find that they engage in this work because it is personally fulfilling and because they believe that working for racial justice will produce a better society for all. For racial justice activists, having healthier communities, more empowered citizens, and more humane culture that focuses on compassion and community will provide a better society for all (Warren 2010).

Another reason it is in the interest of whites to dismantle white privilege is economic. It is costly to maintain inequality. Whiteness privileges some whites more than others. It is estimated that an affluent 20 percent of whites reap the benefits of whiteness (Hobgood 2007). Having a labor

WITNESS

"I think it's the price of the soul. You're internally diminished when you dominate other people or when you're trying to convince yourself you're not dominating others" (Warren 2010:88).

WITNESS

One of the racial justice activists interviewed by Warren (2010) explains why she believes this work is part of her civil and political responsibility: "We have got to do something about that for the good of democracy. It's just not healthy for a democracy to have that kind of racism at its core" (Warren 2010:85).

force that is divided along racial lines (see Chapter 8) deflates all workers' wages. The prison industrial complex (see Chapter 9) disproportionately incarcerates racial minority males. The mass incarceration of minority males becomes self-perpetuating in that they become the face of crime, leaving white criminals privileged in that they are not immediately suspect. However, whites are disadvantaged by the mass incarceration of minorities simply because more and more tax dollars go toward incarcerating citizens rather than toward supporting schools, for instance.

References

"AC Milan Players Respond to Racist Chants by Walking off Field, Match against Pro Patria Ends." 2013. *Huffington Post*, January 3. Retrieved May 2, 2013 (http://www.huffingtonpost.com/2013/01/03/ac-milan-players-racist-chants-walk-off-pro-patria_n_2403497.html).

Alba, Richard. 1990. *Ethnic Identity: The Transformation of White Americans*. New Haven and London: Yale University Press.

Almaguer, Tomas. 1994. *Racial Fault Lines: The Historical Origins of White Supremacy in California*. Berkeley: University of California Press.

Bailey, Stanley R. 2008. "Unmixing for Race Making in Brazil." *American Journal of Sociology* 114(3):577–614.

Bonilla- Silva, Eduardo. 2006. *Racism Without Racists: Color-Blind Racism and the Persistence of Racial Inequality in the United States*, 2nd ed. Lanham, MD: Rowman and Littlefield.

_____. 2010. *Racism Without Racists: Color-Blind Racism and Racial Inequality in Contemporary America*, 3rd ed. Lanham, MD: Rowman and Littlefield.

Burlew, A. K. and L. R. Smith. 1991. "Measures of Racial Identity: An Overview and a Proposed Framework." *Journal of Black Psychology* 17(2):53–71.

Bush, Melanie. 2011. *Everyday Forms of Whiteness: Understanding Race in a Post-Racial World,* 2nd ed. Lanham, MD: Rowman and Littlefield.

Cassidy, Laurie M. and Alex Mikulich, eds. 2007. *Interrupting White Privilege: Catholic Theologians Break the Silence*. Maryknoll, NY: Orbis Books.

Dalton, Harlon. 2008. "Failing to See." Pp. 15–18 in *White Privilege: Essential Readings on the Other Side of Racism,* 3rd ed., edited by P. Rothenberg. New York: Worth Publishers.

Dees, M. and J. Corcoran. 1996. *Gathering Storm: America's Militia Threat*. New York: HarperCollins.

Feagin, Joe R., Hernan Vera, and Pinar Batur. 1995. *White Racism: The Basics*. New York and London: Routledge.

Fitzgerald, Kathleen J. 2007. *Beyond White Ethnicity: Developing a Sociological Understanding of Native American Identity Reclamation*. Lanham, MD: Lexington Books.

Foley, Neil. 2008. "Becoming Hispanic: Mexican Americans and Whiteness." Pp. 49–60 in *White Privilege: Essential Readings on the Other Side of Racism*, 3rd ed., edited by P. Rothenberg. New York: Worth Publishers.

Fox, Helen. 2001. *When Race Breaks Out: Conversations About Race and Racism in College Classrooms*. New York, Washington, DC: Peter Lang Publishers.

Frankenberg, Ruth. 1993. *White Women, Race Matters: The Social Construction of Whiteness*. Minneapolis: University of Minnesota Press.

Gallaher, Carolyn. 2003. *On the Fault Line: Race, Class, and the American Patriot Movement*. Lanham, MD: Rowman and Littlefield.

Haney Lopez, Ian F. 2006. "Colorblind to the Reality of Race in America." *Chronicle of Higher Education*, November 3. Retrieved July 24, 2013 (http://chronicle.com/article/Colorblind-to-the-Reality-of/12577).

Hanrahan, Mark. 2013. "Segregated Prom: Wilcox County, GA, High School Students Set up First Integrated Prom." *Huffington Post*, April 4. Retrieved April 14, 2013 (http://www.huffingtonpost.com/2013/04/04/segregated-prom-wilcox-county-ga-high-school_n_3013733.html).

Helms, Janet. 1990. "Toward a Model of White Racial Identity Development." Pp. 49–66 in *Black and White Racial Identity: Theory, Research and Practice*, edited by J. Helms. Westport, CT: Praeger.

Hobgood, Mary Elizabeth. 2007. "White Economic and Erotic Disempowerment: A Theological Exploration in the Struggle against Racism." Pp. 40–55 in *Interrupting White Privilege: Catholic Theologians Break the Silence*, edited by L. M. Cassidy and A. Mikulich. Maryknoll, NY: Orbis Books.

Hughey, Matthew. 2010. "The (Dis)Similarities of White Racial Identities: The Conceptual Framework of 'Hegemonic Whiteness.'" *Ethnic and Racial Studies* 33(8):1289–1309.

_____. 2012. *White Bound: Nationalists, Anti-Racists, and the Shared Meanings of Race*. Stanford, CA: Stanford University Press.

Ignatiev, Noel. 1995. *How the Irish Became White*. New York, London: Routledge.

Jacobson, Matthew Frye. 1998. *Whiteness of a Different Color: European Immigrants and the Alchemy of Race*. Cambridge, MA: Harvard University Press.

Kendall, Francis. 2006. *Understanding White Privilege: Creating Pathways to Authentic Relationships Across Race*. New York: Routledge.

Kivel, Paul. 2008. "How White People Can Serve as Allies to People of Color in the Struggle to End Racism," PP. 127–136 in *White Privilege: Essential Readings on the Other Side of Racism,* 3rd ed., edited by P. Rothenberg. New York: Worth Publishers.

Korgen, Kathleen Odell. 1998. *From Black to Biracial: Transforming Racial Identity Among Americans*. Westport, CT: Praeger.

Leonhardt, David. 2013. "Hispanics, the New Italians." *New York Times*, April 20. Retrieved May 20, 2013 (http://www.nytimes.com/2013/04/21/sunday-review/hispanics-the-new-italians.html?pagewanted=all&_r=0).

Lopez, Ian Haney. 1996. *White By Law: The Legal Construction of Race*. New York: New York University Press.

McDermott, Monica and Frank L. Samson. 2005. "White Racial and Ethnic Identity in the United States." *Annual Review of Sociology* 31:245–261.

McIntosh, Peggy. 2008. "White Privilege: Unpacking the Invisible Knapsack." Pp. 97–102 in *White Privilege: Essential Readings on the Other Side of Racism*, 3rd ed., edited by P. Rothenberg. New York: Worth Publishers.

McIntyre, Alice. 1997. *Making Meaning of Whiteness: Exploring Racial Identity With White Teachers*. Albany: State University of New York Press.

Millman, Jennifer. 2008. "Slavery Ties: Bush's Long-Held 'Family Secret.'" *DiversityInc.com*, February 20. Retrieved July 11, 2013 (http://www.juneteenth.us/news7.html).

Murray, Gail S. 2004. *Throwing Off the Cloak of Privilege: White Southern Women Activists in the Civil Rights Era*. Gainesville: University Press of Florida.

Nagel, Joane. 1996. *American Indian Ethnic Renewal: Red Power and the Resurgence of Identity and Culture*. New York and Oxford: Oxford University Press.

Newton, Nell Jessup. 1999. "Indian Claims for Reparations, Compensation, and Restitution in the United States Legal System." P. 41 in *When Sorry isn't Enough: The Controversy over Apologies and Reparations for Human Injustice*, edited by R. L. Brooks. New York: New York University Press.

Oliver, Melvin L. and Thomas M. Shapiro. 1995. *Black Wealth/White Wealth: A New Perspective on Racial Inequality.* New York, London: Routledge.

Parker, Robin and Pamela Smith Chambers. 2007. *The Great White Elephant: A Workbook on Racial Privilege for White Anti-Racists.* Mount Laurel, NJ: Beyond Diversity Resource Center.

Pinho, Patricia de Santana. 2009. "White but Not Quite: Tones and Overtones of Whiteness in Brazil." *Small Axe: A Caribbean Journal of Criticism* 29:39–56.

Resnicow, K. and D. Ross-Gaddy. 1997. "Development of a Racial Identity Scale for Low-Income African Americans." *Journal of Black Studies* 28(2):239–254.

Rockquemore, Kerry Ann and David Brunsma. 2002. *Beyond Black: Biracial Identity in America.* Thousand Oaks, CA: Sage Publications.

Rodriguez, Victor M. 2005. "The Racialization of Mexican Americans and Puerto Ricans: 1890s–1930s." *CENTRO Journal* 17(1):71–105.

Rothenberg, Paula S. 2008. *White Privilege: Essential Readings on the Other Side of Racism,* 3rd ed. New York: Worth Publishers.

Rubin, Lillian. 1994. *Families on the Fault Line.* New York: Harper Perennial.

Sokol, Jason. 2006. *There Goes My Everything: White Southerners in the Age of Civil Rights, 1945–1975.* New York: Vintage Books.

Stein, Howard and Robert F. Hill. 1977. *The Ethnic Imperative: Examining the New White Ethnic Movement.* University Park: Pennsylvania State University Press.

Telles, Edward. 2009. "The Social Consequences of Skin Color in Brazil." Pp. 9–24 in *Shades of Difference: Why Skin Color Matters*, edited by E. N. Glenn. Stanford, CA: Stanford University Press.

Terry, Robert W. 1970. *For Whites Only.* Grand Rapids, MI: William B. Eerdmans Publishing.

Thompson, John. 1984. *Studies in the Theory of Ideology.* Cambridge, UK: Polity.

Warren, Mark R. 2010. *Fire in the Heart: How White Activists Embrace Racial Justice.* Oxford, New York: Oxford University Press.

Waters, Mary. 1990. *Ethnic Options: Choosing Identities in America.* Berkeley, CA: University of California Press.

"'White Privilege' Lesson in Delavan-Darien High School Class in Wisconsin Draws Ire." 2013. *Huffington Post*, January 16. Retrieved May 2, 2013 (http://www.huffingtonpost.com/2013/01/16/white-privilege-class-at-_n_2489997.html?view=print&comm_ref=false).

Williams, Linda Faye. 2003. *The Constraint of Race: The Legacies of White Skin Privilege in America.* University Park: The Pennsylvania State University Press.

Wise, Tim. 2005. *White Like Me: Reflections on Race from a Privileged Son.* Brooklyn, NY: Soft Skull Press.

_____ . 2005. "Oh, Give Me A Home." *Alternet*, March 10. Retrieved July 25, 2013 (http://www.alternet.org/story/21469/oh,_give_me_a_home).

_____ . 2008. "Membership Has Its Privileges: Thoughts on Acknowledging and Challenging Whiteness." Pp. 107–110 in *White Privilege: Essential Readings on the Other Side of Racism,* 3rd ed. New York: Worth Publishers.

Zellner, Bob and Constance Curry. 2008. *The Wrong Side of Murder Creek: A White Southerner in the Freedom Movement.* Montgomery, AL: New South Books.

Discussion Questions

1   What is white privilege?

2   What are the differences between assimilation and pluralization?

3   Name a few of the groups that were not previously considered white but are now considered white?

4   Becoming white and becoming middle class are interconnected. Why?

5   Do all whites enjoy the same privileges of white privilege?

CHAPTER 3

Institutional Racism

The Cumulative Pipeline of Persistent Institutional Racism

Rashawn Ray

M elvin Kohn declares that "a truly sociological social psychology can settle for no less than systematic effort towards understanding the processes by which the major social institutions of any society affect members of that society" (1989: 32). This section of the anthology focuses on how race functions on an institutional level. Neighborhoods, schools, and the labor market are where we spend most of our time. As social institutions, these macro-level structures collectively operate to determine our attitudes, perceptions, and interactions. Below I briefly discuss how institutional conditions shape attitudes and perceptions and determine interactions. Then, I highlight some key empirical findings on neighborhoods and communities, education, and the labor market. Finally, I focus on media as an institution that will continue to grow in importance as Generations X and Y progress through the life course.

Institutional Racism, Social Structures, and Normative Institutional Arrangements

As discussed throughout this anthology, racism is a social system that conveys an ideology of inferiority, which is often affiliated with individual- and group-level prejudice and discrimination. Similar to sexism, racism alters social systems and various normative institutional arrangements whereby the entire institution become racialized. This leads to a divergence in various outcomes such as lower educational outcomes (Lewis 2010), lower occupational prestige (Oliver and Shapiro 1995; Bertrand and Mullainathan. 2004), relatively deprived neighborhoods (Sewell 2010), schools, and hospitals, and worse mental and physical health outcomes (Gilbert and Leak 2010).

Hunt and colleagues (2000) make a convincing argument that we should not assume that factors operate similarly across racial groups in work, neighborhood, family, and education contexts.

As indicative of the works in this anthology, race functions on three main levels—1) Micro-level through individual, face-to-face interaction; 2) Meso-level through processes, mechanisms, and normative institutional arrangements; and 3) Macro-level through institutions such as education, the criminal justice system, and the health care system. The social structure refers to aspects of the larger social system that are bounded or determinative patterns of social relationships. Social structures and social processes are organized by institutions such as government, communities, and media which are situated in particular mainstream discourses (Becker and McCall 1990). Discourses become apparent via normalized and accepted institutional practices. These discourses are constantly up for discussion and challenged by various groups and normative institutional arrangements.

Normative institutional arrangements are situated in between the micro- and macro-level of analysis and focus on the accepted arrangement of relationships within social institutions. Furthermore, they are boundaries that shape social interactions and establish control over social environments (Ray and Rosow 2009 in this anthology), and one structural mechanism that should be of importance to scholars interested in race and intersectionality research. Normative institutional arrangements identify social contexts whereby certain behaviors are more or less acceptable, certain structures hold individuals more or less accountable for their treatment of others, and attitudes and perceptions may be altered. Such arrangements represent taken-for-granted assumptions that are external, exist outside of individuals, constraining, and enabling.

Here is an example of the influence of normative institutional arrangements. Hagan, Shedd, and Payne (2005) investigate the impact the size of racial groups in educational settings has on youth's perceptions of police contact. They find that there are breach points or cleavages wherein Blacks and Latinos perceive more police contact when the White population at their school is 15–30 percent. These effects start to diminish when the White population is 0 to 15 percent and 30–45 percent. Collectively, these findings highlight the importance of normative institutional arrangements on perceptions. Below I discuss specific institutions and some key dimensions that make them social entities.

Social Institutions and Important Dimensions of Social Life

Neighborhoods and Communities

A neighborhood is a geographically localized community within a city, town or suburb. A community is defined as a group of individuals living in the same locality and under the same government or power structure. Suburbs are generally located on the outskirts of cities. Urban is typically associated with city life or culture such as Washington D.C, Tokyo, Japan, Frankfurt,

Germany, or Durban, South Africa. Rural is generally associated with country life or culture. Although Whites live in cities and minorities live in rural areas, these two terms often have racial undertones where urban means minority and rural means White.

Since most countries have different definitions for what classifies as urban or rural, comparisons on a global scale can become convoluted. In the United States, an incorporated city is legally defined as a government entity with powers delegated by the state and county and created and approved by the voters of the city. A neighborhood, on the other hand, is typically an unincorporated community with no governmental powers. In Sweden and Denmark, a village of 200 people is counted as an urban population, but it takes a city of 30,000 to be considered urban in Japan. Most other countries fall somewhere in between. Australia and Canada use a population of 1,000, Israel and France use 2,000 and the United States and Mexico call an area of 2,500 residents urban.

In Sewell's (2010)—"A Different Menu: Racial Residential Segregation and the Persistence of Racial Inequality"—she candidly discusses how a majority of the neighborhoods in the United States and around the world are actually ghettos and a result of institutional forms of apartheid. Apartheid is the policy or practice of political, legal, economic, and/or social discrimination against individuals of a particular group. Apartheid is mostly associated with South Africa. However, Massey and Denton (1993) argue that we are encountering an American Apartheid right here in the United States with ghettos as the central physical marking. Generally, a ghetto is a section of a city occupied by a minority group who live there because of legal and institutional discrimination and/or social and economic pressure. Ghettos are normally formed in three ways: 1) when members of a particularly group voluntarily choose to live with their own group; 2) when the majority group uses compulsory violence, hostility, or legal barriers to force minority group members into particular areas; or 3) when majority group members are willing and/or able to pay more than minority group members to live with their own group and exclude minority group members.

What is so intriguing about the term "ghetto" is just how racialized it has become. "Ghetto" has now transcended its literary definition to be used figuratively to describe how individuals act (e.g., urban, thug-like, hard, Black) or to strictly label the poor geographic areas that have a large proportion of a particular group such as Black or Latino housing projects. Ghettos are often categorized as drug infested, downtrodden, poor, crime-riddled, and Black. The word ghetto was originally used to refer to Venetian neighborhoods in Italy where Jews were forced to live. The term came into widespread use during World War II and primarily referenced Nazi ghettos. In addition to Black and Jewish ghettos, there are "rural ghettos" that refer to Indian reservations as well as mobile home parks and farm housing tracks that are mostly inhabited by Whites. Interestingly, based on the actual definition of ghetto, suburbs that are predominately one race can also be considered ghettos.

According to Massey and Denton (1993), however, only one group has historically and continuously experienced ghettoization—Blacks. Despite what many individuals think, most Blacks did not choose or develop ghettos. Instead as Sewell (2010) highlights, coordinated institutional acts of discrimination and uncoordinated individual acts of discrimination were utilized to facilitate that certain housing markets would be denied to Blacks in order to create spatial segregation. Neighborhood associations were formed to prevent Blacks from moving into certain neighborhoods. These neighborhood associations continuously lobbied law makers to implement zoning restrictions to exclude Blacks. Restrictive covenants were formed that established no entry into certain neighborhoods for Blacks. Restrictive covenants were contractual agreements signed by neighborhood tenants who agree not to sell, rent, lease, or allow certain groups (i.e., Blacks) to occupy property in a particular neighborhood.*

Since Blacks were excluded from certain neighborhoods, they were relegated to others. Contrary to ghettos current arrangement, ghettos limited to Blacks had excessively high renter prices. Thus, White real estate companies and agents had an invested interest to create more of these urban ghettos. White real estate agents would go door to door warning Whites of the "Black invasion" so that they could increase prices and rent to needy Blacks (Massey and Denton 1993). This is called redlining. Redlining is the practice of denying or increasing the costs of essential services such as banking, insurance, health care, grocery stores, and public transportation. The term redlining derives from Chicago in the 1960s where banks actually utilized a red line to mark on a map where they would not give out loans to residents or invest in the community.

On the other side of the ghettoization of Blacks, many Whites flocked to the suburbs. This is commonly termed "White flight." White flight is the departure of Whites from places perceived to be populated by minority group members because of the fear that crime will increase, education quality will decrease, and property values will decrease.** Now, gentrification is commencing in many urban areas across the country including Memphis, Los Angeles, Detroit, Philadelphia, and New Orleans. Gentrification is a process in which low-cost, physically deteriorated neighborhoods experience physical renovation and an increase in property values, along with an influx of wealthier residents who typically displace the prior residents.

Patillo (2007) provides a fascinating empirical examination of middle class Blacks who are often situated in neighborhoods and public spaces between working class and poor Black neighborhoods and middle and upper class White neighborhoods. Patillo finds that middle class Blacks act as middlemen between their lower class Black counterparts and the White power structure in Chicago. Unlike a majority of their middle class predecessors, Patillo contends that many middle class Blacks have the ability to influence power structures to direct resources toward under-funded areas. Considering that sociological research frequently classifies Blacks as a monolithic group, Patillo's research is important in that it highlights mechanisms that draw attention to the heterogeneity of Blacks.

---

* The U.S. Supreme Court finally outlawed restrictive covenants in 1948. Still, residential segregation continued around the country on a local level.
** *Why Can't We Live Together* is a good documentary illuminating White flight and its implications and consequences.

Education

As Lewis and Pattison (2010) discuss, education has always been viewed as the "great equalizer." People think that education can solve most of the issues related to racial inequality. This is because most people actually believe that schools are equal and that students are "good" and "bad" instead of schools being "good" and "bad."

Kozol (1991) shows that there are actually "bad" schools, a fact that continues to go under-emphasized. He masterfully documents the woes of inner-city schools in East St. Louis, Missouri, Chicago, Illinois, New York City, New York, Camden, New Jersey, Washington, D.C. and San Antonio, Texas. Kozol paints a portrait of inner-city life as dilapidated, under-funded, under-staffed, under-resourced, overcrowded, and unsanitary. On the other hand, suburban and/or county schools typically have an abundance of resources including a low teacher-student ratio, computers, media stations, and up-to-date science equipment. These schools typically have at least twice as much funding as the schools described in Kozol's study. Due to significant inequalities that result from an unequal distribution of funds for school, which are collected primarily from property taxes, Kozol (2005) argues that schools are placed on unequal grounds that generally fall along racial lines. Kozol (2005) argues that school funding is the primary reason for racial differences in academic achievement. In addition to what I discuss above, Lewis and Pattison (2010) draw attention to the implications racial inequality has for the Black/White achievement gap and perceptions of reasons for this gap historically and currently.

The Labor Market, Socioeconomic Status, and Wealth

Scholars in the 1970s predicted that Blacks would finally flourish and begin to assimilate into the middle class (Wilson 1978). However, many of these predictions became null and void in the 1980s. Some scholars argue the influx of crack cocaine and the culture of poverty are reasons why Blacks seem to be lagging behind educationally and economically. Conversely, Oliver and Shapiro (1995) document how President Reagan's policy agenda increased inequality in the 1980s. Similar policies in the George W. Bush administration reduced Clinton's strides of the 1990s and have widened the economic gap among young adults in America. Oliver and Shapiro display that wealth is primarily located in the intergenerational transmission of family wealth and investments. This accumulation of wealth, however, is highly structured by race. Since homes in predominately Black neighborhoods are often under-appreciated and deemed a lower standard than homes in predominately White communities, most Blacks do not have wealth comparable to their White counterparts. As a result, Black families and Black communities have incurred a significant loss of wealth over time.

So why is wealth more important than income for determining racial inequality? Wealth highlights patterns of inequality that go unnoticed by income (Conley 2000). Blacks and Whites face different structures of investment opportunities that have historical and contemporary implications for the intersections of race and class (Massey and Denton 1993; Oliver and Shapiro 1995; Sewell 2010). Through the Sociology of Wealth, Oliver and Shapiro display how social interactions and life outcomes establish a unique set of social circumstances that structure racial inequality.

The Sociology of Wealth includes three main concepts including the "racialization of state policy," "economic detour," and the "sedimentation of racial inequality." The "racialization of state policy" refers to how state policies impair the ability for many Blacks to accumulate wealth. Oliver and Shapiro argue that this racialization can be traced from slavery up to the present and reportedly cost the current generation of Blacks an estimated $82 Billion. The next generation of Blacks is estimated to be behind Whites by $93 Billion in wealth accumulation. Second, "economic detour" highlights the law restrictions that prevented Blacks from navigating the economic open market. This resulted in less business ownership among Blacks. Third, the "sedimentation of racial inequality" highlights the cumulative effects Blacks have faced in social institutions including lower wages in the labor market, poorer schools (Lewis and Pattison 2010), and neighborhood segregation (Sewell 2010). Over time, this sedimentation becomes ingrained in the social structure. Oliver and Shapiro contend that a racial wage tax has accumulated and established two different worlds among middle class Whites and middle class Blacks.

Below, I present statistics to further illuminate the inequalities in the labor market, socio-economic status, and wealth. A White applicant in the lowest income bracket was more likely to get a mortgage loan than a Black applicant in the highest income bracket. Blacks in the highest income bracket, compared to Whites in the highest income bracket, were denied mortgage loans three times as often. Under-qualified White women are three times more likely than over-qualified Black women to get a job. For every dollar owned by the White middle class, the Black middle class only owns 15 cents. Put another way, for every $100 owned by Whites, Blacks only own $8-$19 (see Oliver and Shapiro 1995). As Bertrand and Mullainathan (2004) show in this anthology, individuals with Black sounding names are 50 percent less likely than those with White sounding names to get a job. As a final note, Pager's (2004) study in this anthology is always a compelling case. Using interactive field experiments, Pager (2003) explores discrimination against minorities and ex-offenders in a low-wage market. She finds that a racial advantage is given to White applicants with a criminal record over Black applicants without a criminal record. Not only do Whites without a criminal record get hired more than Blacks, but Whites with a criminal record get hired more than Blacks without a criminal record.

Mass Media

Due to the influx of the internet and its entities such as YouTube, Facebook, MySpace, and Twitter, most individuals believe that they actually have good interpretations of social life and various racial groups. Stein (1983: 285) refers to media as "a variety of modes by which senders can record information and/or experiences and transmit them to a large audience fairly rapidly." Forms of media include film, TV, internet, radio, newspapers, magazines, and books. Much of the media, however, is simply a competing curriculum for reality. Professional communicators are frequently overshadowed by amateur communicators on YouTube, blogs, and the like. In the virtual world, the media market can be so saturated that the professional communicators whose main goal is surveillance and reporting go unnoticed. In this regard, I believe that scholars and educators have the ability to show the distinctions between professional and amateur communicators and inform students about how to seek accurate portraits of social life.

There needs to be more research on the implications that modes of mass media have on attitudes and perceptions. Future research can focus on how blogs translate into racial attitudes and have consequences for prejudice and discriminatory behavior. On the other hand, the internet may have under-emphasized qualities that can decrease forms of prejudice.

Supplemental Readings and Resources

Becker, Howard and Michael McCall. 1990. *Symbolic Interaction and Cultural Studies*. Chicago: University of Chicago Press.

Bobo, Lawrence D. and Victor Thompson. 2006. "Unfair by Design: The War on Drugs, Race, and the Legitimacy of the Criminal Justice System." *Social Research* 73: 445–472.

Bowser, Rene. 2001. "Racial Profiling in Health Care: an Institutional Analysis of Medical Treatment Disparities." *Michigan Journal of Race and Law* 7: 79–133.

Browne-Marshall, Gloria. 2007. *Race, Law, and American Society: 1607 to Present*. Routledge.

Conley, Dalton. 2000. "40 Acres and a Mule: The Black-White Wealth Gap in America." *National Forum* 80: 21–24.

Cummings, Jason L and Pamela Braboy Jackson. 2007. "Race, Gender, and SES Disparities in Self-Assessed Health, 1974–2004." *Research on Aging* 30: 137–168.

Engel, Kathleen C. and Patricia A. McCoy. 2008. "From Credit Denial to Predatory Lending: The Challenge of Sustaining Minority Home Ownership." In *Segregation: The Rising Costs for America* (Eds.). James H. Carr, Nandinee K. Kutty. Routledge.

Farley, John E. and Gregory D. Squires. 2005. "Fences and Neighbors: Segregation in 21st Century America." *Contexts* 4: 33–39.

Feagin, Joe R. and Bernice McNair Barnett. 2004. "Success and Failure: How Systematic Racism Trumped the Brown v. Board of Education Decision." *University of Illinois Law Review*. 1099–1130.

Feagin, Joe R. and Karyn D. McKinney. 2003. "The Physical Health Consequences of Racism." Pps. 65–93 in *The Many Costs of White Racism*. Oxford: Rowman and Littlefield Publishers.

Hagan, John, Carla Shedd, and Monique R. Payne. 2005. "Race, Ethnicity, and Youth Perceptions of Criminal Injustice." *American Sociological Review* 70: 381–407.

Hoberman, John. 1997. *Darwin's Athletes: How Sport has Damaged Black America and Preserved the Myth of Race*. New York: Houghton Mifflin.

Jackson, Pamela Braboy and Jason L. Cummings. 2009. "The Health of the Black Middle Class." In *The Handbook of the Sociology of Health, Illness, & Healing: Blueprint for the 21st Century*. (Eds.). Bernice Pescosolido, Jack Martin, Jane McLeod, and Anne Rogers. NewYork: Springer Publishers.

Kozol, Jonathon. 1991. *Savage Inequalities*. New York: HarperCollins.

Kozol, Jonathan. 2005. "Still Separate, Still Unequal: America's Educational Apartheid." *Harper's Magazine*.

Massey, Douglas and Nancy Denton. 1993. *American Apartheid: Segregation and the Making of the Underclass*. Harvard University Press.

McCall, Leslie. 2001. "Sources of Racial Wage Inequality in Metropolitan Labor Markets: Racial, Ethnic, and Gender Differences," *American Sociological Review* 66: 520–541.

Orfield, Gary and Chungmei Lee. 2004. "Brown At 50: King's Dream Or Plessy's Nightmare?" *The Civil Rights Project: Harvard University*.

Stein, Gloria. 1983. "The Effective Use of Mass Media in Sociology Education: Confronting the Competing Curriculum." *Teaching Sociology*.

Tashiro, Cathy. 2005. "The Meaning of Race in Health Care and Research." *Pediatric Nursing* 31, 3/4: 208–210, 305–308.

Tatum, Beverly. 2003. *Why Are All the Black Kids Sitting Together in the Cafeteria*.

Discussion Questions

1   Name the three main levels in which race functions in a society?

2   What are social structures, and how do they influence race relations?

3   What are the two main institutions that have persistent institutional racism?

4   How do social systems portray inequalities as related to the labor market, socioeconomic status, and wealth?

5   What role are scholars and educators required to play in providing students with accurate narratives of social life?

CHAPTER 4

Affirmative Action and Racism

Affirmative Action

Inequality in America: Race, Poverty and fulfilling Democracy promises

Stephen Caliendo

History of Affirmative Action in America

The legal rights of persons of color—specifically those of African descent—to avoid discrimination emanate from the Fourteenth Amendment to the US Constitution. Passed as one of the three Civil War amendments, it includes a constitutional provision that guarantees citizens' rights be upheld and protected by the state governments, as well as the federal government. This amendment is at the center of many legal and theoretical conflicts relating to civil rights and civil liberties in the United States. Whereas the first ten amendments to the Constitution (the Bill of Rights) were believed to apply only to the federal government for much of our nation's history, a gradual incorporation of those constitutional provisions by the courts to apply to the states through the Fourteenth Amendment has resulted in more widespread protections for citizens. With respect to racial nondiscrimination, a series of Supreme Court cases has helped to clarify these protections, including the *Brown v. Board of Education* case that halted legally mandated racial segregation of public schools. Recall from Chapter 4, however, that the Court's decision in *Brown* pivoted on the psychological harm that was done to students of color as a result of being segregated from whites. It left open the question of what rights whites had with respect to actions by government and private institutions to increase diversity and/or account for historical injustice when making decisions that involved the selection of individuals for various positions.

A series of executive and legislative measures have also been enacted, beginning with New Deal–era requirements for avoidance of racial discrimination by employers and in public works programs[1] in the early part of the twentieth century. As we have seen, the most meaningful and sweeping antidiscrimination legislation has been the Civil Rights Act of 1964. Title VI of that law prohibits discrimination on the basis of race, color, or national origin by any entity that receives federal financial assistance; Title VII has clear language indicating that discrimination on the basis of sex is similarly prohibited.[2]

It is important to keep in mind the substantive difference between having a policy of nondiscrimination, which can only be enforced through legal proceedings in which someone complains of and proves that discrimination occurred, and policies of preferential treatment, which are designed to proactively address systemic inequality. The latter category of policies fall under the umbrella of affirmative action. In the 1960s, during the height of the civil rights movement, President Lyndon Johnson instigated an affirmative action policy through an executive order to force federal agencies to be attentive to their practices in hiring and awarding contracts with an eye toward avoiding discrimination.[3] Similar policies were adopted at the state level, and institutions of higher education began to use a variety of mechanisms to diversify the student body and to recognize that colorblind merit admission policies were by their nature disadvantageous to students who faced barriers to achieving those ostensibly objective markers (e.g., grade point average, board exam scores, ability to write a strong essay) that other applicants did not face (see Chapter 4).[4]

The friction generated by affirmative action policies stems from the reality that positions, whether in colleges or for employment, often reflect a zero-sum game—there are a set number of openings, with more applicants than opportunities. Traditional notions of meritocracy that are key aspects of American cultural identity suggest that individuals should compete based on their abilities and hard work and that factors that lie beyond the individual's control should never be taken into consideration.[5] The assumption of meritocracy, however, requires a relatively level playing field (or equal starting line, depending on the metaphor applied), which does not reflect the reality of American racial history. As the cartoon in Figure 4.1 suggests, whites were willing to deny access and opportunity to African Americans for centuries, and though now all Americans generally agree that racial discrimination (let alone slavery) is inappropriate, we are not nearly as willing to consider the consequences of persistent disadvantage that have arisen from those centuries of exclusion.

It is not difficult to understand why there is resistance. The limitation of the cartoon, of course, is that the same two characters appear in each of the six panes. Although the cartoonist needed to use this technique to be concise and convey a powerful message, he is unable to capture the important temporal dynamic that arises from current generations of whites claiming that they "never owned a slave." In the cartoon, the white racist in the first four panes is the same as the person who recognizes in the last two that racial prejudice and discrimination are wrong. Because the character equates racism (which is systemic) and prejudice (which is interpersonal), however, he refuses to take actions that would help to rectify past wrongs. He also feels that doing so would be equally improper because it relies on considerations of race. The notion that any consideration of race is racist has helped to perpetuate systems of disadvantage. Whites,

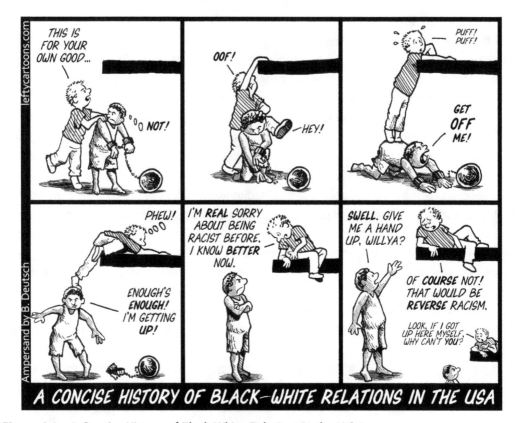

Figure 4.1   A Concise History of Black-White Relations in the U.S.A.

Source: Barry Deutsch, Amptoons.com (via Le yCartoons.com).

who still overwhelmingly control the levers of power in the United States, have been led to believe that the real racists are those who advocate a sophisticated consideration of systemic racism in public policymaking and public discourse.

On the other hand, affirmative action programs should not be viewed as the solution to America's racist past. We have had various forms of affirmative action policies in place for half a century, and as we have discovered, we are far from having a society where all races and ethnicities have the same opportunities for success. We have, however, made great progress in that time on a number of fronts, and while it would be improper to assume that affirmative action policies were solely responsible for that, dismissing them out of hand is also unwise. Instead, in order to appreciate the nuance and complexities of this controversial issue, we consider three Supreme Court cases that have given shape to affirmative action policy in the United States.

From Davis to Ann Arbor to Austin

The first meaningful test of affirmative action policy in the United States came when Allan Bakke, who is white, complained about being denied admission to the University of California–Davis medical school in 1973 and again in 1974. The program, he claimed, was unconstitutional because it denied him the opportunity to compete for all of the available seats in the incoming class. Each year, the school admitted one hundred applicants but had two separate admission programs. One program, which had eighty-four seats, was open to applicants of any race, ethnicity, or educational background. The other program was reserved for applicants who identified themselves as "economically and/or educationally disadvantaged" or members of a racial minority group. The benefit of being considered under the set-aside program was that one would not be compared to applicants in the other program and that the grade point average cutoff that applied to applicants in the other program was not in effect. Bakke's scores were higher than several of the students who were admitted under the second program, which meant that if he would have been permitted to compete for those seats, he would have been admitted. Though whites who were economically or educationally disadvantaged were eligible for consideration (Bakke was neither), none had been admitted in the four years that the program was in place. On this basis, Bakke argued that he was being denied equal protection under the Fourteenth Amendment by the state of California because of his race.

In *Regents of the University of California v. Bakke*,[6] the Supreme Court agreed with Bakke and ruled that such quota programs were unfair to whites (and unconstitutional), but the Court was clear that other types of programs that took race or other systemic disadvantage (including gender) into consideration were permissible. Specifically, the Court pointed to the plan that Harvard University used in admission, which considered racial minority status as a plus factor as part of a formula that contains a number of criteria for consideration. Justice Powell, who wrote the opinion for the Court, noted that race, as well as other characteristics, was part of the diversity that is valued in higher education. This established race as a factor standard that many institutions of higher education still use in admissions decisions.[7] It was precisely this type of plan that was challenged twenty-five years later when the Court heard the next case dealing with affirmative action in higher education.

In 2003 the Court considered two cases simultaneously, both relating to the University of Michigan. In *Gratz v. Bollinger*,[8] the Court struck down the policy that the university used for undergraduate admissions, but in *Grutter v. Bollinger*,[9] the Court upheld the policy being used by the law school. In essence, the Court felt that awarding twenty points to underrepresented racial and ethnic groups in the undergraduate program was disproportionate[10] and that institutions should take a more holistic approach to admissions decisions with respect to diversity. In the law school case, however, the Court found that the policy invoked a narrowly tailored approach to consider race in admissions decisions in a way that was consistent with its desire to have a diverse incoming class in order to enrich the educational experience. Because the law school did

BOX 4.1

Representing:

Justice Clarence Thomas

Only the second African American to be appointed to the US Supreme Court, Clarence Thomas has opposed racial preferences and affirmative action throughout his career. While critics argue that he benefited from affirmative action policies, Thomas has consistently claimed that he was harmed by the policy because he felt that it placed a stigma on him when he graduated from Yale University.

Thomas was born in rural Georgia in 1948 and grew up in the sort of abject poverty described in Chapter 3. There was no sewage system or paved roads. Thomas's mother worked as a housekeeper and accepted church charity to make ends meet. He learned to value education from his grandfather, with whom he lived during his formative years. Thomas was not insulated from racism; he dropped out of seminary in Missouri and even supported work of the Black Panthers while an undergraduate at Holy Cross. President Reagan appointed Thomas to a position in the Department of Education and later at the Equal Employment Opportunity Commission. After serving on the US Court of Appeals for a year, he was appointed by President George H. W. Bush to replace Justice Thurgood Marshall, who successfully argued the *Brown v. Board of Education school* desegregation case before the Supreme Court as a lawyer and who was the first African American to serve on the Court.

While Thomas clearly benefited from racial preferences on a number of occasions throughout his career, the humiliation he felt when he applied for jobs after graduating from Yale Law School stuck with him. That experience has affected his attitudes about affirmative action generally, as well as his ruling on racial preferences cases such as *Grutter v. Bollinger and Gratz v. Bollinger* (see below). Besides the stigmatization argument, Thomas believes that affirmative action programs in education are not effective because they do not guarantee assistance for minority students who may not be prepared to compete. Further, he agrees with those who argue that racial integration may not necessarily be beneficial to students of color. In fact, he has noted that forced integration suggests an underlying racism that "anything that is predominantly black must be inferior."

Opponents of racial preferences celebrate Thomas as a champion with credibility on the subject, while proponents dismiss him as a hypocrite and an opportunist. What is clear, however, is that Thomas's ideas about affirmative action have been shaped by his life experiences, and his justifications do not fall neatly in line with most of the people who agree with him on the issue. In many ways, Thomas embodies the complexity of an issue that has been oversimplified in American public discourse.[a]

---

a "Clarence Thomas," The Oyez Project, http://www.oyez.org/justices/clarence_thomas; Ariane de Vogue, "'Silent' Justice Outspoken on Affirmative Action," ABC News, September 30, 2007, http://abcnews.go.com/TheLaw/story?id=3667079; Maureen Dowd, "Could Thomas Be Right?" *New York Times*, June 25, 2003, http://www.nytimes.com/2003/06/25/opinion/could-thomas-be-right.html?src=pm.

not define diversity solely in terms of race or ethnicity and could award weight to an applicant's rating based on other factors that would enhance diversity, the Court, in a 5–4 decision, upheld the program. Justice Sandra Day O'Connor, who wrote the opinion, indicated that she hoped and expected that such policies would not be necessary in another twenty-five years (see Box 4.2). It is difficult to look into the future to determine the degree to which such policies will be necessary. Though rates of college graduation for African Americans are slowly increasing,[11] the gap between white student graduation rates and those of African Americans and Latinos[12] still exist. More relevant to this issue, however, is the degree to which students of color would be granted admission to colleges if affirmative action plans were not in place.

It did not take twenty-five years for the Court to come back to the issue this time. On October 10, 2012, the Supreme Court heard oral arguments in *Fisher v. University of Texas at Austin*.[13] Abigail Fisher, a white woman who was rejected by the University of Texas at Austin, complained that she had been denied equal treatment under the law as a result of the university's affirmative action policy. The Obama administration, as well as fourteen states, urged the Court to uphold racial preferences in college admissions.[14] At central issue in *Fisher* was whether colleges and universities had taken the Court's advice from *Grutter*, narrowing their use of racial preferences, or whether, as one scholar speculated, they have taken the *Grutter* decision "as a signal that court supervision of preferences would be lax."[15] Before the case was decided, some suspected that the Court would be more clear about how "disadvantage" must be defined so that economically challenged whites are not discriminated against and affluent applicants of color are not advantaged in such programs.[16] In the end, the Court vacated (set aside) the lower court's decision that the University of Texas's policy was constitutional. Justice Anthony Kennedy argued in his majority opinion that the 5th Circuit Court of Appeals did not apply strict scrutiny in its analysis of the program and ordered it to do so. He noted that for the policy to withstand constitutional muster, the burden was on the university to show that attempts to attain a diverse student body were "narrowly tailored to that goal." Opponents of affirmative action viewed the ruling as a victory (because it failed to uphold the existing policy), but so did supporters (because the Court did not rule that considering race in admission was unconstitutional).[17] Irrespective of how the Supreme Court eventually rules on this issue, we are left with two important and interrelated considerations.

First, affirmative action in college (or graduate/professional school) admissions is not a guarantee of a degree or a job. Once a student is admitted, he or she needs to do the same work as any other student to be successful. Given the tremendous disparities in K–12 education, many students of color who are admitted under affirmative action programs are not as well prepared for college as their white counterparts. In this way, such programs are not an effective interruption of the cycle of disadvantage, as they are essentially setting up those students for failure. Second, white students who attend underfunded schools are at a disadvantage if colleges do not consider economic or educational disadvantage in their admission process.[18] It has been argued that middle-class students of color who attend strong high schools also gain entrance under

BOX 4.2

Representing:

Justice Sandra Day O'connor

Three years before she retired from the US Supreme Court, Sandra Day O'Connor wrote one of the most relevant opinions regarding affirmative action in a generation. A Republican state legislator from Arizona, O'Connor was the first woman in the United States to be minority leader of a state senate and the first woman to serve on the Court.

O'Connor was born to rancher parents in southeastern Arizona during the Great Depression. The ranch had no electricity or running water until she was seven years old. O'Connor was sent to boarding school so that she had a chance for a quality education. She attended Stanford for her undergraduate degree and law school. She was appointed to the Arizona Court of Appeals for two years prior to taking her seat on the Supreme Court in 1981.

In *Grutter v. Bollinger*, O'Connor wrote for a 5–4 majority that the University of Michigan's law school admissions program, which takes racial minority status into account when making decisions, was constitutional and advanced the cause of providing for a better education through a diverse student body. She added that in twenty-five years, hopefully, racial preferences in higher education would be unnecessary. Seven years after that ruling, O'Connor wrote an essay clarifying that her "twenty-five years" remark was not meant to be a deadline, as many opponents of affirmative action inferred (and promised to hold the Court to that mark). What she meant was that social scientists should reexamine the educational benefits of diverse student bodies at that time.

While the Court has the opportunity to be counter-majoritarian (and thus protect minority rights), research has demonstrated that it rarely makes decisions that run contrary to public opinion on salient issues. George Washington University law professor Jeffrey Rosen notes that when the Court decided the *Bakke* case in 1978, public opinion was against affirmative action, so it was not surprising that the decision constrained efforts to increase racial minority enrollments in higher education. By 2003, however, when the University of Michigan cases were decided, the public was much more divided on the issue, which is consistent with the 5–4 decision in *Grutter*, as well as the decision in the companion case, *Gratz*, that limited affirmative action programs. We may never know the degree to which O'Connor or the other justices took public opinion into consideration as they reviewed the cases (and they may not know themselves), but such nuance in decisions reminds us that judges and justices, though they are not directly accountable to the people, are important aspects of representation in the United States.[a]

a   Thomas R. Marshall, *Public Opinion and the Supreme Court* (Boston: Unwin Hyman, 1989); Jeffrey Rosen, "Affirmative Action and Public Opinion," *New York Times*, May 23, 2011, http://www.nytimes.com/room-fordebate/2011/05/22/is-anti-white-bias-a-problem/affirmative-action-and-public-opinion; "Sandra Day O'Connor," Oyez Project, http:// www.oyez.org/justices/sandra_day_oconnor; Peter Schmidt, "Sandra Day O'Connor Revisits and Revives Affirmative-Action Controversy," *Chronicle of Higher Education*, January 14, 2010, http://chronicle.com/article/Sandra-Day-OConnor-Revisit/63523/.

affirmative action programs, and while that is not the intent of such programs (because those students can compete in a colorblind system), we must be careful not to extrapolate these few cases too broadly. As we have seen, race and poverty are still closely related in the United States, and even minority students from financially secure families face subconscious prejudice in schools in the form of tracking.[19] One study estimated that admission of racial minority students to the most selective colleges would be reduced by more than half without racially conscious affirmative action programs.[20]

Affirmative Action Beyond the Classroom

Affirmative action receives the most attention as it pertains to college and graduate/professional school admission, but it is important to consider its effect on employment and housing separately. Neither of these areas presupposes that individuals have a college education, so even if affirmative action programs are effective in higher education, they do not always lead to equality in housing opportunities or employment (the other two primary elements of the cycle of disadvantage). Further, even if a person who faced systemic disadvantage early in life obtains a college degree, subconscious (if not overt) racial prejudice is still a relevant factor in housing, as well as in hiring (see Chapters 3 and 5, respectively).

Affirmative action policies in employment work a bit differently than they do in higher education. Employers do not necessarily have a battery of comparable items to judge applicants by, as college admissions officials do, nor do employers usually have a set number of openings with all applicants submitting by a deadline. Consequently the sort of rankings and comparisons that are part of college admissions are not appropriate or possible for employers. Instead, employers monitor diversity in terms of hiring and promotion and, where necessary, develop policies to address deficiencies.[21] Most of the time such policies are voluntary, but occasionally a court orders a business to use affirmative action as a result of a lawsuit.[22] Hiring quotas based on race are illegal, yet many Americans (particularly whites) are suspicious about their use and have a personal story about someone in their family who was denied employment (or perceived that he or she was denied employment) for being white.

This disconnect is partially psychological in the sense that whites often have a nagging suspicion that they are being discriminated against in favor of persons of color, but it is also warranted in the sense that many companies have aggressive targets or goals in terms of diversity that tread dangerously close to the quota line (or at least feel that way to white applicants). Title VII of the Civil Rights Act of 1964[23] was designed to prohibit discrimination against persons of color in the workforce. The bill, as well as subsequent Court decisions (such as *Griggs v. Duke Power Company* 1971),[24] is clear that it is not enough for employers not to *intend* to discriminate (which would be a difficult measure to prove); they must proactively avoid discrimination. Proactively avoiding discrimination, however, is not the same as affirmative action. That standard merely represents a call for equal opportunity that is intentionally protected. Affirmative action programs, such as that which was at issue in the Court's 2009 *Ricci v. DeStefano*[25] decision, go farther by instituting procedures that actively seek racial and ethnic (or gender) diversity.[26]

With respect to housing, there are no formal affirmative action policies. Most of the effort in housing has been to ensure that persons of color are not discriminated against, but with respect to sales and rentals, there is no governmental mandate or widespread practice of ensuring diversity in neighborhoods. As noted in Chapter 3, there were efforts to increase homeownership among African Americans and Latinos through the mortgage agencies Fannie Mae and Freddie Mac (these nicknames refer to the Federal National Mortgage Association and the Federal Home Loan Mortgage Corporation, respectively), but those agencies were placed into conservatorship due to the housing crisis in 2008, meaning that the federal government took control of them. As a result, there is uncertainty as to the effect on minority borrowers if they must rely on private banks to lend without the backing of the US government.[27]

Affirmative Action Ballot Initiatives and Referendums

Measuring public opinion about affirmative action can be difficult, as is capturing public sentiment on any issue relating to race. Americans are sensitive to accusations of being racially prejudiced, and white Americans in particular tend to be concerned with being accused of being racist when they are not conscious of harboring any racial animosity. Most Americans favor affirmative action programs when asked directly and in the abstract, but when asked whether it is worth paying a price of disadvantaging whites to help minorities, a majority respond that it is not. Further, when asked specifically about "programs that give preferences in hiring, promotions and college admission," only preferences for the handicapped have a majority of support.[28] Further, some analysis has found that support for women receiving preferential treatment for affirmative action is greater than that for racial and ethnic minorities[29] and that white women have benefited most from affirmative action programs.[30] There can also be an interest effect such that women[31] and racial minorities[32] are more likely than men and whites, respectively, to prefer affirmative action programs. Further, whites who oppose affirmative action with respect to racial minorities often support it when it is alternately framed as a benefit to women. As might be expected, attitudes toward both types of affirmative action are related to prejudices toward women and racial minorities.[33, 34]

When voters have had the opportunity to weigh in on affirmative action through ballot initiative or referendum, they have mostly supported bans on race-conscious policies in hiring and school admission. The first state to adopt such a ban was California, which won approval of Proposition 209 in 1996. Prop 209, as it is known, is an amendment to Article I of the California constitution and reads as follows: "The state shall not discriminate against, or grant preferential treatment to, any individual or group on the basis of race, sex, color, ethnicity, or national origin in the operation of public employment, public education, or public contracting."[35] On its face, of course, the language is entirely race neutral and protects persons of all races and ethnicities from discrimination. The measure, though, was explicitly a response to California's affirmative action policies, and it ignores historical, systemic disadvantage for women and persons of color, assuming that each Californian starts at roughly the same point and therefore can be assured fair, unbiased competition for open positions.

As expected, Prop 209 started a trend. In 1997, Washington State passed Initiative 200; in 2006, the Michigan Civil Rights Initiative passed; in 2008, Nebraska voters passed Initiative 424; and in 2010, the Arizona Civil Rights Initiative was approved by voters. All of these measures were pushed and supported by California businessman Ward Connerly, who is multiracial (see Box 4.3). While three of his anti–affirmative action initiatives failed to be approved for ballots in 2008, the only one to fail that year was in Colorado (in an extremely close vote).[36]

To more clearly understand the dynamic of increased support for affirmative action programs that benefit women versus those that benefit persons of color, it is useful to consider some of the difference between legal challenges to affirmative action policies and ballot-based efforts to eliminate the practice. The plebiscite language almost always includes gender, as well as race, color, ethnicity, and national origin, but legal challenges are almost always narrowly targeted at advantages to persons of color (even though, as noted above, white women have benefited disproportionately from these programs). For example, the language for the Michigan measure in 2006 banned "affirmative action programs that give preferential treatment to groups or individuals based on their race, gender, color, ethnicity or national origin for public employment, education or contradicting purposes."[37] In the landmark University of Michigan cases that went before the US Supreme Court, though, whites brought the suits, alleging that the policies were unfairly beneficial to persons of color.[38] In cases that involve alleged discrimination, courts have different standards in determining whether a law relating to sex is constitutional as compared with a law relating to race. Sex-related issues are subjected to intermediate scrutiny, while race-related issues must pass strict scrutiny. This means that government policies that result in preferences or discrimination based on race are very difficult to sustain because the government must demonstrate that it has a compelling interest in having a law that on its face (i.e., without taking historical factors into consideration) discriminates and that the policy in place is narrowly tailored to achieve that interest. With respect to sex, however, government must only show that the law "further[s] an important government interest by means that are substantially related to that interest."[39] Accordingly, affirmative action policies that benefit women specifically are more likely to withstand legal scrutiny than those that specifically aim to address racial discrimination.[40]

Perhaps this is not surprising. Americans want to live in a race-neutral meritocracy and believe that we do. Many of us have friends (or at least friendly acquaintances) of different races and ethnicities. Most of us do not recognize racial resentment in ourselves, we celebrate Martin Luther King Day, and we do not use racial epithets, even when we are angry. Absent a purposeful

BOX 4.3

Representing:

Ward Connerly

As founder and president of the American Civil Rights Institute,[a] Ward Connerly advocates for equal treatment of American citizens irrespective of race or ethnicity. He is the author of two books: *Creating Equal: My Fight Against Race Preferences*[b] and *Lessons from My Uncle James: Beyond Skin Color to the Content of Our Character.*[c]

Connerly is most widely known for supporting affirmative action bans in a number of states since the mid-1990s. Rather than lobbying representatives to sponsor legislation and advocate for passage, he used the plebiscite option that is available in twenty-four states. In some states, ballot measures must be passed by state legislatures before they can be presented to the public for a vote, but in other states, signatures can be collected for presentation, thus bypassing elected officials altogether. Ballot initiatives or referendums are not permissible at the federal level under the US Constitution.

After a high-profile victory in his home state, California, he helped usher in similar bans in Michigan, Washington, Arizona, and Nebraska. Several other attempts failed to win ballot placement, and one (in Colorado) failed. In 2003, Connerly backed California Proposition 54, which would have amended the state constitution to prohibit using racial classifications at all. It was soundly defeated, garnering only about 36 percent of the vote. Connerly claimed that classifying people by race or ethnicity is antiquated and divisive, but opponents persuasively argued that the measure would have hindered medical treatment that sometimes is more effective when tailored to specific ethnic or racial groups.

Though his record of success is mixed, Connerly has been a vocal champion of the vision of American society that Martin Luther King imagined. Critics claim that his vision of a colorblind society, while laudable, is premature and that America has yet to do the hard work to get us to a place where we can be judged not on the color of our skin but on the content of our character. Connerly is of mixed racial descent, and he has said that the continual race mixing in the United States is making racial classifications irrelevant. Such a view challenges the reality of racism in the United States today, but it is consistent with the fact that race is a social, not a biological, construct. While we cannot know for sure how long it will take for America to truly be majority-minority (in terms of number of citizens, as well as power balance), it seems inevitable that sooner or later, the United States will be characterized by a numerical minority of whites. When that happens, we can expect another shift in the way we talk about race and racism in America.[d]

---

a http://www.acri.org.

b Ward Connerly, *Creating Equal: My Fight Against Race Preferences* (San Francisco, CA: Encounter).

c Ward Connerly, *Lessons from My Uncle James: Beyond Skin Color to the Content of Our Character* (San Francisco: Encounter).

d National Conference of State Legislatures, "Initiative, Referendum and Recall," 2011, http://www.ncsl.org/default.aspx?tabid=16600; Tanya Schevitz, "Prop. 54 Defeated Soundly/State Initiative on Racial Privacy Raised Issues about Health, Education," *San Francisco Chronicle*, October 8, 2003, http://www.sfgate.com/politics/article/Prop-54-defeated-soundly-State-initiative-on-2583626.php; "Ward Connerly," American Civil Rights Institute, 2007, http://www.acri.org/ward_bio.html; Zevloff, "After Colorado Loss, Ward Connerly May Pull the Plug on Affirmative-Action Bans."

recognition and consideration of the complexities described in this book, the language of these ballot proposals fits neatly with our core values and beliefs about what America *should* be.

The primary difference between proponents of bans on affirmative action policies and supporters of affirmative action is the degree to which they are willing to acknowledge the systemic effects of historical discrimination and prejudice. Neither Ward Connerly nor Jesse Jackson[41] hates America or is trying to leverage personal gain from the policies they champion. They may disagree about the degree to which discrimination persists, the potential stigmatizing effect on minorities as a result of the programs, the value of racial diversity in the workplace and schools, and the degree to which whites are harmed by racially conscious policies, but it would be difficult to argue that either man does not have the best interest of the country at heart.

Reasonable people can (and do) disagree about the ability of affirmative action programs to appropriately rectify systemic disadvantages or lead to more racial equality. To be considered to be reasonable, however, each of us must seriously and honestly reflect on the various ways that we may be advantaged or disadvantaged by a system that is rooted in fundamental inequality. Most Americans would agree that a colorblind—or at least color neutral—society would be preferable, but we are unable to wish away the realities of the lingering racism that continues to characterize American society.

Summary

Legal rights aside, most Americans (not just whites) do not really understand how affirmative action programs are designed, what they are intended to do, or whether they are effective. An honest, holistic appraisal reveals that the evidence of the effectiveness of such programs is inconclusive. Anecdotally, we can point to individuals who were provided opportunities (and were able to capitalize on them). It is more difficult to measure the long-term psychological effects on whites, many of whom feel as if they are at a disadvantage for college admission and employment, and minorities, some of whom might interpret acceptance under these programs as a tacit indicator of their unworthiness[42] (see Boxes 4.1 and 4.3). Under these circumstances, we need to decide whether affirmative action programs do more harm than good or, put another way, whether America would be a more just and equitable nation if we did not have them.

Ultimately, affirmative action programs serve more as a bandage than a cure, with most proponents believing that removing such programs would exacerbate the inequality that still exists.[43] Others believe that affirmative action programs will lead to a colorblind, gender-neutral society.[44] Opponents, however, believe that the bandage is keeping the wound from healing properly. From any perspective, it is clear that a permanent solution to America's persistent racial and economic inequality must be found elsewhere.

Notes

1 Terry H. Anderson, *The Pursuit of Fairness: A History of Affirmative Action* (New York: Oxford University Press, 2004); Anderson, "The Strange Career of Affirmative Action," *South Central Review* 22, no. 2 (2005): 110–129; Carl E. Brody, "A Historical Review of Affirmative Action and the Interpretation of Its Legislative Intent by the Supreme Court," *Akron Law Review* 29 (1996): 291–337; Ira Katznelson, *When Affirmative Action Was White: An Untold History of Racial Inequality in Twentieth-Century America* (New York: Norton, 2005).

2 Brody, "Historical Review of Affirmative Action."

3 James W. Button and Barbara A. Rienzo, "The Impact of Affirmative Action: Black Employment in Six Southern Cities," *Social Science Quarterly* 84, no. 1 (2003): 1–14, as cited in Faye J. Crosby, Aarti Iyer, and Sirinda Sincharoen, "Understanding Affirmative Action," *Annual Review of Psychology* 57 (2006): 585–611.

4 For an in-depth study of affirmative action in higher education admission, see William Bowen and Derek Bok, *The Shape of the River: Long-Term Consequences of Considering Race in College and University Admissions* (Princeton: Princeton University Press, 2000).

5 Steven N. Durlauf, "Affirmative Action, Meritocracy, and Efficiency," *Politics, Philosophy, and Economics* 7, no. 2 (2008): 131–158; H. Roy Kaplan, "Racial Inequality and 'Meritocracy': A Closer Look," *Racism Review,* April 22, 2011, http://www.racismreview.com/blog/2011/04/22/racial-inequality-and-meritocracy-a-closer-look/.

6 438 US 265, http://www.law.cornell.edu/supct/html/historics/USSC_CR_0438_0265_ZS.html.

7 US Commission on Civil Rights, "The Commission, Affirmative Action, and Current Challenges Facing Equal Opportunity in Education," March 2003, http://www.usccr.gov/aaction/ccraa.htm, n7.

8 539 US 244, http://www.law.cornell.edu/supct/html/02-516.ZS.html.

9 539 US 306, http://www.law.cornell.edu/supct/html/02-241.ZS.html.

10 The scale used for ranking was 150 points; a score of 100 was needed to guarantee admission. Twelve points were awarded to applicants who had a perfect score on the Scholastic Aptitude Test (SAT), three points for an outstanding essay, and twenty points for being a scholarship athlete. A perfect grade point average was worth eighty points. Walter E. Williams, "Affirmative Action or Racism," George Mason University, January 27, 2003, http://econfaculty.gmu.edu/wew/articles/03/aa.html.

11 "Black Student College Graduation Rates Inch Higher but a Large Racial Gap Persists," *Journal of Blacks in Higher Education*, 2007, http://www.jbhe.com/preview/winter07preview.html.

12 Bill and Melinda Gates Foundation, "Low Hispanic College Graduation Rates Threaten U.S. Attainment Goals," March 18, 2010, http://www.gates foundation.org/media-center/Press-Releases/2010/03/Low-Hispanic-College-Graduation-Rates-Threaten-US-Attainment-Goals.

13 570 US__ http://www.law.cornell.edu/supremecourt/text/11-345.

14 "New York, 13 Other States Back Affirmative Action Policy," *(Memphis) Commercial Appeal*, August 14, 2012, http://www.commercialappeal.com/news/2012/aug/14/ny-13-other-states-back-affirmative-action-policy/.

15 Richard Sander and Stuart Taylor Jr., "Why the Court Wants to Try Again," *Washington Post*, September 30, 2012, http://www.washingtonpost.com/opinions/supreme-court-wants-another-shot-at-affirmative-action/2012/09/30/82cd260e-0b28-11e2-bb5e-492c0d30bff6_story.html.

16 David Leonhardt, "Rethinking Affirmative Action," *New York Times*, October 13, 2012, http://www.nytimes.com/2012/10/14/sunday-review/rethinking-affirmative-action.html.

17 Katey Psencik, "Both Sides Claim Victory in Fisher v. UT," *USA Today*, June 25, 2013, http://www.usatoday.com/story/news/nation/2013/06/25/fisher-ut-supreme-court/2457939/.

18 In the wake of *Fisher*, some affirmative action advocates have shifted their attention to socioeconomic status and away from race as a direct consideration. Bill Keller, "Affirmative Reaction," *New York Times*, June 9, 2013, http://www.nytimes.com/2013/06/10/opinion/keller-affirmative-reaction.html. It is important to keep in mind, though, that considering income would have a different result than considering wealth. Using zip codes might achieve the desired result (given the robust economic and racial segregation in the United States) without violating constitutional principles relating to white students' civil rights. David Leonhardt, "The Liberals Against Affirmative Action," *New York Times*, March 9, 2013, http://www.nytimes.com/2013/03/10/sunday-review/the-liberals-against-affirmative-action.html.

19 Sam Barr, "Weighing In: Class-Based Affirmative Action Good, but Arguments Against Race-Based Affirmative Action Still Bad," *Harvard Political Review*, December 11, 2010, http://hpronline.org/hprgument/weighing-in-class-based-affirmative-action-good-but-arguments-against-race-based-affirmative-action-still-bad/.

20 Bowen and Bok, *Shape of the River*, chap. 2.

21 Faye J. Crosby et al., "Affirmative Action: Psychological Data and the Policy Debates," *American Psychologist* 58, no. 2 (2003): 93–115.

22 Barbara F. Reskin, *The Realities of Affirmative Action in Employment* (Washington DC: American Sociological Association, 1998).

23 The full text of the bill as amended is available at http://www.eeoc.gov/laws/statutes/titlevii.cfm.

24 In this case, the Court ruled that ostensibly race-neutral policies (such as an IQ test and the require-ment of holding a high school diploma at a time when far fewer African Americans than whites did so) that are not directly related to the job to be performed are unconstitutional if they cause a "disparate impact" on a protected class of citizens, according to Title VII of the Civil Rights Act of 1964. 401 US 424, http://www.law.cornell.edu/supct/html/historics/USSC_CR_0401_0424_ZO.html.

25 In this case, twenty firefighters (nineteen of whom were white) who had passed a test for promotion sued the city of New Haven, Connecticut, for invalidating the results of the test because no African Americans qualified for promotion. The city claimed that it did so out of fear of a lawsuit by the black firefighters. The Court ruled, in a 5–4 decision, that the city violated Title VII of the Civil Rights Act of 1964 by denying promotions to the twenty firefighters who earned them by passing the test. 557 US___. Available at http://www.law.cornell.edu/supct/html/07-1428.ZS.html.

26 Crosby et al., "Affirmative Action," 94–95.

27 National Public Radio, *Tell Me More*, "End of Fannie Mae, Freddie Mac Will Affect Minorities," February 15, 2011, http://www.npr.org/2011/02/15/133777142/End-Of-Fannie-Mae-Freddie-Mac-Will-Affect-Minorities.

28 PollingReport.com, "Race and Ethnicity," 2011, http://www.pollingreport.com/race.htm.

29 David C. Wilson et al., "Affirmative Action Programs for Women and Minorities: Expressed Support Affected by Question Order," *Public Opinion Quarterly* 72, no. 3 (2008): 514–522.

30 Richard J. Hill, "Minorities, Women, and Institutional Change: Some Administrative Concerns," *Sociological Perspectives* 26, no. 1 (1983): 17–28; Tim Wise, "Is Sisterhood Conditional? White Women and the Rollback of Affirmative Action," *NWSA Journal* 10, no. 3 (1998): 1–26.

31 Lawrence Bobo, "Race, Interests, and Beliefs about Affirmative Action," *American Behavioral Scientist* 41, no. 7 (1998): 985–1003; David A. Kravitz and Judith Platania, "Attitudes and Beliefs About Affirmative Action: Effects of Target and of Respondent Sex and Ethnicity," *Journal of Applied Psychology* 78, no. 6 (1993): 928–938; Linda J. Sax and Marisol Arredondo, "Student Attitudes Toward Affirmative Action in College Admissions," *Research in Higher Education* 40, no. 4 (1999): 439–459; but see Dawn Michelle Baunach, "Attitudes Toward Gender-Based Affirmative Action," *Sociological Focus* 35, no. 4 (2002): 345–362.

32 Baunach, "Attitudes Toward Gender-Based Affirmative Action"; Sax and Arredond, "Student Attitudes Toward Affirmative Action in College Admissions"; Dara Z. Strolovitch, "Playing Favorites: Public Attitudes Toward Race-and Gender-Targeted Anti-discrimination Policy," *NWSA Journal* 10, no. 3 (1998): 27–53.

33 James R. Kluegel and Eliot R. Smith, "Affirmative Action Attitudes: Effects of Self-Interest, Racial Affect, and Stratification Beliefs on Whites' Views," *Social Forces* 61, no. 3 (1983): 797–824; Amy C. Steinbugler, Julie E. Press, and Janice Johnson Dias, "Gender, Race, and Affirmative Action:

Operationalizing Intersectionality in Survey Research," *Gender & Society* 20, no. 6 (2006): 805–825; Steven A. Tuch and Michael Hughes, "Whites' Racial Policy Attitudes in the Twenty-First Century: The Continuing Significance of Racial Resentment," *Annals of the American Academy of Political and Social Science* 634 (2011): 134–152.

34 Other demographic characteristics have also been found to affect attitudes about affirmative action. For instance, one study found that working women who have daughters are more likely to support affirmative action programs for women than those who do not, though there was no such effect for men with daughters. Anastasia H. Prokos, Chardie L. Baird, and Jennifer Reid Keene, "Attitudes About Affirmative Action for Women: The Role of Children in Shaping Parents' Interests," *Sex Roles* 62 (2010): 347–360.

35 "Proposition 209: Text of Proposed Law," 1996, http://vote96.sos.ca.gov/Vote96/html/BP/209text.htm.

36 Naomi Zevloff, "After Colorado Loss, Ward Connerly May Pull the Plug on Affirmative-Action Bans," *Colorado Independent*, November 7, 2008, http://coloradoindependent.com/14617/ward-connerly-may-pull-the-plug. For an overview of plebiscite measures to eliminate affirmative action, see Jessica Larson and Stephen Menendian, "Anti-Affirmative Action Ballot Initiatives," Kirwan Institute for the Study of Race and Ethnicity, Ohio State University, 2008, http://research.kirwaninstitute.org/publications/anti-affirmative_action_ballot_initiatives_report.pdf.

37 Justin Miller, "Ballot Wording Called Fair," *Michigan Daily*, January 9, 2006, http://www.michigandaily.com/content/ballot-wording-called-fair.

38 In *Gratz* v. *Bollinger* (the undergraduate program case), Jennifer Gratz and Patrick Hamacher brought suit; in *Grutter* v. *Bollinger* (the law school program case), Barbara Grutter brought suit. All three litigants are white, and two of the three (at least one in each case) are female.

39 Legal Information Institute, "Strict Scrutiny," 2010, http://www.law.cornell.edu/wex/strict_scrutiny.

40 For this reason, the Court's upholding of the University of Michigan Law School's policy is particularly noteworthy in *Grutter*.

41 Reverend Jackson has been a vocal supporter of affirmative action policies. He drafted a statement after attending oral arguments for the University of Michigan cases at the US Supreme Court in 2003, which can be read here: http://www.inmotionmagazine.com/opin/supreme.html.

42 Bowen and Bok, *Shape of the River*.

43 See, for instance, Cornel West, *Race Matters* (New York: Vintage, 1993).

44 James P. Sterba, *Affirmative Action for the Future* (Ithaca, NY: Cornell University Press, 2009).

Discussion Questions

1   What is affirmative action?

2   How did affirmative action become a law?

3   Does the assumption of meritocracy create a level playing field for all racial groups in America?

4   In what two areas other than education is affirmative action not implicitly applied?

5   Describe some of the legal challenges of upholding affirmative action when referring to disadvantaged persons of color?

CHAPTER 5

Miseducation of Racism in the US

Teaching Historical Understanding with Christopher Columbus

Benjamin Justice

Context: TE Elementary, TE Secondary, K–6, 7–12, University

NCSS Standards: I (Culture), II (Time, Continuity, and Change), VI (Power, Authority, and Governance)

INTASC Standards: 1 (Subject Matter), 4 (Instructional Strategy)

Topics: history, historical understanding, Christopher Columbus, indigenous peoples, historical figures, historical content knowledge, multiple perspectives, creating teaching materials, jig-saw, children's literature

I'm a big fan of Christopher Columbus. Not the man, the phenomenon. Columbus plays a major role in how historians, teachers, and popular media talk about the past. For the big winners of the Atlantic encounter—those Europeans who settled North America and accumulated vast wealth—the story has typically been told as a triumph, a grand narrative with a happy ending. For those people who lost in the exchange—the people of Africa, the Americas, and others—the story is a disaster. The moment when Columbus touched land in the Caribbean marks the beginning of one of the greatest shifts in human history: the appropriation of the land and resources of two continents by the people of a third; the depopulation by accident or disease, or, some argue, by conscious policy, of tens of millions of people in North and South America; the abduction and wanton killing of tens of millions of Africans to work as slaves on that "new land." In any case, triumph, disaster, or pivotal moment, Columbus, more than any other historical figure I have yet encountered, can serve to create the necessary cognitive dissonance for future social studies teachers to unlearn what society tells them history is for, what heroes are made of, and how social studies instruction can be a force for inequality and racism or, instead, for democracy and thoughtful inquiry.

I devote an entire session to Columbus in each of my two social studies methods courses. What follows is a description of how we examine Columbus (the phenomenon) as a complicated historical and cultural symbol. The first case is an elementary methods course where I ask students to consider how an alternative reading of the Columbian encounter troubles the traditional representation of Columbus as a hero. The second case, a secondary methods course, utilizes Seixas' (2000) and Segall's (2006) curricular and disciplinary representations to ask students to question how they will design and teach curriculum about a complicated historical and cultural figure. In both cases, the primary goal is not to indoctrinate students into one line of thinking or another—Columbus as hero or Columbus as villain, for example. Rather, the goal is to disrupt the notion that there can be a single, definitive narrative of the Columbian encounter, and that fashioning such a narrative is not only an act of interpretation, it is an imposition of the present onto the past.

Elementary Methods Course

In my course "Teaching Social Studies in the Elementary School," Columbus fits into a broader discussion about history and hero worship. Throughout the course I ask students to wrestle with related notions in social studies curriculum and pedagogy: how does social studies convey notions of justice and injustice, racism and antiracism? What does it mean to understand something and how can we teach for understanding? And what the heck is social studies anyway?

In preparation for the Columbus class, I assign "The True Importance of Christopher Columbus," a chapter from Loewen's *Lies My Teacher Told Me* (1996), and "Unsung Heroes" and "Teaching About Unsung Heroes" from Au, Bigelow, and Karp's (2007) *Rethinking Our Classrooms*, Vol. 2. I also assign groups of students a particular children's book related to the Atlantic encounter, including Yolen's *Encounter* (1996), Dorris's *Morning Girl* (1992), Conrad's *Pedro's Journal* (1999), Fritz's *Where Do You Think You're Going, Christopher Columbus?* (1997), and Roop and Roop's *Christopher Columbus* (2001). In their weekly essays written in preparation for class, many students express outrage that, according to Loewen, Columbus oversaw the enslavement, torture, rape, and eventual genocide of the people he encountered. Some argue that Loewen is exaggerating. A few make the case that replacing Columbus the hero with Columbus the villain is equally problematic: we cannot judge people in the past by contemporary standards.

In my actual lesson plan I try to model what would be effective approaches to Columbus in an elementary classroom. I ask students to coteach portions of the class with me, and this past year the students began by making a web map of the word *hero*, on the board, plotting words that people associate with that concept. They then asked their classmates to name personal heroes from their own childhoods and then explain their choices. In a large group discussion we examined the historical perspective that Loewen articulates about Columbus. I began by asking students for their gut reactions to the piece. I then asked them to identify Loewen's argument and to evaluate his evidence. One of Loewen's claims is that the mythical Columbus is ubiquitous, and to that end I had students meet in jig-sawed book-review groups to share their particular book with others who had not read it. Groups looked for how each of their books jibed with the evidence Loewen presents, and then picked their most and least favorite.

Nearly all groups selected *Morning Girl* or *Encounter* as the best of the lot, and this raised an important question. Both books are highly fictionalized accounts of Columbus's encounter with the Taino people, based on almost no historical evidence. I challenged their choices. If Loewen's argument is that the Columbus myth relies on lies and withheld information, how can *Morning Girl* and *Encounter* be excellent books? Many hands shot up, and the two students who spoke made the point that seemed to speak for all the hands: These two books may be fiction, but they offer something kids almost never get: an indigenous perspective on Columbus.

Discussion

My goal is that my student teachers will understand the tension between doing good, ethically responsible history and using history as political tool. This understanding should lead, I hope, to the recognition that history has multiple, equally valid perspectives on the one hand, and also depends on the use of good evidence and clear reasoning on the other. Teaching kids "the facts" is sometimes a subversive act, but can also be a repressive one. Making the choice to teach Columbus as a hero is not a neutral decision, but a biased one which negates the historical record and the perspectives of many Americans. An uncritical view of Columbus as an unscrupulous villain has similar problems. My recent addition of the *Rethinking Classrooms* pieces on hero worship has, I hope, added to students' understanding of what it means to pluck a hero from history, and the very limited way that Columbus functions in that capacity. This year's children's literature jigsaw indicated that most of the class, at least, understood that Native Americans had perspectives as valid as European ones, and that we as historians need to navigate among these and other ways of seeing the past.

Secondary Methods Course

Unlike the elementary student teachers, the men and women in this course typically hold BAs in history or other social studies-related fields. In my course "Analysis of Social Studies Curriculum," which comes at the end of our EdM program, I ask students to dig into the underlying theory of the fields of history and social studies. Columbus provides a chance for them to grapple with ways in which historical narratives serve political ends; but it also provides an opportunity to see how scholarship changes over time, how scholars actually do history, and how the many other academic disciplines within social studies can converge.

I design the lesson in the same fashion as the elementary class. In advance I assign the Loewen chapter to all students and assign particular groups select pages from scholarly books on the encounter. Each year I try to update the list, and this year it will include: *Cortés and Montezuma* (Collis, 1954); *The Broken Spears* (Leon-Portilla, 1962); *The Columbian Exchange* (Crosby, 1972); and *Guns, Germs, and Steel* (Diamond, 1997). We begin class by discussing Loewen. After students share their gut reactions, we dig into questions of evidence and argument. I focus the discussion less on Loewen's argument that Columbus is mistaught in textbooks than his claim that the Columbus myth is inherently White-supremacist. In this group of students, only a few argue that Columbus should be a national hero, and accuse naysayers of being hypercritical, too liberal, or America haters. As the discussion unfolds, I challenge them to answer the question: Is Loewen's argument about Columbus the final word, or are there alternatives?

I then break students into groups to discuss their book assignment with others who read the same. I ask them to identify the argument, the evidence, the strengths and weaknesses, and report back to the class. On the board, I chart group responses to each book, including a new concept, "unit of analysis" (a unit of analysis is the building block of a historical argument). As groups discuss their books, they see how units of analysis have changed with each scholarly argument: Collis looks at great men; Leon-Portillo focuses on national groups from a native perspective; Crosby examines flora and fauna; and Diamond looks at the biggest unit yet: the geographic distribution of humans across the planet for the last 10,000 years (this book is more anthropology than history). Students concede that each book makes excellent use of evidence, is convincing, and tries to "revise" scholarship that came before it. Each has strengths as well as weaknesses. And yet, each is so completely different!

As my culminating activity, I create jigsaw groups that consist of representatives from each book group. I charge these new groups with developing an actual curriculum for the encounter between Europe, Africa, and the Americas. I use Peter Seixas's (2000) three models for social studies instruction. Some groups must write a "best story" textbook entry. Others must create a curriculum using either a disciplinary or postmodern approach. Each group reports back and we debrief. The disciplinary groups usually have the easiest time. They identify primary source documents, come up with interesting activities, and aim to help children develop their own interpretations of the past. The postmodern groups typically emphasize Internet research into the politics of Columbus Day, looking at how various people and groups seek to construct narratives of Columbus as a political act. One year the postmodern group designed an activity where kids critically analyze their textbooks. Every year, the group in charge of writing a textbook entry has the hardest time. Their struggle highlights many of the problems inherent in the production of ostensibly "neutral" historical narratives: How can one story of the past suffice?

Discussion

My goal for this Columbian encounter is that students will understand the process of how history gets made, and in so doing, better understand what social studies is really about: identifying genuine social questions or problems and using reasoned inquiry (through disciplines such as history) to generate answers. In the case of the Columbus phenomenon, any narrative of who Columbus was is a product of a series of choices—of units of analysis, of which evidence to include and exclude, of where the story begins and ends, of whose perspective we take. In this way of thinking, Columbus is neither a villain nor a hero, but a work in progress.

References

Segall, A. (2006). What's the purpose of teaching a discipline, anyway? The case of history. In A. Segall, E. E. Heilman, & C. H. Cherryholmes (Eds.), *Social studies—The next generation: Re-searching in the postmodern* (pp. 125–139). New York: Lang.

Seixas, P. (2000). "Schweigen, die kinder!" or, does postmodern history have a place in the schools. In P. Stearns, P. Sexias, & S. Wineberg (Eds.), *Knowing, teaching, and learning history: National and international perspectives* (pp. 19–37). New York: New York University Press.

Teaching Resources

Elementary Methods Course

Au, W., Bigelow, B. & Karp, S. (Eds). (2007). *Rethinking our classrooms: Teaching for equity and social justice* (Vol. 1). Williston, VT: Rethinking Schools.

Bigelow, B. (Ed.). (2001) *Rethinking our classrooms: Teaching for equity and social justice* (Vol. 2). Williston, VT: Rethinking Schools.

Conrad, P. (1999). *Pedro's journal: A voyage with Christopher Columbus.* New York: Scholastic.

Dorris, M. (1992). *Morning girl.* New York: Hyperion.

Fritz, J. (1997). *Where do you think you're going, Christopher Columbus?* New York: Putnam & Grosset.

Loewen, J. (1996). *Lies my teacher told me: Everything your American history textbook got wrong.* New York: Simon & Schuster.

Roop, P., & Roop, C. (2001). *Christopher Columbus (in their own words).* New York: Scholastic.

Yolen, J. (1996). *Encounter.* New York: Harcourt Children's Books.

Secondary Methods Course

Collis, M. (1954). *Corté s and Montezuma.* London: Faber & Faber.

Crosby, A. (1972). *The Columbian exchange: Biological and cultural consequences of 1492.* Westport, CT: Greenwood Press.

Diamond, J. (1997). *Guns, germs, and steel: The fates of human societies.* New York: Norton.

Hoxie, F. E. (1992, December). Discovering America: Ani. *The Journal of American History, 79*(3), 835–840.

Leon-Portilla, M. (1962). *The broken spears: The Aztec account of the conquest of Mexico.* Boston: Beacon Press.

Discussion Questions

1   How is Christopher Columbus a complicated historical and cultural figure?

2   Why is there a dissonance with the Christopher Columbus of the past and the one we need for the future?

3   Describe the experiences of the "Natives" from their point of view?

4   The truth about history is that one story cannot suffice. It is all about understanding the process of how history is made and identifying the problems with it. How true is this statement?

5   "Christopher Columbus is neither a hero nor a villain but a work in progress." Discuss.

Braided Histories and Experiences in Literature for Children and Adolescents

María Paula Ghiso, Gerald Campano, and Ted Hall

This study examines how intergroup histories and experiences are represented in children's literature to foster social justice inquiry.

"'There's no unraveling the rope. We're all in this together.'"
—Louise Erdrich (Goodman & Erdrich, 2008)

Louise Erdrich's (2008) novel *The Plague of Daves* traces how a community copes with the traumatic legacy of the vigilante lynching of four innocent Native Americans on a reservation town in North Dakota. Drawing on an actual historical hanging of a thirteen-year-old in 1897, the novel depicts the not-always-obvious intergenerational impact of murder and injustice, while employing elements of magical realism to conjure possibilities of survival and healing. It also explores difficult issues about identity and shared history. Midway through the novel, one of the main protagonists, Evelina, reflects on her own and others' hereditary implication in the original violent episode and thinks to herself, "Now that some of us have mixed in the spring of our existence both guilt and victim, there is no unraveling the rope" (p. 243). The image of a tangled rope that cannot be unraveled, thematically linked to the noose, is a grim symbol for intergroup history and experience. Yet, it is also an honest and unflinching metaphor, especially when understood within a larger national record that not only includes the conquest of indigenous communities but also the degradations of chattel slavery and Jim Crow. The past cannot be undone, Erdrich seems to suggest, and will forever dangle before our efforts to progress.

Maria Paula Ghiso, Gerald Campano and Ted Hall, "Braided Histories and Experiences in Literature for Children and Adolescents," *Journal of Children's Literature*, vol. 38, no. 2, pp. 14-22. Copyright © 2012 by Children's Literature Assembly.

The Gordian knot of shared history does not imply a unidirectional backward orientation, a need to exhume the past at the expense of the future. Evelina's thoughts, and life, also connote the possibility of growth and regeneration. The younger generations are in the "spring of … existence" and, reminiscent of the poet Derek Walcott's (1998) characterization of his own Creole inheritance as the "soldering of two great worlds, like the halves of a fruit seamed by its own bitter juice" (p. 64), the soil of their mixed heritage has been cross-pollinated with the seed of "both guilt and victim." These youths embody the insight that "the other" may not be so absolutely other, but rather inheres—culturally, historically, and often physiologically—within us by virtue of our shared humanity. Taking full measure of the past is necessary for a fertile future, which entails the ethical revelation that not only are we implicated in one another's histories but in fact our futures are also ineluctably intertwined, despite efforts to segregate our experiences; or, as commented on by Erdrich (who is of Ojibwe, German, and French descent) in an interview about the novel, "We're all in this together" (Goodman & Erdrich, 2008).

This article explores how children's literature might provide a resource for students to explore how we are indeed "all in this together." This question has significance because, following Erdrich, we believe that a nuanced understanding of our togetherness is a necessary precondition for the interrelated processes of redressing past injustices, surviving the present, and working toward a better future. At some point in their education, students—if they are fortunate—may have the opportunity to read adult novels such as *The Plague of Doves,* most likely as part of a high school or college curriculum. Yet, children's literature remains a primary vehicle for intellectual and imaginative maturation, and it is thus important to ask whether younger students have the opportunity to transact with books that represent and raise questions about shared experiences and cooperation across social, cultural, and linguistic boundaries. We examine three promising texts from our larger study that provide a platform for investigating braided histories. Through these books, we illustrate ideological shifts in representation and draw out potential theoretical and pedagogical implications.

Theoretical Perspectives

Researchers have noted the importance of youth engaging with literature that reflects their identities and provides opportunities for honing critical sensibilities (e.g., Cai, 1997; DeNicolo & Fránquiz, 2006; Harris, 2003; Wolf, 2004). For example, the recent *Handbook of Research on Children's and Young Adult Literature* (Wolf, Coats, Enciso, & Jenkins, 2011) includes chapters with LGBT themes (Blackburn & Clark, 2011), Latino/a literature (Fránquiz, Martínez-Roldán, & Mercado, 2011), the history and development of African American children's literature (Bishop, 2011), and the politics of representing Native American experiences (Bradford, 2011). Additionally, there is a burgeoning body of children's literature authors—many of them also included in the handbook—who strive to provide a greater range of cultural representations, as well as capture how some of these identities overlap. Jacqueline Woodson described her blended identities as "I'm a writer who's black; I'm a writer who's female; I'm a writer who's gay. Those different identities weave themselves into the writing. But I'm not just one of those things" (Patton, 2006, p. 48).

Despite progress in the publishing field, children's literature does not fully reflect the world of many 21st-century schools, which increasingly house students who communicate in numerous languages, claim multiple identities, and often have ties that extend beyond our nation's borders (Campano & Ghiso, 2011). One possible avenue for addressing students' identities is the continued commitment to providing texts that echo students' experiences and portray a multiplicity of cultural, linguistic, and migratory representations within any given community. The project of expanding the canon to include the "dense particularities" (Mohanty, 1997, p. 130) of specific group experiences needs to continue with vigor. However, it may be equally important to examine how our "differences are intertwined" (Mohanty, 1997, p. 130): how various communities' histories and experiences do not merely occupy insular spaces but have also been, and continue to be, braided in ways that both reinforce power asymmetries and promote intergroup social, political, and imaginative cooperation.

This article draws on theoretical frameworks that attempt to navigate two ostensibly opposite, but really quite compatible, tendencies: the Scylla of a postmodern relativism and multiculturalism, in which students may acknowledge one another's cultural spaces and celebrate differences but not probe deeply into either structural inequality or social cooperation; and the Charybdis of an idealized notion of common humanity that transcends difference. Our study is inspired by interdisciplinary frameworks that include realist theories of identity (e.g., Mohanty, 1997; Moya, 2000) that value people's perspectives and identities as a source of knowledge, intersectional approaches to understanding multiple oppressions (e.g., the Black feminist work of Collins [2008]), and cultural identity as blended and pluralized (Ramazani, 2001). Our conceptual and empirical project considers how children's literature might promote a curriculum that allows students' particular experiences to have an integrity of their own while simultaneously being in conjunction with others' histories and narratives (Campano, 2007).

Methods

This article draws from a larger study that examines 100 quality multicultural children's literature texts. We sought to explore the following question, How and to what extent does children's literature address the topic of shared histories, identities, and experiences? This included investigating whether the texts capture multicultural identities and how, what conceptions they foster about human rights, and the ideological implications for the types of experiences represented. The texts selected for analysis were designated by the Children's Literature and Reading Special Interest Group of the International Reading Association (2007) as "Notable Books for a Global Society" (para. 2). Each year's booklist consists of 25 K–12 texts published the year before that span fiction, nonfiction, and poetry and which meet the criteria for promoting global understandings. Criteria include authentic representation of cultural groups and sociopolitical issues, avoidance of stereotypes, interaction between and within cultures, and the extent to which the text can serve as a platform for critical reflection and response (Children's Literature and Reading, 2011). These booklists were chosen because they encompass multiple group experiences and also overlap with other children's literature distinctions, such as the Coretta Scott King Award. We used the four lists that were the most recent at the start of this study for our analysis, 2007–2010.

Beginning with open coding (Strauss & Corbin, 1998) by each researcher independently, we examined the verbal and, where applicable, visual text (illustrations, photographs, diagrams) for each of the children's literature examples, attending to character, plot, setting, and theme. We noted, for instance, who was present and absent, how each character or group was positioned in relation to others, how each group's experience intersected with another's, and whether there was mention of power asymmetries (e.g., colonization) and/or evidence of coalition building. After the independent review of the texts, we conferred to share our perspectives and form conceptual categories of how children's literature texts address shared histories and experiences through the constant comparative method (Glaser & Strauss, 1978).

This article focuses on a subset of our findings—a robust category of promising texts that provide insights into how communities and individuals are implicated in one another's circumstances, struggles, and progress. We highlight three representative examples—*Denied, Detained, Deported: Stories from the Dark Side of American Immigration* by Ann Bausum (2009), *Moses: When Harriet Tubman Led Her People to Freedom* by Carole Boston Weatherford (2006), and *After Gandhi: One Hundred Years of Nonviolent Resistance* by Anne Sibley O'Brien and Perry Edmond O'Brien (2009)—and detail the ideological implications inherent in their depictions of intergroup experience. As scholars and former schoolteachers of South American, Filipino European, and African American descent, respectively, we have had many conversations about the importance of solidarity across communities. We have also wondered what educational resources are available to help cultivate what historian Marable (2009) described as "the cultural contexts for multiracial, multiclass coalitional politics" (p. xxvii). The books we discuss below offer a promising start.

Denied, Detained, Deported: Stories from the Dark Side of American Immigration

From the onset, Bausum's text juxtaposes the mythology of the United States as a refuge for those seeking freedom and a better life with the contradictory nature of official policies that have excluded and oppressed certain immigrant groups. This overlay is vividly captured in the opening images and the text of the endpages. A photograph of the Statue of Liberty, the iconic symbol of the United States as a nation of immigrants, is superimposed with two parallel poems: the statue's inscription on the left-hand side and a poem by Naomi Shihab Nye on the right that

As scholars and former schoolteachers of South American, Filipino European, and African American descent, respectively, we have had many conversations about the importance of solidarity across communities.

blends this original inscription with caveats that speak to how different immigrant groups have fared with regards to the American Dream: "Give me your tired, your poor / but not too tired, not too poor" (p. 7).

Bausum explores these contradictions and exclusions through specific cases from U.S. immigration history: the Chinese Exclusion Act; a profile of the *St. Louis,* a ship that sought refuge from the Nazis just before World War II; Japanese internment camps; the story of Emma Goldman, an anarchist who was deported for ideological reasons; and Mexican-U.S. border and labor relations. Through beautifully rendered photographs and historical documents, the text puts a human face to those who are most vulnerable in times of crisis and documents how geopolitical dynamics, such as war and the economy, fuel nativism and fear of the other.

Denied, Detained, Deported makes use of visual imagery as part of a countertext to the traditional immigration narrative. One photograph, for instance, features a cluster of individuals in the foreground, their backs to the reader, waving at the Statue of Liberty in the distance. At first glance, it may appear to be one of the familiar renderings of immigrants arriving in the new land—a symbol of the asylum of the United States—but the small caption alerts readers that this is an image of individuals being deported because of their political ideologies. Another striking visual superimposes words from a speech by President Franklin Delano Roosevelt urging Congress to repeal the Chinese Exclusion Act, in which he proclaimed, "We must be big enough to acknowledge our mistakes of the past and to correct them" (n.p.), onto a photograph of a Japanese internment camp that he had approved the year prior. The multimodality of the book captures the contradictory experiences of America's aspirations to live up to its professed ideals, an issue that harkens to our nation's founding, when "all men are created equal" did not include women or people of African descent.

In looking back at history, *Denied, Detained, Deported* makes explicit links between past cases and more contemporary events, such as the profiling of Muslim Americans after September 11, 2001, and the xenophobic sentiments aimed at Latino workers, particularly Mexican Americans. The text ends with an immigration timeline that weaves together various episodes in American history, emphasizing that a particular moment that seems so unique and flooded with emotion is actually part of a pattern in which the reader can discern links across communities. This linkage is expressed earlier in the book when one of the passengers onboard the *St. Louis* lamented how they were denied entry while attempting to escape from the Nazis, whereas Cubans fleeing Castro were welcomed with refugee status. A friend onboard the *St. Louis* responded, "I like to think [that] because of us is why they let them in" (p. 59). Although Bausum profiles specific historical events and figures, the interconnections imbue the text with a universalism, leaving the reader thinking that the tables can turn on any community and that no group is immune from being stigmatized or scapegoated. This is the vulnerability that we share as human beings. These experiences also create hope that there can be progress.

Moses: When Harriet Tubman Led Her People to Freedom

Weatherford's picture book takes place in pre-Civil War, rural southeastern Maryland. Readers follow Harriet Tubman's escape from slavery to freedom in Philadelphia and her subsequent return to guide others on the journey. A source of strength—and a primary emphasis of the book—is her spiritual calling. Known as "the Moses of her people," Tubman is likened to the biblical Moses, and her work leading slaves to freedom is likened to the Exodus narrative (a theme in African American history and culture), which recounts the Israelites' suffering as Egyptian slaves and Moses leading them out of bondage. Metaphorically, Tubman is given the name Moses because she represented deliverance in the imagination of her people. In exploring this connection, Weatherford makes links across religious and historical traditions toward social justice ends.

Through realistically rendered nighttime settings, illustrator Kadir Nelson depicts how Harriet Tubman used the cover of darkness to stay out of reach of surveillance, an artistic choice that also indexes how the night was the time for traveling because of the restrictions imposed during the day by slavery. The visual setting is Tubman's nocturnal journey, when she networked with abolitionists and liberated others via the Underground Railroad. The author and illustrator present the historic reality that collaboration is a possibility at night, which implies that people who aided others in the project of liberation had much to risk as well. This setting points to the invisible histories and shared experiences detailed in the book.

Weatherford subtly chronicles the importance of nondescript, minor actors as instrumental in Harriet Tubman's success, suggesting that she was active in creating coalitions across class, race, and culture. On one such occasion in her journey, Harriet Tubman must find cover and sees a farmer and his wife. She remembers that the farmer's wife "spoke to her and was always nice to her" (n.p.), and Tubman reaches out to them. Given historical knowledge of the context, we can assume that the farmer and

The multimodality of the book captures the contradictory experiences of America's aspirations to live up to its professed ideals, an issue that harkens to our nation's founding, when "all men are created equal" did not include women or people of African descent.

his wife are White because of their class status in 19th-century rural Maryland. They provide cover, and other unnamed characters similarly aid the cause: a couple who give her a ride in a carriage and a man who hides her in his boat. These three instances implicitly speak to how people outside of particular oppressed communities have been willing throughout history to be allies in the struggle for liberation. For example, Frederick Douglass ardently participated in the Women's suffrage movement of the late 19th century. More recently, it brings to mind theologian Rabbi Abraham Joshua Heschel and his endearing friendship with Dr. Martin Luther King Jr., which developed during many of the Freedom Marches at the height of the civil rights movement. Importantly, Weatherford does not name the minor characters in the narrative. Their anonymity does not diminish Harriet Tubman's agency, but rather signals how any struggle for social change involves varied networks of support.

Community is not a given, however; it is judiciously created across sectarian boundaries among people with a shared vision. Weatherford writes, "Harriet knows that most strangers will turn her in, not help her" (n. p.). For Harriet Tubman, coalitional networks involved a high-stakes reading of the world that anticipates the perspectives of Freire (1983) in order to know where to seek support. These understandings were rooted in her own family. During a moment of uncertainty in the narrative, Tubman hears from God, who encourages her to look within herself for answers: "your father taught you to read the stars, predict the weather, and make cures from berries" (n. p.). Community ties give her the knowledge to navigate her surroundings, and also result in a new collective purpose once she has reached her destination, for "freedom brings new woes" (n. p.). Weatherford portrays Harriet Tubman as weeping at the table after reaching freedom in the North, longing to restore her family and community. The definition of liberation as collective—no one is fully free until everyone is free—is deeply rooted in African American culture, passed down intergenerationally. This idea becomes the catalyst for her participation in the Underground Railroad during the remaining years of her life.

After Gandhi: One Hundred Years of Nonviolent Resistance

Anne Sibley O'Brien and Perry Edmond O'Brien bring together 16 social movements from across the world, including events that have garnered less attention in children's literature, such as the Aboriginal rights movement in Australia, student activism in Tiananmen Square, and protests against the Iraq War. The authors note that their goal is not to write a history book but to portray social justice struggles that capture what they believe to be living legacies of pacificism—as they quote Gandhi, "lamppost[s] on the road" (p. 9) of a global project for human rights. The book is set up in chronological order beginning in 1908; each chapter details an episode from a particular social movement and then provides contextualizing information about that event and the leaders typically associated with it. From the opening lines of the first vignette, intergroup experience is highlighted: "Some three thousand Indian men had gathered—Muslim, Hindu, and Christian. Some wore English-style suits and hats; others were dressed in traditional Indian tunics and turbans or rectangular caps. They had come to break a law" (p. 8).

The text takes as its narrative starting point the power of the collective, the coming together across differences of religion and tradition to take peaceful action against institutional racism. Throughout the global contexts and struggles featured, *After Gandhi* juxtaposes, both in the verbal text and through its illustrations, such group representations with portraits of individuals associated with specific movements. For instance, the aforementioned opening follows an illustration depicting a faceless mass of people, sketched in vigorous strokes with individuals barely distinguishable from one other, gathered around a fire where they have come in protest to burn identification papers. It is not until 10 pages later that readers encounter a close-up image of Gandhi. This pattern is repeated throughout the book, featuring, for instance, a rendering of the 1963 church bombing in Birmingham, Alabama, followed later by a drawing of Martin Luther King Jr. The panoramic representation of crowds with blurred faces underscore the vast number of anonymous people involved in collective projects for change.

One way to understand this oscillation between the vivid, up close portraits and the faceless masses in collective struggle is through Foucault's (1977) conceptualization of the author function. He argues that individuals are not the sole authors of their ideas and experiences, but the product of larger discourses and dynamics happening in society. The opening illustrations of the lampposts on the struggle for social justice and the iconic portraits that follow situate particular figures within the social and political context: The text highlights the movements that speak through such individuals and through which they speak.

The collective images also call attention to the structural inequalities and oppressive circumstances at the root of these social movements. Each chapter opening illustration pauses an active scene, allowing the reader to inspect the situation more closely and reflect on the circumstances of context. One example is the 1965 Great Delano Grape Strike, described by the authors as "an action of two unions, the mostly Mexican NFWA [National Farm Workers Association] and another group that was mostly Filipino workers" (p. 74). On the right-hand side of the two-page spread stands a crowd of protesters, their faces obscured, a sign reading "Huelga" (Strike) held aloft. The crowd is engulfed in a cloud of dust, and a tractor looms nearby. The ensuing narrative details how tractors "churn[ed] up clouds of brown dust" over the strikers in an effort to break the resistance of the farmworkers, while the protesters tried to encourage hired strikebreakers to join their struggle. The text continues: "Again and again, for nearly an

We are left to contend with profound issues related to ethics, social justice, and what it means to live and participate in a democratic society.

hour, the tractors backed up and drove at them, until every protester was completely covered with dirt. They refused to budge" (p.71).

The illustration and accompanying description bring into stark relief the dehumanizing and violent nature of the inequalities being protested and the notion of resistance as holding one's ground—that not acting is a form of action. Similar vignettes throughout the book portray the details of oppression as well as pacifism and noncompliance as a form of resistance: White students in Moore, Australia, who blocked the entrance to the town pool to protest its exclusion of Aboriginal children while townspeople threw garbage, rocks, and broken bottles at them; a crowd of Catholic and Protestant peace marchers who protested religious division in Belfast and, when attacked with rocks, bricks and bottles, protected themselves by opening their umbrellas; a bus scene in which Rosa Parks is in the background, her gaze turned from the reader, while in the foreground a policeman looms aggressively over her with a club in his hand and his back to readers. We are left to contend with profound issues related to ethics, social justice, and what it means to live and participate in a democratic society.

Discussion

In an issue of the journal *Daedalous* themed "On Cosmopolitanism," philosopher Nussbaum (2008) draws on several figures who are prominent in the books that we feature in this article, including King and Gandhi, to delineate the contours of what she terms "a globally sensitive patriotism" (p. 78). A revision of an earlier position advocating for the primacy of cosmopolitanism in a comprehensive ethical and political doctrine, Nussbaum argues that it is necessary to "draw on symbol and rhetoric, emotional memory and history" (p. 93) associated with patriotism for progressive ends, less they be monopolized by a political agenda of intolerance and fear. One way to think about the texts highlighted in this article is that they provide a reservoir of symbols, emotions, and memory for students to transact with in order to both confront the trauma of the past—the braided rope—and become edified by the ways that people have worked together for change. These texts are promising because they signal what we have identified as four shifts in representation (see Figure 6.1), which we detail below, that can serve as a platform for understanding and investigating our shared experiences.

Although what we looked for when selecting children's literature texts for analysis was a greater emphasis on intergroup, rather than exclusively intragroup, histories and on instances of commonality and cooperation, we also found these to be coextensive with other changes in orientations. First, the books share a move from focusing on the individual to emphasizing the collective. As we examined in earlier sections, this characteristic is concretely exemplified in *After Gandhi,* as key figures in global movements for peace are portrayed as part of larger collective struggles. The individuals profiled in *Denied, Detained, Deported* are everyday people who responded courageously to their time. These characterizations are interwoven with commentary

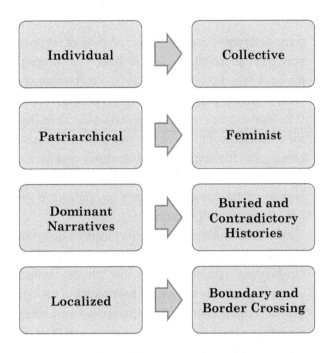

FIGURE 6.1 Shifts in representation in promising children's literature texts

on social policies and events, past and present. The timeline at the end of the book reinforces how the particular circumstances depicted in the text fit together within a larger pattern of U.S. immigration history. In *Moses: When Harriet Tubman Led Her People to Freedom,* Weatherford portrays the anonymous underground who aided in the collective abolitionist movement; that they remain unnamed in the text points to the many who constituted networks of support. Not unrelated to this notion of collectivities is the shift from patriarchical to feminist orientations, which challenge the "great man" version of history, in which social change is the result of the efforts of individual charismatic leaders (often male). While the books certainly profile many individuals, they also highlight cooperative social struggle and the role that women played, such as the Mothers of the Disappeared in Argentina.

The promising texts also display a shift from focusing on dominant narratives to delineating buried and contradictory histories. Set against the ideological backdrop of the American Dream, *Denied, Detained, Deported* profiles individuals for whom America is not a refuge. In the United States, known as the Land of the Free, not everyone was counted as free, a reality that is under-scored in Weatherford's *Moses. After Gandhi* brings to the forefront a range of political struggles from around the world that seldom receive treatment in children's literature. The books that we featured break away from a simplified gloss on historical events and instead provide coun-ternarratives that expose the contradictory and complex nature of struggles for social justice amid structural inequalities. One dominant narrative disrupted in the texts is the notion that

These texts provide fertile ground for inquiring how experiences are interwoven, how people are/have been included or excluded, and ultimately, how they create coalitions for positive social change.

stark differences are the cause of conflict; instead, the books evidence how, throughout history, people have been scapegoated and persecuted for what Freud characterized as "the narcissism of minor differences" (as cited in Jacoby, 2011, p. xiii). One rich example is the detailed rendering of U.S.–Mexico border relations in *Denied, Detained, Deported* that emphasizes the colonization of Mexico, the link between the two economies for over a century, and the populations of Mexicans who have always lived within the United States. Unlike the us/ them polarizing rhetoric prevalent in immigration media discourse, the text highlights the similarities and intricate links between both nations.

We also identified a shift from localized group representations to ones that denote boundary and border crossing. *Denied, Detained, Deported,* for example, reminds readers that the phenomenology of immigration involves constantly navigating the politics of national borders and that the United States is constituted by those who were considered "other" and who were themselves subject to exclusionary policies at home and colonizing practices abroad. *After Gandhi*'s weaving together of events from around the world emphasizes how social justice ideas have circulated across political borders, challenging notions of national exceptionalism. *Moses* situates Tubman's agency, and her coalitional networks, on the border between the North and the South, which may have been as wide a gulf as between nations. These texts do not characterize identity as static but, to echo Anzaldúa (1999), as a "borderland" that is actively negotiated.

In presenting characterizations of group histories in ways that complicate and extend conventional renderings of children's literature themes, the books remind us that historical narrative is always an interpretive act. These texts provide an opportunity for investigating "historical truths ... [that] cannot be sugarcoated" (Harris, 2003, p. 124) as well as potential sites of connection across experiences. It is important to situate such endeavors within an inquiry stance (Cochran-Smith & Lytle, 2009), in which the books become part of a larger exploration of social justice movements in the past and perhaps even in students' own lives. These texts provide fertile ground for inquiring into how experiences are interwoven, how people are/ have been included or excluded, and ultimately, how they create coalitions for positive social change.

Conclusion: Literature as a Platform for Inquiry into Our Shared Histories

We conclude by discussing a picture book, too recently published to be included in our main study, that beautifully captures many of the shifts that we have identified: *We Are America: A Tribute from the Heart* by Walter Dean Myers (2011) and illustrated by his son Christopher Myers. In a move similar to Nussbaum's, author and illustrator frame the book as a tribute that reclaims patriotism in terms of its social justice and abolitionist legacies. The cover and frontmatter also depict the Statute of Liberty and contain images of discovery and westward expansion: an iconographical constellation that sets readers' expectations for a conventional narrative of American exceptionalism and manifest destiny. This triumphalism is immediately complicated in the author's note, in which Walter Dean Myers describes his witness to the aftermath of the September 11, 2001, terrorist attack, the "collective grief" and "outrage," as well as the "spate of patriotism" (n. p.) that to him often felt jingoistic and exclusionary. The book was inspired by his desire to "take responsibility" and represent a more inclusive America, accounting for the "many millions [who] chose to come to our shores or, if they did not arrive by choice, how they still have prevailed" (n. p.).

Christopher Myers's colorful, mural-like illustrations make connections across histories and experiences. Sometimes parallels are made between oppressions. One particularly poignant visual blends images of a lashed slave, the massacre of Wounded Knee, and the Japanese internment. Others capture an American sense of hope and possibility, whether in a Whitmanesque juxtaposition of the explorer John Smith sailing alongside a Haitian refugee boat or a panoramic view of workers who built the nation, including brickmakers, Chinese laborers of the intercontinental railroad, and Detroit automakers. The illustrations are accompanied by quotes from the nation's foundational texts, such as the Treaty of Paris, the Declaration of Independence, and the Constitution, as well as some of its most eloquent leaders, such as Patrick Henry, Abraham Lincoln, Frederick Douglass, and Barbara Jordan. The endpage is a quilt of individual profiles (e.g., Gertrude Stein, Thomas Jefferson, Dolores Huerta, Kalpana Chawla, Helen Keller, Maria Tallchief) that convey an inclusive, pluralistic national history and vision.

The "we" in *We Are America* reinforces the notion presented by all of our promising texts, that "we're all in this together." They invite students to enter the symbolic contest and participate in interpreting and defining our shared narratives, metaphors, and legacies. This involves directly confronting a past that has not been sanitized, neither its tragic nor more edifying episodes, in order to define our present and imagine a better future, together. Continuing to represent various experiences as insular may perpetuate unproductive dichotomies in the curriculum. We believe children's literature that emphasizes shared histories and stories can play a key role in educating students about cultural understandings and misunderstandings. Such texts enable children to see representations of social cooperation and the interconnectedness of humanity while also fostering critical discernment and empathetic sensibilities about the ways in which difference is often produced by inequality. This pedagogical and inquiry project is elegantly expressed in the artist's note to *We Are America,* in which Christopher Myers shares vignettes from his biological and adoptive grandparents, from varied descents and walks of life, all actively asking, "What is America, and what will I make of it?" (n. p.). Reflecting on the picture book as a means of answering these questions, he concludes, "in some way the beauty of this country is its open-endedness, the question mark of it. Where other places in the world end in periods, neat packets of sealed identities, we end in possibilities" (n. p.).

References

Anzaldúa, G. (1999). *Borderlands/La Frontera: The new mestiza* (2nd ed.). San Francisco, CA: Aunt Lute Books.

Bishop, R. S. (2011). African American children's literature: Researching its development, exploring its voices. In S. A. Wolf, K. Coats, P. Enciso, & C. A. Jenkins (Eds.), *Handbook of research on children's and young adult literature* (pp. 225–236). New York, NY: Routledge.

Blackburn, M. V., & Clark, C. T. (2011). Becoming readers of literature with LGBT themes: In and out of classrooms. In S. A. Wolf, K. Coats, P. Enciso, & C. A. Jenkins (Eds.), *Handbook of research on children's and young adult literature* (pp. 148–163). New York, NY: Routledge.

Bradford, C. (2011). Reading indigeneity: The ethics of interpretation and representation. In S. A. Wolf. K. Coats, P. Enciso, & C. A. Jenkins (Eds.), *Handbook of research on children's and young adult literature* (pp. 331–342). New York, NY: Routledge.

Cai, M. (2002). *Multicultural literature for children and young adults: Reflections on critical issues.* Westport, CT: Greenwood Press.

Campano, G. (2007). *Immigrant students and literacy: Reading, writing, and remembering.* New York, NY: Teachers College Press.

Campano, G., & Ghiso, M. P. (2011). Immigrant students as cosmopolitan intellectuals. In S. A. Wolf, K. Coats, P. Enciso, & C. A. Jenkins (Eds.), *Handbook of research on children's and young adult literature* (pp. 164–176). New York, NY: Routledge.

Children's Literature and Reading Special Interest Group of the International Reading Association. (2011). *Notable books for a global society.* Retrieved from http://www.clrsig.org/nbgs_books.php

Cochran-Smith, M., & Lytle, S. L. (2009). *Inquiry as stance: Practitioner research for the next generation.* New York, NY: Teachers College Press.

Collins, P. H. (2008). *Black feminist thought: Knowledge, consciousness, and the politics of empowerment* (2nd ed.). New York, NY: Routledge.

DeNicolo, C. P., & Fránquiz, M. E. (2006). "Do I have to say it?": Critical encounters with multicultural children's literature. *Language Arts, 84(2),* 157–170.

Erdrich, L. (2008). *The plague of doves.* New York, NY: HarperCollins.

Foucault, M. (1977). What is an author? In D. F. Bouchard (Ed.), *Language, counter-memory, practice: Selected essays and interviews* (pp. 113–138) (D. F. Bouchard & S. Simon, Trans.). Ithaca, NY: Cornell University Press.

Fránquiz, M. E., Martínez-Roldán, C., & Mercado, C. I. (2011). Teaching Latina/o children's literature in multicultural contexts: Theoretical and pedagogical possibilities. In S. A. Wolf, K. Coats, P. Enciso, & C. A.

Jenkins (Eds.), *Handbook of research on children's and young adult literature* (pp. 108–120). New York, NY: Routledge.

Freire, P. (1983). The importance of the act of reading. *Journal of Education, 165*(1), 5–11.

Glaser, B. G., & Strauss, A. L. (1978). *The discovery of grounded theory: Strategies for qualitative research.* Chicago, IL: Aldine.

Goodman, A., & Erdrich, L. (2008, June 6). *Native American writer and independent bookseller Louise Erdrich* [Interview]. Retrieved from http://www.democracynow.org/2008/6/6/native_american_writer_and_independent_book

Harris, V. J. (2003). The complexity of debates about multicultural literature and cultural authenticity. In D. L. Fox & K. G. Short (Eds.), *Stories matter: The complexity of cultural authenticity in children's literature* (pp. 116–134). Urbana, IL: National Council of Teachers of English.

Jacoby, R. (2011). *Bloodlust: On the roots of violence from Cain and Abel to the present.* New York, NY: Free Press.

Marable, M. (2009). *Beyond black and white: Transforming African-American politics* (2nd ed.). New York, NY: Verso.

Mohanty, S. P. (1997). *Literary theory and the claims of history: Postmodernism, objectivity, multicultural politics.* Ithaca, NY: Cornell University Press.

Moya, P. M. L. (2000). Postmodernism, "realism," and the politics of identity: Cherríe Moraga and Chicana feminism. In P. M. L. Moya & M. R. Hames-García (Eds.), *Reclaiming identity: Realist theory and the predicament of postmodernism* (pp. 67–101). Berkeley, CA: University of California Press.

Nussbaum, M. C. (2008). Toward a globaly sensitive patriotism. *Daedalus, 137(3),* 78–93.

Patton, J. R. (2006, April). Jacqueline Woodson: Poetry in motion. *Teaching Pre K–8, 36* (7), 46–48.

Ramazani, J. (2001). *Hybrid muse: Postcolonial poetry in English.* Chicago, IL: University of Chicago Press.

Strauss, A., & Corbin, J. (1998). Basics *of qualitative research: Techniques and procedures for developing grounded theory* (2nd ed.). Thousand Oaks, CA: Sage.

Walcott, D. (1998). *What the twilight says: Essays.* New York, NY: Farrar Straus & Giroux.

Wolf, S. A. (2004). *Interpreting literature with children.* Mahwah, NJ: Lawrence Erlbaum.

Wolf, S. A., Coats, K., Enciso, P., & Jenkins, C. A. (Eds.). (2011). *Handbook of research on children's and young adult literature.* New York, NY: Routledge.

Children's Literature Cited

Bausum, A. (2009). *Denied, detained, deported: Stories from the dark side of American immigration.* Washington, DC: National Geographic Society.

Myers, W. D. (2011). *We are America: A tribute from the heart.* (C. Myers, Illus.). New York, NY: HarperCollins.

O'Brien, A. S., & O'Brien, P. E. (2009). *After Gandhi: One hundred years of nonviolent resistance.* (A.S. O'Brien, Illus.). Watertown, MA: Charlesbridge.

Weatherford, C. B. (2006). *Moses: When Harriet Tubman led her people to freedom.* (K. Nelson, Illus.). New York, NY: Hyperion.

Discussion Questions

1   Why do we need to explore difficult issues about identity and shared history in America?

2   How and to what extent does children's literature address topics on shared histories, identities, and experiences?

3   How do the contradictory experiences of the American dream live up to the nation's founding ideal of all men created equal?

4   The experiences of America's braided histories move from focusing on the individual to emphasizing the collective. How true is this statement?

5   Historical perspective is always an interpretative act. How true is this statement?

PART II

RACISM AGAINST MINORITY GROUPS

Introduction

Discrimination against ethnic minorities is a violation of human rights. Everyone should be equal in the face of the law. In 1977, the federal government adopted new sets of standards for defining racial and ethnic categories, which led to the formalization of five racial groups in the US. These categories were socio-political constructs. A careful look at these groups aids in our understanding of how racism and other forms of oppression operate.

Native Americans make up at least one percent of the population. In the late nineteenth century Native American Boarding schools were developed with the aim "To kill the Indian and save the man." (Churchill, 2004) Hence, many Native American children were taken away and inducted into European culture. Native American stereotypical images, mascots, and nicknames were developed for sports teams in the name of good clean fun. This once-thriving group that numbered over 10 million persons with 700 languages have been reduced to less than half of a percent of their original size after colonialization. Most Native American tribes have become extinct or are near extinction.

Much like the Native Americans are a group politically known as Hispanics. The Latino population originally occupied a unique position in the racial and ethnic hierarchy of the United States. It was the annexation of the Southwest that brought about the citizenship of the Latino population in the US and, in effect, deemed them as an "honorary white" population. This group has been defined based on greater than twenty countries having a common culture rooted in the Spanish language. Hispanics are by the far the fastest growing racial group in the United States.

Discrimination is a major threat to the existence of African Americans. Their entrance as slaves into the Americas has posed great dysfunction in society. African Americans' history of slavery undermines their ability to develop strong bonds with conventional institutions like the educational and legal systems. Discrimination against African Americans has been largely due to stereotypes. Negative media depiction, historical stereotypes, and ethnocentric biases have all contributed to make blackness synonymous with criminality. This remains a norm in white America.

In the wake of World War II, Asian Americans were considered traitors in the bombing of Pearl Harbor by the Japanese. The term "Yellow Peril" was resuscitated, and Japanese Americans were forced into concentration camps. In 1982, after the death of Vincent Chin, Anti-Asian sentiments reached a fever pitch. The Vincent Chin case came to mean more to Asians. It represented the racial hatred, scapegoating, and discrimination Asian Americans have endured since they set foot on American soil. This case proved that Americans from China, Japan, Korea, the Philippines, Southeastern Asia, India, and other Asian regions can make a powerful impact when they work together.

Interracial marriages were illegal in thirteen states until 1967 when the Supreme Court overturned a judgement in the case of *Loving v. Virginia*. The law prevented whites from marrying African Americans or Native Americans. Mixed-race children, then referred to as "mulattoes," were stigmatized and were subjected to some informal social sanctions. They were given a separate racial status. By the 1930s, the "one-drop rule" was in existence, which meant a single-drop of black blood made a person black. Biracial and Multiracial children now refer to themselves as "biracial and multiracial" eliminating the color line.

CHAPTER 6

Racism against American Indians

The Native American Experience

Racism and Mascots in Professional Sports

Krystal Beamon and Chris M. Messer

E arly European contact with Native American tribes resulted in cultural and physical **genocide.** According to the 2010 census, Native Americans make up less than 1 percent of the total population of the United States of America. This once thriving group that numbered over 10 million persons and spoke over 700 languages prior to colonization is projected to make up less than 0.5 percent of the American population by 2050 (Schaefer 2011). Today, the culture and language of many tribes are extinct, with tribal elders, anthropologists, and other scholars fighting to preserve and pass on remnants of both for future generations. Compared to other racial and ethnic groups, Native Americans have the highest rates of poverty, alcoholism, and suicide, and the lowest rate of educational attainment (Center for Native American Youth 2012).

The term Native American refers to an extremely diverse group of people. Although similarities exist, each tribe has a distinct culture with varying customs, religious and spiritual beliefs, kinship and political systems, and history. Due to the wide use of stereotypes in the media, isolation of Native Americans on reservations, and the invisible nature of mixed-raced Native Americans in urban areas, most Americans conceive of "Indians" in a very narrow manner. **Pan-Indianism,** or the growing solidarity among Native Americans, has created a tendency to focus less on tribal heritage and more on common injustices that Native Americans face as a whole. A key source of frustration relates to a set of cultural stereotypes that narrowly depict Native Americans as a remnant of history filled with savagery. More specifically, according to many pan-Indian civil rights groups, the commercialization of Native American images and the use of Native American mascots perpetuate a minimalistic understanding of their diverse experiences and cultures (Nuessel 1994; Williams 2007). It's important first to discuss the historical presence of Native Americans in sport, and later, the surfacing of mascots that depict Native American images.

Native Americans in Sports

Historically, Native American tribes have been physically active in games and athletics. Traditional Native American sports such as stickball, lacrosse, archery, running, and canoeing were often connected to spiritual, political, or economic worldviews (King 2004). They were important in training children, and the outcomes often held ritual significance. In the late 19th century, Native American boarding schools were developed with aims to "kill the Indian and save the man," taking Indian children out of their homes away from their families and indoctrinating them with European language, culture, religion, and sports (Churchill 2004: 14). While many Native Americans continued to participate in traditional games and sports, this forced **assimilation**, a form of ethnic genocide in boarding schools, produced a decline in traditional games.

Organized interscholastic sports were institutionalized by European Americans as a form of cultural control. Sports were used as a tool of domination in which Native American boys learned to see their traditional games as "inferior" and were taught that there were more "civilized" ways to compete. For example, according to Gems, football "taught Indians rules, discipline, and civilization" (1998: 146), which were considered European American virtues. The White headmasters perceived sports as an effective tool in channeling males into more acceptable European roles and behavior. As an unintended consequence, many boarding schools fielded successful athletic teams in football and baseball, taking on and winning against collegiate powerhouses such as Harvard and Syracuse between 1900 and 1932 (Haggard 2004).

The Carlisle Indian School and Haskell Institute produced exceptional athletes, such as Jim Thorpe, who is considered one of the most versatile athletes in American history. A Sac and Fox tribal member, Thorpe played professional baseball, football, and basketball and also won gold medals in the 1912 Olympics for the pentathlon and decathlon. He attended the Haskell Institute in Lawrence, Kansas as a youth (Wheeler 1979). As Gems (1998) notes, athletic participation at such schools allowed Native Americans in the early 1900s to assert their racial identity,

> by providing a collective memory of self-validation and the creation of kindred heroes as they successfully tested themselves against the beliefs of Social Darwinism and dispelled notions of white dominance ... In that sense football proved to be not only an assimilative experience, but a resistive and liberating one as well.

> (Gems 1998: 148)

Nonetheless, there was an obvious absence of Native American athletes reaching national success between World War II and the 1964 victory of Billy Mills at the Olympic Games (King 2004). Mills began running at the Haskell Institute in Kansas as a youth and became the second Native American to win a gold medal at the Olympics (Jim Thorpe was the first). His win in the 10,000-meter run was unexpected as he competed against a world record holder from Australia, Ron Clarke (Mills 2009). Mills often discussed why many traditional Native Americans did not participate fully in organized sports. Mills believed that engaging in a sporting program that does not acknowledge cultural heritage creates a fear among Native American athletes, a fear of going too far into White society and losing one's "Indianness" while participating in mainstream sports (Simpson 2009: 291).

In 1968, the American Indian Movement (AIM) was launched in Minneapolis, Minnesota and soon thereafter spread across the country. The movement sought to address problems affecting the Native American community such as poverty, police harassment, and treaty violations. During its initial stages, the movement was known for its pan-Indian philosophy and protests. Perhaps the most famous protest occurred in 1973 at Wounded Knee, South Dakota at the Pine Ridge Indian Reservation. Armed members of the movement occupied the area in protest at Native American poverty and U.S. government treaty violations. The event culminated in a 71-day standoff with federal law enforcement and ended only after two Native Americans were killed (Banks and Erdoes 2004). Today, AIM continues to fight against the same problems of poverty and treaty violations and also actively protests the use of Native American mascots (American Indian Movement n.d.).

Other organizations such as the National Indian Athletic Association (NIAA), founded in 1973, and the Native American Sports Council (NASC), founded in1993, were created to promote athletic participation and excellence among Native American athletes throughout North America. Today, the NASC sponsors sports leagues and provides training and other forms of support to potential Olympians. These organizations support the development of Native Americans through fitness, community involvement, and boosting self-esteem (Kalambakal 2004). Formerly a colonial tool used to force Native American children of both sexes to reject their heritage and adopt European-American cultural norms, these athletic organizations employ sports to steer youngsters in a positive direction and reduce the high rates of suicide, drug and alcohol use, and gang activity on the reservations (Kalambakal 2004). Through both the NIAA and NASC, sports education, sports camps, and clinics have led to an increase in Native American participation in mainstream sports in the Olympics, college, and professional sports; however, this "trend has yet to produce the numbers experienced during the early twentieth century" (Haggard 2004: 226).

Native American athletes are hardly visible in contemporary sports. Aside from a few teams and individual athletes in segregated Indian schools, Native American sport participation has been limited by many factors. Poverty, poor health, lack of equipment and facilities, and a lack of cultural understanding by those who control sports, as well as academic unpreparedness and negative academic stereotypes of Native American student-athletes, has limited the non-reservation sports opportunities of these athletes (Simpson 2009). This cultural group remains underrepresented as athletes at all levels despite the obvious talent and the popularity of basketball on Native American reservations. However, this talent garnered recent attention with the story of two sisters on the University of Louisville's women's basketball team, which finished as the national championship runner-up in 2013. Shone and Jude Schimmel were raised on the Umatilla Reservation in Oregon and were considered exceptional local talent. Playing a style they call "rez ball," the sisters captivated local audiences growing up. Their national success has led to an explosion of interest in basketball among the local reservation youth and a sense of pride among Native Americans in general (Block 2013).

Youth sports are associated with forms of capital including social capital that can advantage Native youth. For example, children and youth who participate in organized sports perform better academically, are less likely to drink or do drugs, have higher self-esteem, and lower rates of obesity and diabetes (Bailey 2006; Broh 2002; Eitle and Eitle 2002; Ewing et al. 2002; Pate et al. 2000). Native Americans are underrepresented in youth sport leagues and have higher rates of alcoholism, high school dropout, suicide, obesity, and diabetes than any other minority group (Bachman et al. 1991; Center for Native American Youth 2012; Gray and Smith 2003). Greater participation may be a valuable resource for Native American youth.

Native Americans also remain underrepresented at the elite levels. In NCAA Division I, II, and III sports, Native American men and women make up 0.4 percent of student-athletes (NCAA 2012b). As illustrated in Figure 7.1, White men and women make up the largest majority of NCAA Division I, II, and III student-athletes in most sports, while Native Americans are widely underrepresented in all sports. In fact, even in lacrosse, a sport thought to have roots in the Cherokee traditional game "stickball," Native American men and women make up less than 0.5 percent of collegiate players. The highest representation of Native American NCAA student-athletes is seen in softball, where Native American women make up 0.7 percent of all players.

While they are underrepresented as students on college campuses along with most minority groups, Native Americans are far less represented as collegiate athletes compared to Blacks and Hispanics. In fact, the most visible representation of Native American culture in popular commercialized sports is found among mascots. In addition to the many professional sports teams, hundreds of high schools and close to 100 universities have Native American images for mascots and nicknames—not to mention the countless little league and peewee teams that follow suit using these images to represent their teams. Along with class and access issues in youth sports, these disparaging mascots may be linked to the lack of participation of Natives in youth sports and the benefits that go along with participation.

Figure 7.1   NCAA Student-Athlete Racial Composition by Selected Sport 2010–2011

	All sports (Division I)	Football	Basketball	Track and field	Soccer	Baseball	Softball	Lacrosse
White Men	62.5	55.1	43.5	64.9	68.5	84.7		88.2
White Women	70.6		55.7	66.2	80.7		81.1	88.2
Black Men	29.4	35.4	45.5	21.6	7.2	3.9		2.7
Black Women	16		32.7	20.4	3.7		5.8	2.8
Hispanic Men	4.2	3	2.8	4.6	9.9	5.6		1.5
Hispanic Women	4.2		3	4.1	5.6		6	2.1
Native American Men	0.4	0.5	0.2	0.4	0.2	0.4		0.3
Native American Women	0.4	0.7	0.4	0.4	0.3		0.7	0.2
Asian Men	2		0.5	1.4	1.6	0.9		0.9
Asian Women	2.4		0.8	1.4	1.5		1.2	1.2

Source: Lapchick 2011

Contemporary Racism in Sports: Native American Symbols as Mascots

Native American mascots have remained a common fixture in the world of athletics at all levels from peewee leagues to professional teams. The Washington Redskin has been the mascot of one of the most popular NFL teams, located in our nation's capital, since 1932. The term is considered a disparaging reference to many Native American people. According to Stapleton (2001), "redskin" is a term with a 400-year history and first emerged in sport during a time when the American government actively sought to assimilate Native Americans. In his book *Skull Wars*, Thomas (2000) writes,

> There is today no single word more offensive to Indian people then the term "redskins," a racial epithet that conjures up the American legacy of bounty hunters bringing in wagon loads of Indian skulls and corpses—literally the bloody dead bodies were known as "redskins"—to collect their payments.
>
> (p. 204)

Although many Native Americans are offended by the term, 88 percent of Americans surveyed oppose a name change for the team (Sigelman 2001).

In a survey of the top 10 most common team mascots, most were birds or beasts of prey, with the exception of two: "Warriors" and "Indians" (Franks 1982). The only two nickname categories that are not predatory animals refer to Native Americans. Many would ask, what's the problem? Are we not honoring indigenous people for being such fierce warriors?

To perceive Native Americans through the eyes of mascots and sports nicknames creates a myopic and inaccurate version of the rich traditions, culture, history, and contemporary existence of the population. Native American mascots are based on the stereotypical "Cowboy and Indian" Wild West images of America's indigenous peoples, with no regard for the diverse cultures and religious beliefs of tribal groups. This manner of stereotyping Native Americans began very early upon European contact. Colonizers portrayed "Indians" as "barbaric," "wild," "bestial," and most of all "savage" (Berkhofer 1978). In fact, Americans' view of "Indians" as predatory beasts has been ingrained from the inception of our nation. George Washington wrote that "Indians" were "wolves and beasts who deserve nothing from whites but total ruin," and President Andrew Jackson stated that troops should seek out "Indians" to "root them out of their dens and kill Indian women and their whelps" (Stannard 1992: 240–41). Racist and dehumanizing descriptions produced mass fear of Native Americans as an entire race or category of people. This fear negates the concept of "honoring" tribes as the basis for naming teams as fierce warriors or other Native American-derived images.

As America grew, these stereotypes were used to justify the systematic genocide of Native Americans, as they were seen as a threat to the safety of colonizers. These images remain a part of American culture, as many Americans continue to visualize the image of a "savage warrior" with feathers and war paint when thinking of Native Americans. One can go into any costume shop and find a Native American costume complete with tomahawk and a feathered headdress. These images have become embraced by **popular culture** and controlled by the **dominant group** instead of Native Americans themselves.

Activism around Native American Imagery

Native American mascots and the use of Native American imagery in advertising and branding (i.e., Land O'Lakes butter, Sue Bee honey, Jeep Cherokee, Crazy Horse Malt Liquor, Winnebagos) grew during the era of racial segregation and legalized discrimination in America (Meerskin 2012). The use of Native American peoples as mascots ranges from generic titles such as Indians, Braves, Warriors, or Savages to specific tribal designations such as Seminoles, Apaches, or Illini. These have been prevalent since the turn of the century, at a time when Little Black Sambo, Frito Bandito, and other racially insensitive branding was commonplace in "less enlightened times" (Graham 1993: 35). While Little Black Sambo and Uncle Rastus have long since been abandoned, the equally insensitive **Chief Wahoo** remains. These images exaggerate physical and cultural aspects of Native Americans and reduce them to one stereotypical representation: savage warrior.

The fight to remove the stereotypical images of Native American mascots and nicknames in sport has been active for nearly four decades. It occurred alongside the **civil rights movement** of the 1960s as the **National Congress of American Indians (NCAI)** began to challenge the use of stereotypical imagery in print and other forms of media (Staurowsky and Baca 2004). The use of Native American mascots also fell under attack when this campaign was launched in 1968. NCAI contended that the use of Native American imagery was not only racist but further reproduced the perception of Native American peoples as sub-human. By 1969 universities began to respond, as Dartmouth College changed its nickname from "the Indians" to "Big Green." Many followed suit, including the universities of Oklahoma, Marquette, and Syracuse, which all dropped Indian nicknames in the 1970s. Currently, an estimated 1,000 academic institutions have relinquished use of Native American mascots or nicknames.

Other institutions have resisted and remain invested in retaining their racist mascots. Close to 1,400 high schools and 70 colleges and universities have refused to cede to calls for change (Staurowsky and Baca 2004). Although Native Americans protest at every home opener with signs that read "We are human beings, not Mascots," MLB's Cleveland Indians maintain the use of the caricatured Chief Wahoo. The Washington Redskins have lost trademark protection, but continue to fight through litigation to maintain the use of the team's mascot. The University of Illinois Fighting Illini fought to maintain their mascot, **Chief Illiniwek**, amid major controversy for over a decade before finally retiring the chief in 2007. The Florida State Seminoles also maintain the use of their Native American imagery, citing an endorsement from the Seminole tribe as justification. All argue that they are honoring the history of Native Americans by using them as mascots. For example, the Cleveland Indians proclaim that the team's designation was chosen to honor the first Native American to play professional baseball, Louis Francis Sockalexis. The University of Illinois argued that their mascot was an honor to the extinct tribe that once inhabited the state. Although Florida State University has been given "permission" to maintain the use of its mascot and nickname by the Seminole tribe and its chief, "there are American Indians protesting outside every Florida State game, including some Seminole people. They say the mascot looks like a Lakota who got lost in an Apache dressing room riding a Nez Perce horse" (Spindel 2002: 16).

Many organizations using Native American designations argue that some Native American individuals and tribal groups have no issue with the use of the mascots and indeed feel a sense of pride. And many fans of these teams agree. In his study of local public opinion, Callais (2010) found that supporters of retaining Native American mascots base their position on maintaining tradition and promoting a color-blind society through a tribute to Native Americans.

While some individual tribes and persons may approve of this practice, all major Native American organizations have denounced it and called for a cessation of the use of their images as mascots, nicknames, and in the branding of products. Mascots are "manufactured images" of Native Americans, and their continued promotion results in a loss of power to control use of those images.

Indigenous mascots exhibit either idealized or comical facial features and "native" dress, ranging from body-length feathered (usually turkey) headdresses to more subtle fake buckskin attire or skimpy loincloths. Some teams and supporters display counterfeit Indigenous paraphernalia, including tomahawks, feathers, face paints, and symbolic drums and pipes. They also use mock Indigenous behaviors such as the tomahawk chop, dances, chants, drumbeats, war-whooping, and symbolic scalping.

(Pewewardy 1999: 2)

These images were manufactured by their respective schools, universities, and teams. They were created in the minds of those who established them during a time of racial hatred, stereotyping, and when Native Americans were seen as a threat (Callais 2010). The "costumes" of the mascots are derived from stereotypical and widely oversimplified views of a diverse group of people. In reality, each feather and bead, the facial paint, and especially the dances have a distinct, significant, deeply spiritual, and religious meaning to each tribal group. Particular dances mark "the passage of time, the changing of the seasons, a new status in a person's life" and "dancing expresses and consolidates a sense of belonging" (Spindel 2002: 189). In the eyes of many Native Americans, to put on the "costume" and perform a "war dance" at halftime is to mock their religion. How would it go over to have a team designated the "Black Warriors" with a mascot named Chief Watutsi dressed in a loincloth dancing around with a spear? While this mascot would not probably last a single day, Native Americans have been unable to have the use of their images stopped, despite a 40-year struggle to do so.

All in Fun?

Charlene Teters, the Native American activist who called national attention to the University of Illinois fighting Illini, describes how her children reacted when they first witnessed Chief Illiniwek in the documentary *In Whose Honor* (Rosenstein 1997). She describes her son sinking into his chair as he tried to become "invisible." One of the primary arguments against the use of Native American mascots is how it affects children of all races, but especially Native American children. The flippant and inaccurate depiction of Native American culture and identity "causes many young indigenous people to feel shame about who they are as human beings" (Pewewardy 1999: 342). These feelings become a part of the identity and self-image of Native American children, working together with the objective experiences of poverty and deprivation to create low self-esteem and high rates of depression (Pewewardy 1999). One in five Native American youth attempts suicide before the age of 20. In fact, suicide is the second leading cause of death for Native American youth between the ages of 15 and 24 (Center for Native American Youth 2012). This is two and a half times higher than the national average. While there are many factors that contribute to this statistic, such as poverty and drug and alcohol abuse, the use of Native American mascots further damages the self-image of Native American youth. Mascots dehumanize Native Americans and present images, sacred rituals, and other symbols in a way that negates the reverence instilled in Native children, thus negatively impacting their self-esteem. In fact, the American Psychological Association (2001) states emphatically that the use of Native American mascots perpetuates stigmatization of the group and has negative implications for perceptions of self among Native American children and adolescents.

For non-indigenous children, the use of Native American stereotypes as mascots perpetuates the mythical "Cowboys and Indians" view of the group. In a study conducted by Children Now, most of the children studied were found to perceive Native Americans as disconnected from their own way of life (Children Now 1999). Debbie Reese, a Nambe' Pueblo who travels across the country educating children and teachers concerning Native American stereotypes, recounts the many times that children described native people as "exotic," "mythical," or "extinct" and asked if she drove cars or rode horses (Spindel 2002: 224). Most Americans do not come into meaningful contact with traditional Native Americans very often, if at all. Thus, these stereotypical images of mascots and mythical beings are how we learn about Native American culture. Unfortunately, they disallow Americans from visualizing "Indians" as real people, but encourage viewing them as fierce warriors or even clowns dancing around with tomahawks, war paint, and feathered headdresses.

Children and adults alike are profoundly influenced by stereotypical images. The **stereotype threat** is a popular social psychological theory that has been researched empirically since introduced to the literature in 1995 (Steele and Aronson 1995). Claude Steele, a Stanford University professor of social psychology, defines a stereotype threat as "the pressure that a person can feel when she is at risk of confirming, or being seen to confirm a negative stereotype about her group" (Steele and Davies 2003: 311). For instance, when women are reminded that they are women, they perform poorly on math tests due to the stereotype that women are not good at math (Spencer, Steele, and Quinn 1999). Applied to the stereotypical images of Native Americans perpetuated through mascots, these violent and trivialized images may be associated with the lowered self-images of Native youth or the current statistic in which violence accounts for 75 percent of deaths among Native Americans between the ages of 12 and 20 (Center for Native American Youth 2012).

The use of Native American mascots is an example of institutional discrimination. Chief Wahoo and other such images have become as American as baseball itself. They are ingrained into the interworking of our society and its institutions. Major societal institutions such as the economy, sports, and education discriminate against Native Americans by continuing to denigrate living human beings through mascots and team designations. Perhaps if the elite levels of sport (professional and intercollegiate) terminated their use of Native American mascots and raised awareness on the issue, K–12 schools would follow suit. This could serve as an instructional piece for schools as they confront the issue of stereotyping, a process that begins early in one's childhood.

The U.S. Civil Rights Commission released a statement in 2001 condemning the use of Native American mascots. In fact, the National Congress of American Indians, American Indian Movement, National Education Association, National Association for the Advancement of Colored People (NAACP), countless state and local school boards, and the American Psychological Association have all issued similar resolutions. Such images and symbols have been found to perpetuate stereotypes and stigmatization, and negatively affect the mental health and behaviors of Native American people (American Psychological Association 2001). As stated by Native American activist Dennis Banks, "what part of ouch do they not understand?" (Rosenstein 1997).

Conclusion

The issues that Native Americans currently experience in sport—underrepresentation and stereotyping—bring us back to the image of sport as contested terrain. While many believe that the use of Native American mascots is a way of paying tribute, many Native Americans themselves battle to gain more control over the portrayal of their own identity. Athletes are often portrayed as "savages" and "animals," images that Native Americans have fought hard to be disassociated from. And while universities and professional teams generate millions of dollars from the sale of merchandise using Native American imagery, "real" Native Americans remain one of the most impoverished racial groups in society. With a group that experiences disproportionately high rates of dropout, obesity, and suicide, perhaps more effort should be spent on encouraging Native American youth athletics participation, which may help reduce these very problems. Furthermore, their heightened level of participation in sport could also result in society adopting a more positive outlook and understanding of Native Americans, an identification that goes beyond equating Native Americans and sports with mascots.

References

American Indian Movement. n.d. "National coalition on racism in sports and media." Accessed online at http://www.aimovement.org/ncrsm/index.html

American Psychological Association. 2001. "An emergency action of the board of directors: Resolution against racism and in support of the goals of the 2001 United Nations world conference against racism, racial discrimination, xenophobia, and related intolerance." Accessed online at http://www.apa.org/pi/racismresolution.html

Bachman, Jerald, John Wallace, Patrick O'Malley, Lloyd Johnston, Candace Kurth, and Harold Neighbors. 1991. "Racial/Ethnic differences in smoking, drinking, and illicit drug use among American high school seniors, 1976–89." *American Journal of Public Health, 81*, 372–77.

Bailey, Richard. 2006. "Physical education and sport in schools: A review of benefits and outcomes." *Journal of School Health, 76*, 397–401.

Banks, Dennis, and Richard Erdoes. 2004. *Ojibwa warrior: Dennis Banks and the rise of the American Indian Movement*. Norman, OK: University of Oklahoma Press.

Berkhofer, Robert. 1978. *White man's Indian: Images of American Indians from Columbus to the present*. New York: Random House.

Block, Melissa. 2013. "Two sisters bring Native American pride to women's NCAA." *NPR*. Retrieved April 8, 2013 (http://www.npr.org/2013/04/08/176597459/two-sisters-bring-nativeamerica-bride-to-womens-ncaa)

Broh, Beckett. 2002. "Linking extracurricular programming to academic achievement: Who benefits and why?" *Sociology of Education, 75*, 69–95.

Callais, Todd. 2010. "Controversial mascots: Authority and racial hegemony in the maintenance of deviant symbols." *Sociological Focus, 43*, 61–81.

Center for Native American Youth. 2012. "Fast facts on Native American youth and Indian Country." Accessed online at http://www.aspeninstitute.org/sites/default/files/content/upload/1302012% 20Fast%20Facts.pdf

Children Now. 1999. "A different world: Native American children's perceptions of race and class in the media." Accessed online at http://www.childrennow.org/uploads/documents/different_world_native_americans_1999.pdf

Churchill, Ward. 2004. *Kill the Indian, save the man: The genocidal impact of American Indian residential schools*. San Francisco, CA: City Lights Books.

Eitle, Tamela, and David Eitle. 2002. "Race, cultural capital, and the educational effects of participation in sports." *Sociology of Education, 75*, 123–46.

Ewing, Martha, Lori Gano-Overway, Crystal Branta, and Vern Seefeldt. 2002. "The role of sports in youth development." Pp. 31–47 in *Paradoxes of Youth and Sport*, ed. Michael Margaret Gatz, Michael Messner, and Sandra Ball-Rokeach. Albany, NY: State University of New York Press.

Franks, Ray. 1982. *What's in a nickname? Exploring the jungle of college athletic mascots*. Amarillo, TX: Ray Franks Publishing.

Gems, Gerald. 1998. "The construction, negotiation, and transformation of racial identity in American football: A study of Native and African Americans." *American Indian Culture and Research Journal, 22*, 131–50.

Graham, Renee. 1993. "Symbol or stereotype: One consumer's tradition is another's racial slur." *The Boston Globe* (January 6): 35.

Gray, Amy, and Chery Smith. 2003. "Fitness, dietary intake, and body mass index in urban Native American youth." *Journal of American Dietetic Association, 103*, 1187–91.

Haggard, Dixie. 2004. "Nationalism." Pp. 224–26 in *Native Americans in sports*, ed. Richard King. Armonk, NY: Sharpe Reference.

Kalambakal, Vickey. 2004. "National Indian Athletic Association." P. 223 in *Native Americans in sports*, ed. C. Richard King. Armonk, NY: Sharpe Reference.

King, C. Richard. 2004. *Native Americans in sports*. Armonk, NY: Sharpe Reference.

Meerskin, Debra. 2012. "Crazy Horse malt liquor and athletes: The tenacity of stereotypes." pp. 304–10 in *Rethinking the color line*, ed. C. Gallagher. New York: McGraw Hill.

Mills, Billy. 2009. *Wokini: A Lakota journey to happiness and self-understanding,* New York: Hay House.

National Collegiate Athletic Association. 2012b. "Race and gender demographics." Accessed online at http://web1.ncaa.org/rgdSearch

Nuessel, Frank. 1994. "Objectionable sport team designations." *Names, 42*, 101–19.

Pate, Russell, Stewart Trost, Sarah Levin, and Marsha Dowda. 2000. "Sports participation and health-related behaviors among U.S. youth." *Archives of Pediatrics and Adolescent Medicine, 154*, 904–11.

Pewewardy, Cornel. 1999. "The deculturalization of indigenous mascots in U.S. sports culture." *The Educational Forum, 63,* 342–47.

Rosenstein, Jay (dir.). 1997. *In whose honor?* [Film]. New Day Films.

Schaefer, Richard. 2011. *Racial and ethnic groups* (10th edn.). Upper Saddle River, NJ: Pearson.

Sigelman, Lee. 2001. "Hail to the Redskins? Public reactions to a racially insensitive team name?" Pp. 203–209 in *Contemporary issues in the sociology of sport,* ed. A. Yinnakis and M. Melnic. Champaign, IL: Human Kinetics.

Simpson, Kevin. 2009. "Sporting dreams die on the 'Rez.'" Pp. 285–91 in *Sport in Contemporary Society*, ed. D. Eitzen. Boulder, CO: Paradigm.

Spencer, Stephen, Claude Steele, and Diane Quinn. 1999. "Stereotype threat and women's math performance." *Journal of Experimental Social Psychology, 35,* 4–28.

Spindel, Carol. 2002. *Dancing at halftime: Sports and the controversy over American Indian mascots.* New York: New York University Press.

Stannard, David. 1992. *American holocaust: Columbus and the conquest of the New World.* New York: Oxford University Press.

Stapleton, Bruce. 2001. *Redskins: Racial slur or symbol of success?* San Jose, CA: Writers Club Press.

Staurowsky, Ellen, and Lawrence Baca. 2004. "Mascot controversy." Pp. 201–204 in *Native Americans in sports,* ed. C. Richard King. Armonk, NY: Sharpe Reference.

Steele, Claude, and Joshua Aronson. 1995. "Stereotype threat and the intellectual test performance of African Americans." *Journal of Personality and Social Psychology, 69,* 797–811.

Steele, Claude, and Paul Davies. 2003. "Stereotype threat and employment testing." *Human Performance, 16,* 311–26.

Thomas, David. 2000. *Skull wars: Kennewick man, archaeology, and the battle for Native American identity.* New York: Basic Books.

Wheeler, Robert. 1979. *Jim Thorpe, world's greatest athlete.* Norman, OK: University of Oklahoma Press.

Williams, Dana. 2007. "Where's the honor: Attitudes toward the 'Fighting Sioux' nickname and logo." *Sociology of Sport Journal, 24,* 437–56.

Discussion Questions

1 Who were the Native Americans, and how are they depicted in history books?

2 What was the purpose of Native American Boarding schools?

3 Why did many traditional Native Americans not participate in sports?

4 Why are Native American Mascots a common fixture in the world of athletics?

5 "All in fun" has been the claim for using Native American names and mascots in sports. How does that argument hold?

CHAPTER 7

Racism Against Chican@/Latin@

Race, Racialization and the Latino Populations in the United States

Tomás Almaguer

The Racialization of Latinos in the United States

The Latino population has historically occupied a unique position in the racial and ethnic hierarchy of the United States. It is important to assess how Latinos have been racialized over time and the various ways that they have complicated how we think about race. When *Racial Formation in the United States* was published in 1986, the federal government's standards for defining racial and ethnic groups had recently been reformulated. In 1977 the Office of Management and Budget's Statistical Policy Division and Office of Information and Regulatory Affairs issued "Directive 15: Race and Ethnic Standards for Federal Statistics and Administrative Reporting." That decree standardized the governmental collection and use of "racial" and "ethnic" statistics in the United States. It provided new operational definitions for the OMB's racial/ethnic cartography of the United States. Directive 15 clearly specified the codification of four major "races"—"American Indian or Alaska Native," "Asian or Pacific Islander," "Black," and "White"—and the delineation of two "ethnic" groups—"Hispanic origin" and "not of Hispanic origin." According to Ruben Rumbaut, "Since that time, in keeping with the logic of this classification system, census data on Hispanics have been officially reported with a footnote indicating that 'Hispanics may be of any race' " (Rumbaut 2009, 24).

These race and ethnic standards were revised in 1977 in response to mounting criticisms of the way these categories were deployed in implementing Directive 15. In that year, the federal government adopted a new set of standards for defining racial/ethnic categories, which led to the formalization of five "racial" groups rather than four.

In essence, the "Pacific Islander" population was disaggregated from the "Asian American" population and placed in a separate racial category. Census 2000 offered respondents for the first time the option of selecting more than one racial designation and reworded the two existing "ethnic" categories as "Hispanic or Latino" and "not Hispanic or Latino." In so doing, the census formally defined an individual of "Hispanic or Latino" background as "a person of Cuban, Mexican, Puerto Rican, South or Central American, or other Spanish culture or origins, regardless of race."

The revisions to Directive 15 in 1977 were the product of intense political contestations and vociferous criticisms from various quarters. In this regard, as Rumbaut discovered, the announcement reporting these changes in the *Federal Register* candidly noted: "The categories in this classification are social-political constructs and should not be interpreted as being scientific or anthropological in nature. ... The standards have been developed to provide a common language for uniformity and comparability in the collection and use of data on race and ethnicity by Federal agencies" (Rumbaut 2009, 25). In his perceptive assessment of these OMB changes, Rumbaut concludes: "The classification of 'Hispanic' or 'Latino' itself is new, an instance of a panethnic category created by law decades ago. But the groups subsumed under that label— Mexicans, Puerto Ricans, Cubans, Dominicans, Salvadorans, Guatemalans, Colombians, Peruvians, Ecuadorians, and the other dozen nationalities from Latin American and even Spain itself—were not 'Hispanics' or 'Latinos' in their countries of origin; rather, they only became so in the United States. That catchall label has a particular meaning only in the U.S. context in which it was constructed and is applied, and where its meaning continues to evolve" (16–17).

Yet many Latinos continue to base their racial identities on the way that the various nationalities were racialized in their country of origin when it was part of the Spanish colonial empire.[1] However, this highly variegated and nuanced racial system clashes with the way racial categories are more starkly drawn and defined in the United States. It appears that Latino immigrants are racialized in one particular way in the Spanish colonial context and then reracialized under the cultural logic of another racial order when they come to this country.

This difficulty in unambiguously racializing the Latino population has a long and complex history in this country that dates back to at least the middle of the nineteenth century when the United States seized control of the American Southwest through the U.S.–Mexico War of 1846–48. For example, it was principally as a result of the annexation of the Southwest that the Mexican population was formally granted U.S. citizenship and, in effect, deemed an "honorary white" population. The nearly 110,000 Mexicanos who remained in the territory ceded by Mexico one year after the ratification of the Treaty of Guadalupe Hidalgo (1848) became U.S. citizens with formally recognized claims to the prerogatives and privileges of whiteness. (Whether they were ever fully or meaningfully extended in the various territories and eventual states is quite another matter altogether).[2]

Clear codification of the racial status of the Mexican population can be seen in the 1850 decennial U.S. census; when the newly conquered Mexican population in the American Southwest was enumerated as "White," as it remained until 1930. In that year, they were summarily removed from the white category and placed in a separate racial designation as "Mexican." By the Great Depression, the number of Mexican people in the United States had grown to more than 1.5 million and had become the source of intense anti-immigrant xenophobia.

By 1940, however, the Mexican population was once again redefined as part of the "white" population and marked as speaking the "Spanish mother tongue." In that year, the federal census classified "persons of Mexican birth or ancestry who were not defined as Indian or some other nonwhite race ... as white." The federal censuses of 1950 and 1960 continued to enumerate Mexicans as "white persons of Spanish surname."[3]

When one spoke of the Latino/Hispanic population in the late 1960s, before the publication of *Racial Formation in the United States,* one still referred primarily to Mexicans. This was at a time before widespread and sustained Puerto Rican, Cuban, or Central American immigration to the United States. After 1960, however, things changed dramatically and quickly. The explosive rise in Latino immigration after 1965 led to the exponential increase in the pan-Latino population in the United States, one not only far larger but also more racially diverse than it had been in prior years.

In 1970 the federal census relied on the category "Hispanic" to capture the tremendous internal diversity of the various Latino nationalities in the United States. It underscored their common "Hispanic" (i.e., Spanish) ethnicity and former status as part of the Spanish colonial world. Having a "common culture" rooted in the Spanish language and Catholic religion was the key ethnic signifier that bound these diverse nationalities into one category.[4] This shared ethnic background is something that none of the other racialized populations have in common that are placed in the discrete racial categories deployed in the United States. None of the groups racialized as "White," "Black," "Asian," Hawaiian/Pacific Islander," or "American Indian" share a common culture solidly anchored in one particular language or religious background. Latinos are thus a unique population in this regard.

By 1970 there were more than 10 million "Hispanics" in the United States. Mexicans were still the largest Latino population, numbering 4.5 million and accounting for nearly 45 percent of Hispanics in the United States at the time. In that year there were also 1.5 million Puerto Ricans; 550,000 Cubans; 1.5 million Central and South Americans; and another million designated as some "Other Spanish" population.

By 1990, a mere twenty years later, the Hispanic population had more than doubled to nearly 22 million. By the time Census 2000 was taken, the Hispanic/Latino population had dramatically risen to 35.2 million and accounted for nearly 12.5 percent of the total U.S. population. Mexicans still remained the largest Latino nationality, comprising 60 percent of the Latino population in that year. They were followed by Puerto Ricans (9.7%), Central Americans (3.5%), South Americans (4.0%), Dominicans (2.3%), and the "Other Hispanic" category (15.7%).

By the time Census 2000 was taken, Latinos had actually surpassed African Americans as the largest racial-ethnic group in the United States. Each accounted for 35 million individuals that year, or approximately 12.5 percent of the total U.S. population. However, by 2007 the number of

Latinos in the United States had dramatically swelled to nearly 45 million, or 15 percent of the total population. In the fifty-year period from 1950 to 2000, the Latino population had dramatically increased from approximately 4 million to over 35 million individuals. Census 2010 data has documented that the Latino population grew from 35.3 million in 2000 to over 50 million in 2010 (U.S. Bureau of the Census 2010). Current population trends suggest that by the year 2050 Latinos will have increased in number to an estimated 128 million people, or 29 percent of the total U.S. population. Demographers predict that they will significantly exceed the total number of all other racial/ethnic groups combined. African Americans, for example, are projected to continue to account for only 13 percent of the national total; while Asian Americas will account for another 9 percent of the U.S. population in 2050 (Rumbaut 2009, 17).

This monumental population increase has been accompanied by a number of profound structural changes that have powerfully impacted our perceptions of race and race relations in the United States. Among these changes worth noting here have been the momentous change in U.S. immigration policy in 1965 (which shifted the focus away from Western Europe and toward Latin America and Asia), the hard-won victories of the Civil Rights Movement (which arguably extended meaningful, first-class citizenship rights to African Americans and other people of color), and the overturning of anti-miscegenation laws, through *Loving v. Commonwealth of Virginia*. That 1967 Supreme Court decision put an end to more than three hundred years of legal prohibitions on interracial marriages in the United States and directly contributed to the recent rise of a growing "multiracial" population. This mixed-race population grew by nearly 30 percent in the from 2000 to 2010 and now comprises approximately 3 percent of the total U.S. population (U.S. Bureau of the Census 2010). If one were to combine this "multiracial" population with the Latino population, approximately 18 percent of the total U.S. population is arguably mixed-race. This is clearly a very recent historical development that has had profound implications for how we understand the meaning of race and for the changing nature of race relations in the contemporary United States.

The Conundrums of Racial Identity Among the Latino Population

We know from the way that Latinos responded to both the race and ethnic questions in Census 2000 that many had difficulty placing themselves in the discrete racial categories used in the federal census. It appears that many Latinos resorted to constructions of racial categories and identities drawn from the Spanish colonial world or simply used their nationality as the basis of their racial identity. In 2000, more than half (52.3%) of the pan-Latino population racially defined themselves as "White." Despite the central role that the Indigenous and African populations played in the Spanish racial regime, it is surprising that so very few Latinos actually identify as either Indian or black. Less than 1 percent defined themselves in 2000 as "American

Indian" or "Alaska Native, Asian, or Native Hawaiian or other Pacific Islander." Only 1.4 percent of Latinos racially defined themselves as "Black," while another 3.9 percent claimed to be of "two or more races" (Candelario 2007a, 345). It is significant that less than 2 percent of the total U.S. population indicated that they were of more than one race. But of those who did, Hispanics were more than three times as likely to report being of "two or more races" than non-Hispanics (Rumbaut 2009, 26–27).

In Census 2000 a person who ethnically identified as "Hispanic" or "Latino" was, in essence, separated from the other five racial categories and then asked to racially define him- or herself based on the OMB's newly reformulated racial categories. Nearly half of the Latino populations when asked to give their racial identity in Census 2000 provided answers that led to their being placed in the "some other race" category. Many Latinos simply used their nationality as a proxy for race by indicating that they were "Chicano," "Cuban," "Puerto Rican," "Dominican," or some another Latino nationality. Others invoked the nuanced racial categories or skin-color designations used in their countries of origin to racially identify themselves.

What is significant here is the large number of Latinos who do not see themselves as falling into any of the discrete racial categories deployed on the federal census. Over 40 percent (41.2%) of Latinos opted to define themselves as belonging to "some other race." For many of these individual, intermediate racial categories such as "mestizo" and "mulato" or color designations such as "trigueño" or "moreno" were written into the space provided.[5]

There are, of course, significant differences among the pan-Latino population in how the different nationalities racially identify themselves. The vast majority of people from Cuba, Uruguay, Argentina, and Chile see themselves as white (75–88%). Panamanians claim the highest percentage of individuals who self-define as black (40.1%), followed by Dominicans, Costa Ricans, and Hondurans (9.4%, 7.2%, and 5.3%, respectively) (Candelario 2007a, 345).

People from the Dominican Republic, El Salvador, and Guatemala are among the most likely to define themselves as being of "some other race." Dominicans, on the other hand, often racially self-identify by invoking the intermediate categories "Indio blanco" and "Indio oscuro," which are among the core racial designations in the Dominican Republic. In Haiti, only the Francophone immigrant population is seen as being black.[6]

Given the prerogatives and entitlements of whiteness extended to both Mexicans and Puerto Ricans as a result of U.S. colonial conquest (the Treaty of Guadalupe Hidalgo in 1848 and the Jones Act in 1917), it is not surprising that both of the two largest Latino groups generally see themselves as a white population.[7] In 2000, approximately 47 percent of both Mexicans and Puerto Ricans racially defined themselves as white.

"Some other race" was the second-largest category enumerated by Mexicans (45.4%) and Puerto Ricans (38.4%) when they were asked to racially identify themselves. Another 10.7 percent of Mexicans and 14.3 percent of Puerto Ricans did not answer the race question. Once again, only a very small number of Mexicans define themselves as "Black" (0.7%). Despite the growing number of indigenous people from Mexico now in the United States, only about 1 percent of

Mexicans racially self-define as "Indian." A smaller number of Puerto Ricans identified themselves as "Indian" (0.5%), while a significant number (5.8%) racially defined themselves as "Black." Both groups made significant use of the "two or more races" category. However, given their mixed-raced ancestry, it is surprising that only 5.2 percent of Mexicans and 7.8 percent of Puerto Ricans claimed more than one racial background.[8]

The Reracialization of Latino Populations in the United States

While this ambiguity in how Latinos racially identify themselves is understandable given that they have straddled two very different racial regimes, they apparently have far less trouble racializing one another. Nowhere is this more apparent than in the ways that the two largest Latino populations have increasingly come into conflict in ways that can be traced to how each group racializes the other. In other words, Mexicans and Puerto Ricans have increasingly come to racially define each other through the lens and logic of the Spanish racial regime that previously ensnared them. They apparently rely on this cultural logic after immigrating to the United States.

Growing evidence of this pattern can be seen in a number of recent ethnographic studies that have explored the often contentious relationship between the two Latino populations. Let us now explore the curious way that this reracialization unfolds and how it complicates the forging of a pan-Latino identity among the various Latino nationalities in the United States.

Some of the most interesting, and troubling, research in Latino studies has produced superb ethnographic studies of multiple Latino populations in areas where they have converged in recent years. Nicolas De Genova and Ana Ramos-Zayas' *Latino Crossings* (2003), De Genova's *Working the Boundaries* (2005), Gina Perez's *The Near Northwest Side Story* (2004), Arlene Davila's *Barrio Dreams* (2004), and Robert Smith's *Mexican New York* (2006) are a few examples of this sophisticated ethnographic research. While each of these scholars addresses a distinct set of issues, all have in the process also documented the increasing tensions between recent Mexican immigrants and Puerto Rican migrants in Chicago and New York City.

De Genova and Ramos-Zayas's powerful book *Latino Crossings* offers the following troubling summary of this contentious intergroup conflict:

> What emerge are competing visions of each group's "civilized" or "modern" qualities in juxtaposition to the other's purported "rudeness" or "backwardness." ... Mexican immigrants often generalized from the allegation that Puerto Ricans were "lazy" to posit variously they were like-wise untrustworthy, deceptive, willing to cheat, disagreeable, nervous, rude, aggressive, violent, dangerous, and criminal. In constructing these racialized images

of the character of Puerto Ricans as a group, Mexicans were implicitly celebrating themselves as educated, well-mannered, and civilized. In contrast, Puerto Ricans frequently elaborated further upon their perceptions of Mexicans as uninitiated into the workings of the sociopolitical system in the United States and inclined to sacrifice their dignity in a desperate quest for work. Puerto Ricans commonly coupled these judgments with allegations that Mexicans, as a group, were submissive, obliging, gullible, naïve, rustic, out-moded, folksy, backward, and predominantly "cultural," in contrast to a vision of themselves as political, principled, sophisticated, stylish, dynamic, urban, and modern. Remarkably, these parallel discourses on the parts of both groups served to sustain their own divergent claims of civility or modernity, in ways that implied their differential worthiness for the entitlements of citizenship. (De Genova and Ramos-Zayas 2003, 83)

While there is considerable merit in De Genova and Ramos-Zayas's characterization of this ethnic tension, I suspect that there is something far more fundamental taking place here than a cultural conflict between two Latino populations. At the core of these tensions are the different ways that each group constructs the meaning of race in its country of origin and how each group reracializes the other in the United States. It is the distinct constructions of race in the Spanish and U.S. colonial contexts that leads to each group viewing the other through the eyes of the two colonial regimes that have largely structured their historical experiences. In other words, Mexicans appear to view Puerto Ricans principally through the lens of how "blackness" is constructed in both Mexico and in the United States. Puerto Ricans, on the other hand, essentially come to view Mexicans through the lens of how "Indianness" is given meaning in Puerto Rico and in the United States. While notions of "civilization" and "modernity" undeniably play a role in these racialized constructions, they do so through the way that blackness and Indianness have been infused with racialized cultural meaning in their distinct historical experiences.

These racialized constructions are the product of the ways that each group has internalized its Spanish colonial world's view of the African and Indigenous populations subjugated in Mexico and Puerto Rico. Added to that foundation, these groups then reracialize each other under the discursive logic that structures the meaning of race in the United States. Mexicans take what they learned from their Spanish colonizers and fuse that with what they quickly learn about the meaning of race in the white supremacist United States. The negative constructions of blackness that Mexican immigrants bring with them from Mexico are exacerbated by the way in which African Americans and black Latinos are racially constructed by the white population in the United States. Puerto Ricans, and also many African Americans, tend to immediately mark and position Mexicans as a largely backward population that they view as fundamentally "Indian."

[...]

Puerto Rican Views of Race in Puerto Rico and the United States

Like ethnic Mexicans, Puerto Ricans in both the United States and the island also invoke a gradational racial hierarchy to mark lines of racial difference among themselves. In his interesting analysis of racial identity among Puerto Ricans, anthropologist Jorge Duany has documented at least nineteen different ways in which Puerto Ricans have racially define themselves on the island. Among these racial categories and skin-color referents are *blanco* (white), *trigueño* (wheat-colored or brunette; usually light mulatto), *moreno* (dark-skinned; usually dark mulatto), *mulato* (mixed-race; rarely used in public); *Indio* (literally, Indian; brown skin with straight hair); *prieto* (dark-skinned; usually derogatory); *negro* (black; rarely used as a direct term of reference); and *negrito* (literally, little black) (Duany 2002b).

Duany maintains that "racialized images of Indians and Africans have dominated how Puerto Ricans imagined their ethnic background" (Duany 2002b, 276). "Puerto Rican identity," he contends, "reveals the systematic overvaluation of the Hispanic element, the romanticization of Taino Indians, and the underestimation of the African-derived ingredients" (280). Like Mexicans, Puerto Ricans also have long and deep investments in their claims to whiteness. For example, in response to the Census 2000 question on race, approximately 48 percent of Puerto Ricans in the United States claimed to be "white," while another 38 percent gave responses that led to their being categorized as belonging to "some other race" (Jung and Almaguer 2004, 72). Despite the widespread racial mixing in their Spanish colonial history, very few Puerto Ricans actually claim to be either "Black" or "Indian" in any significant numbers. Only 5.8 percent of Puerto Ricans identified as "Black," and less than 1 percent as "Indian" in Census 2000 (Jung and Almaguer 2004, 72). Curiously, Duany has shown that the actual number of Puerto Ricans on the island—known as "the whitest of the Antilles"—who identify as "White" has actually grown over the years and was calibrated at over 80 percent in Census 2000 (Duany 2002b, 248).

What is so interesting about the racial classifications deployed among Puerto Ricans is the particular way in which Indianness is socially marked. The preconquest indigenous Taino population has taken on importance in the way that Puerto Ricans have come to racialize Mexicans. Being of Taino ancestry assumes certain social associations that capture the way in which Indianness is infused with racial meaning in Puerto Rico. The dominant characterizations of the Taino, according to Duany, constitute the prototype of Rousseau's "noble savage" (in which these indigenous people are seen as "docile, sedentary, indolent, tranquil, and chaste") (Duany 2002b, 268).

In terms of skin color, the most relied-upon racial descriptions of the Taino is "neither white nor black but brown or 'copper like' and that their intermediate phenotype placed them between Europeans and Africans in moral and ascetic terms" (Duany 2002b, 270). Duany contends that few "standard descriptions of the Taino Indians fail to mention their skin color, physical stature, bodily constitution, hair texture, and facial features. ... For example, one third-grade textbook widely used in Puerto Rico today lists the following 'characteristics of the Taino race': medium build, coppertone skin, black and straight hair, prominent cheekbones, slightly slanted eyes, long nose, and relatively thick lips. These features are sharply contrasted with the phenotypes of both Spaniards and Africans" (270).

In Chicago, Puerto Ricans are quick to acknowledge that Mexicans have a much closer and deeper association with Indianness than do Puerto Ricans. As one informant told De Genova and Ramos-Zayas: "Mexicans have real Indians. We (Puerto Ricans) have Indian blood in our heritage, be we are not *Indian* Indian" (2003, 192). According to sociologist Robert Smith, the racial mapping of Mexican bodies in Indian terms also occurs in New York City (R. Smith 2006).

Arlene Davila also underscores this point in her book *Barrio Dreams*. Therein she acknowledges that Herman Badillo, the Puerto Rican chairman of the board of trustees at the City University of New York and unsuccessful candidate for mayor in 2001, articulated the commonly held view among Puerto Ricans that Mexicans "'came from the hills,' from countries with little tradition of education, and were mostly short and straight haired Indians. These racist comments exposed stereotypes of Mexicans as less educated or unsophisticated 'newcomers,' as opposed the 'urban savviness' of Puerto Ricans" (Davila 2004, 173).

This perception that Mexicans are racially "more Indian" than Puerto Ricans occasionally finds expression in how these Latino groups explicitly racialize one another's gendered bodies. A conversation among young Puerto Rican informants in *Latino Crossings* offers an insightful example of this racialization: "You can tell if someone is Mexican or Puerto Rican by looking at their asses. … Yeah, you see, Puerto Ricans have an ass and Mexicans are flat-assed—they have an Indian ass. … Yeah, Selena was real pretty. She looked Puerto Rican, you know. She had an ass … Women who have big tits have flat asses. If you really want to know if a woman has a flat ass, you look at her chest. That's why you have a lot of Mexican women who are big on top and have no ass" (quoted in Davila 2004, 193).

This ethnographic data documents the troubling way that Latino populations previously ensnared by the Spanish colonial empire have come to view one another in the United States. This brings us back to how Puerto Ricans view the Mexican immigrant population in Chicago as essentially "Indians." It is their construction of the Taino that provides a window on how they have come to construct recent Mexican immigrants. This is, in one respect, just the other side of the way Puerto Ricans are have been constructed as "black" by the Mexican population in Chicago.

Conclusion

This chapter explores the unique way in which the Latino population has been racialized in the United States and situated within its racial and ethnic landscape. I argue that Latinos stand alone among communities of color in the United States in that they are principally defined in ethnic—rather than racial—terms. It is fundamentally on the basis of their common culture (based on the Spanish language and Catholic religion) that they are placed in the "Spanish/Hispanic/Latino" category rather than one discrete racial category. In other words, it is the cultural logic of ethnicity, rather than that of race per se, that leads to placing the multiracial Latino populations in the "Spanish/Hispanic/Latino" ethnic category.

In addition to the unique way that Latinos are located within the racial and ethnic landscape of the United States, I attempt to make sense of the equally curious and troubling way that Latinos have come to racialize one another in areas where they have increasingly settled in the United States. There is mounting ethnographic evidence that Latinos have resorted to stigmatizing one another by using the ways in which racial categories were infused with meaning in the Spanish colonial world. It is in the disparaging ways that Indianness and blackness are given cultural meaning in the countries of origin that we are able to better understand the documented tensions between the two largest Latino populations in the United States. Both Mexicans and Puerto Ricans, both of whom have valorized and made direct claims to the privileges and entitlements of "whiteness," resort to racializing each another by drawing on the most stigmatizing ways that race is defined in both Mexico and Puerto Rico. Mexicans largely denigrate Puerto Ricans on the basis of their African ancestry, while Puerto Ricans denigrate Mexicans based on their putative Indianness.

The complex meaning of race and the particular way that racialization unfolds in the United States is an ever changing sociohistorical process. Nowhere are the ambiguities and vagaries of racial formation in this country more starkly evident than in the case of the Latino population. Making sense of the unique way that race and racialization has been given cultural meaning among Latinos provides yet another window on a process that has been most eloquently articulated in Michael Omi and Howard Winant's seminal work. *Racial Formation in the United States* has enabled us to clearly see that race is fundamentally a sociohistorical category at once fictional and yet also profoundly real in its profound sociological implications.

One of these implications is the particular way that the United States has given cultural meaning to racial designations and attempts to locate various populations within the logic of the racial categories deployed in the United States. It is here that the Latino populations continue to complicate the very logic of the racial formation process in this country. As I show here, there is also mounting ethnographic evidence that Latinos often resort to the way that race was given specific meaning in the Spanish colonial context to racialize one another. It is here, in the troubling convergence of two distinct racial regimes in the lives of the Latino population, that we may illuminate the conundrums and contestations inherent in the racial formation process in the United States.

Notes

1 In this regard, see the canonical study by Ramón Gutiérrez on the way these racial lines were initially drawn in Spanish colonial New Mexico (Gutiérrez 1991). Also see his classic essay "Hispanic Identities in the Southwestern United States" (Gutiérrez 2009).

2 A number of scholars have explored the racialization of the Mexican population after the U.S.–Mexico War. See, for example, Menchaca 2001, 2007; Haas 1995; Almaguer 1994; Foley 1997, 2007; Montejano 1987; Guglielmo 2006; Ruiz 2004; Gómez 2007, 2009.

3 A number of scholars have written about the historical and contemporary ambiguities in the placement of Latinos in the decennial census. See, for example, C. Rodríguez 2000, 2009; and Tienda and Ortiz 1986.

4 See, for example, Portes 2007.

5 For example, I answered the ethnic question on both Census 2000 and Census 2010 by indicating that I was of "Spanish/Hispanic/Latino" origin (I ethnically self-identify as "Chicano"). I then indicated in response to the race question that I was "mestizo" when asked "What is this person's race?" As a result, that particular response led to my being summarily placed in the "Some other race" category.

6 See, in this regard, Candelario 2007b and Torres-Saillant 1998, 2007.

7 The scholarly literature on the claims to whiteness by both Mexicans and Puerto Ricans continues to increase over time. On the Mexican population, for example, see Almaguer 1994; Foley 1997, 2007; Guglielmo 2006; and Menchaca 2007. On Puerto Ricans, see Duany 2002a, 2003, and 2007; Loveman and Muniz 2007; Landale and Oropesa 2002; and Vidal-Ortiz 2004.

8 These figures are based on the use of U.S. Census Public Use Microdata Samples (PUMSs) for 2000 that are gathered in Jung and Almaguer 2004, 72.

Bibliography

Almaguer, Tomás. 1994. *Racial Fault Lines: The Historical Origins of White Supremacy in California*. Berkeley: University of California Press.

Candelario, Ginetta E. B. 2007a. Color Matters: Latina/o Racial Identities and Life Chances. In *A Companion to Latino Studies,* ed. Juan Flores and Renato Rosaldo. Malden, MA: Blackwell.

———. 2007b. *Black behind the Ears: Dominican Racial Identity from Museums to Beauty Shops.* Durham, NC: Duke University Press.

Davila, Arlene. 2004. *Barrio Dreams: Puerto Ricans, Latinos, and the Neoliberal City*. Berkeley: University of California Press.

De Genova, Nicholas. 2005. *Working the Boundaries: Race, Space, and "Illegality" in Mexican Chicago*. Durham, NC: Duke University Press.

De Genova, Nicholas, and Ana Y. Ramos-Zayas. 2003. *Latino Crossings: Mexicans, Puerto Ricans, and the Politics of Race and Citizenship*. New York: Routledge.

Duany, Jorge. 2002a. Neither Black nor White: The Representation of Racial Identity among Puerto Ricans on the Island and in the U.S. Mainland. In *The Puerto Rican Nation on the Move: Identities on the Island and in the United States*. Chapel Hill: University of North Carolina Press.

_____. 2002b. *The Puerto Rican Nation on the Move: Identities on the Island and in the United States*. Chapel Hill: University of North Carolina Press.

_____. 2003. Nation, Migration, Identity: The Case of Puerto Ricans. *Latino Studies Journal* 1 (3): 424–444.

_____. 2007. Nation and Migration: Rethinking Puerto Rican Identity in a Transnational Context. In *None of the Above: Puerto Ricans in the Global Era*, ed. Frances Negron-Muntaner. New York: Palgrave MacMillan.

Foley, Neil. 1997. *The White Scourge: Mexicans, Blacks, and Poor Whites in Texas Cotton Culture*. Berkeley: University of California Press.

_____. 2007. "God Bless the Law, He Is White": Legal, Local, and International Politics of Latina/o and Black Desegregation Cases in Post–World War II California and Texas. In *A Companion to Latino Studies*, ed. Juan Flores and Renato Rosaldo. Malden, MA: Blackwell Publishing.

Gómez, Laura E. 2007. *Manifest Destinies: The Making of the Mexican American Race*. New York: New York University Press.

_____. 2009. Opposite One-Drop Rules: Mexican Americans, African Americans, and the Need to Reconceive Turn-of-the-Century Race Relations. In *How the United States Racializes Latinos: White Hegemony and Its Consequences*, ed. Jose A. Cobas, Jorge Duany, and Joe R. Feagin. Boulder: Paradigm.

Guglielmo, Thomas A. 2006. Fighting for Caucasian Rights: Mexicans, Mexican Americans, and the Transnational Struggle for Civil Rights in World War II Texas. *Journal of American History* 92 (4): 1212–1237.

Gutiérrez, Ramón A. 1991. *When Jesus Came, the Corn Mothers Went Away: Marriage, Sexuality, and Power in New Mexico, 1500–1846*. Stanford: Stanford University Press.

_____. 2009. Hispanic Identities in the Southwestern United States. In *Race and Classification: The Case of Mexican Americans*, ed. Ilona Katzew and Susan Deans-Smith. Stanford: Stanford University Press.

Haas, Lisbeth. 1995. *Conquests and Historical Identities in California, 1769–1936*. Berkeley: University of California Press.

Jung, Moon-Kie, and Tomás Almaguer. 2004. The State and the Production of Racial Categories. In *Race and Ethnicity: Across Time, Space, and Discipline*, ed. Rodney D. Coates. Leiden, The Netherlands: Brill.

Landale, Nancy S., and Ralph Salvatore Oropesa. 2002. White, Black, or Puerto Rican?: Racial Self-Identification among Mainland and Island Puerto Ricans. *Social Forces* 81 (1): 231–254.

Loveman, Mara, and Jeronimo O. Muniz. 2007. How Puerto Ricans Became White: Boundary Dynamics and Inter-census Racial Reclassification. *American Sociological Review* 72 (6): 915–939.

Menchaca, Martha. 2001. *Recovering History, Constructing Race: The Indian, Black, and White Roots of Mexican Americans*. Austin: University of Texas Press.

_____. 2007. Latinos/as and the *Mestizo* Racial Heritage of Mexican Americans. In *A Companion to Latino Studies*, ed. Juan Flores and Renato Rosaldo. Malden, MA: Blackwell.

Montejano, David. 1987. *Anglos and Mexicans in the Making of Texas, 1836–1986*. Austin: University of Texas Press.

Omi, Michael, and Howard Winant. 1986. *Racial Formation in the United States: From the 1960s to the 1980s.* New York: Routledge.

Perez, Gina M. 2004. *The Near Northwest Side Story: Migration, Displacement, and Puerto Rican Families.* Berkeley: University of California Press.

Portes, Alejandro. 2007. The New Latin Nation: Immigration and Hispanic Population in the United States. In *A Companion to Latino Studies,* ed. Juan Flores and Renato Rosaldo. Malden, MA: Blackwell.

Rodríguez, Clara E. 2000. *Changing Race: Latinos, the Census, and the History of Ethnicity in the United States.* New York: New York University Press.

_____ . 2009. Counting Latinos in the U.S. Census. In *Race and Classification: The Case of Mexican Americans,* ed. Ilona Katzew and Susan Deans-Smith. Stanford: Stanford University Press.

Ruiz, Vicki L. 2004. *Morena/o, blanca/o y café con leche:* Racial Constructions in Chicana/o Historiography. *Mexican Studies / Estudios Mexicanos* 20 (2): 343–359.

Rumbaut, Ruben G. 2009. Pigments of Our Imagination: On the Racialization and Racial Identity of "Hispanics" and "Latinos." In *How the United States Racializes Latinos: White Hegemony and Its Consequences,* ed. Jose A. Cobas, Jorge Duany, and Joe R. Feagin. Boulder, CO: Paradigm.

Smith, Robert Courtney. 2006. *Mexican New York: Transnational Lives of New Immigrants.* Berkeley: University of California Press.

Tienda, Marta, and Vilma Ortiz. 1986. "Hispanicity" and the 1980 Census. *Social Science Quarterly* 67 (1): 3–20.

Torres-Saillant, Silvio. 1998. The Tribulations of Blackness: Stages in Dominican Racial Identity. *Latin American Perspectives* 25 (3): 126–146.

_____ . 2007. Afro-Latinas/os and the Racial Wall. In *A Companion to Latino Studies,* ed. Juan Flores and Renato Rosaldo. Malden, MA: Blackwell.

U.S. Bureau of the Census. 2010. *Overview of Race and Hispanic Origin: 2010.* Issued March 2011 http://www.census.gov/prod/cen2010/briefs/c2010br-02.pdf. Accessed January 8, 2012.

Vidal-Ortiz, Salvador. 2004. On Being a White Person of Color: Using Autoethnography in Understanding Puerto Rican's Racialization. *Qualitative Sociology* 27 (2): 179–203.

Discussion Questions

1   How did Latinos become US citizens in the early 1960s?

2   Why was this group of ethnic minorities called "Hispanics" by the federal government?

3   Identify the largest group in the Hispanic community, and give reasons why they became the largest.

4   In analyzing the racial formation of Latinos, describe how racialization unfolds in the United States.

5   Describe how Latino groups define each other based on their "Spanish" ethnicity.

CHAPTER 8

Racism Against African Americans

Racial Discrimination, Negative Stereotypes, Threats and African-American Offending

James D. Unnever and Shaun L. Gabbidon

Racial Discrimination and the General Well-Being of African Americans

The literature is replete with analysis of how African Americans suffer because of their exposure to different aspects of racial discrimination (Blistein, 2009; Gabbidon and Peterson, 2006; Geronimus, Hicken, Keene, and Bound, 2006; Geronimus and Thompson, 2004; Harrell, 2000; Klonoff et al., 1999; Major and O'Brien, 2005). Scholars have studied the effect that racial discrimination has on African Americans on diminished mental health, stress, high blood pressure, cognitive processing, substance abuse, depression, coronary heart disease, and hypertension (for reviews of this literature, see Brondolo, ver Halen, Pencille, Beatty, and Contrada, 2009; Clark, Anderson, Clark, and Williams, 1999; Williams, Neighbors, and Jackson, 2003; Williams, Neighbors, and Jackson, 2008). Yet, nearly all of this research shows the deleterious health-related, not criminogenic (crime-causing), consequences of racial discrimination. Below we briefly review a few studies (the literature is exponential) that show that perceived discrimination has negative effects on the well-being of African Americans regardless of their age, class, or gender.

Keith, Lincoln, Taylor and Jackson (2010) analyzed data from the National Survey of American Life and investigated the relationship between perceived discrimination and depressive symptoms among African American women aged 18–98 years. Keith et al. (2010:48) found that: "discrimination is a major threat to African American women's mental health. They are vulnerable to discrimination, in part, because discrimination undermines their beliefs in mastery making them less psychologically resilient." Perceived racial discrimination was measured with items such as, "called names or insulted," "threatened or harassed," and "followed around in stores," and mastery was assessed with items such as, "no way I can solve problems" and "I have little control over what happens" (see also Odom and Vernon-Feagans, 2010).

African American youth are also vulnerable to the negative consequences of racial discrimination (Seaton, Yip, and Sellers, 2009; Seaton, 2010). Seaton and Yip (2009) analyzed data collected on 252 urban African American adolescents (ages 13 to 18). They found a negative relationship between perceived discrimination and the youth's self-esteem and a positive relationship between perceived discrimination and depressive symptoms. The more these youths perceived racial discrimination, the more likely they were to be depressed and to lack self-esteem. Measures that Seaton and Yip (2009) used to assess perceived discrimination included, "White people have treated you as if you were stupid and needed things explained to you slowly or several times" and "You think you did not receive a school award you deserved because you are Black." Self-esteem was measured with the Rosenberg scale, which included items such as "On the whole, I am satisfied with myself." They measured depressive symptoms using the Center for Epidemiological Studies Depression Scale (CES-D), which included items such as, "I did not feel like eating, my appetite was poor." Relatedly, Brody, Chen, Murry, Ge, Simons, Gibbons, Gerrard, and Cutrona (2006:1183) analyzed three waves of longitudinal data from the Family and Community Health Study and found that perceived discrimination was related "to conduct problems and depressive symptoms among African American youths across late childhood and early adolescence." They used a scale that assessed perceived discrimination over the past year ("a store owner or sales person working at a business treated you in a disrespectful way because you are African American," "someone yelled a racial insult at you because you are African American," and "you encountered Whites who didn't expect you to do well because you are African American").

Furthermore, perceived racial discrimination has been found to diminish the well-being among African American men. African American men have the highest age-adjusted death rate of any group, experience higher rates of preventable illness, and suffer an increased incidence of preventable deaths while having lower alcohol-use rates than white men (Sellers, Bonham, Neighbors, and Amell, 2009). Sellers et al. (2009) analyzed a sample of 399 middle-class, well-educated African American men to assess whether they suffered the deleterious effects of racial discrimination. They used the Jackson and Williams discrimination stress scale (e.g., the men were asked whether because of their race they have been unfairly fired or denied a promotion, unfairly not hired for a job, unfairly stopped by the police, unfairly discouraged by a teacher from continuing education, or unfairly prevented from moving into a neighborhood) and examined whether it was related to their measures of the person's mental health (they used the SF-12 scale to assess mental health). Sellers et al. (2009) found that mental health problems are related to increases in perceived racial discrimination, even among middle-class, well-educated black men. Together, these studies indisputably show that "discrimination ranks in significance with major stressful life events such as divorce, job loss, and death of a loved one" (Sellers et al., 2009:33).

[...]

Racial Discrimination and Weak School Bonds

The data reveal vast differences in the ability of African Americans, especially black males, to achieve educational success. The gap between the high school graduation rates of African Americans and white males is glaring, 47 versus 78 percent. Perhaps more disconcerting, the data show that in some school districts (e.g., Pinellas County, FL and Charleston County, SC) less than 25 percent of African American males graduate from high school (in comparison to over 50 percent of white males) (Schott Foundation for Public Education, 2010).

Our theory asserts that racial discrimination can increase the probability of black offending by undermining the ability of African Americans to develop strong bonds with conventional institutions. We focus on the educational system to illustrate how racial discrimination weakens the ties that African Americans have with institutions because school failure is related to youth offending (Noble, 2006; Zahn, Agnew, Fishbein, Miller, Winn, Dakoff, Kruttschnitt, Giordano, Gottfredson, Payne, Feld, and Chesney-Lind, 2010). For example, Payne (2008:450) reports "that students who are more attached to their school and teachers and more committed to their education and who give more legitimacy to the school rules and norms will be involved in less delinquency." And, Carswell (2007) specifically found that African American students are less likely to engage in delinquency when they have strong bonds with their school. It is also noteworthy that scholars have found that African Americans are as strongly bonded to schools as whites and that the effect of weak school bonds on offending is equivalent for blacks and whites (Cernkovich and Giordano, 1992). Scholars have further found that school failure is related to other life course turning points such as unemployment, which in turn is related to adult offending (see also Baron, 2008; Crutchfield and Pitchford, 1997; Farrington, Gallagher, Morley, Ledger, and West, 1986; Giordano et al., 2007; Uggen, 2000). Hip-hop artist Gang Starr succinctly captures the reason why we focus on education: "The educational system presumes you fail/The next place is the corner then after that jail."

Thus, our thesis is straightforward. We assert that African Americans encounter a unique lived experience within their schools—that is, an experience not shared by whites—that causes them to develop weak bonds with the educational system. We argue that African Americans encounter the many variegated forms of racial discrimination within their schools.

As previously discussed, social bond theory argues that the fundamental cause for why African Americans and whites fail to develop strong ties with conventional institutions (e.g., attachment and commitment), such as with the educational system, is the failure of parents to bond with their children. Therefore, the failure of parents to develop strong ties with their children cascades into the person having difficulties bonding to other institutions such as with their schools and the legal system. As Hirschi (1969:94) states: "The more strongly a child is attached to his parents, the more strongly he is bound to their expectations, and therefore the more strongly he is bound to conformity with the legal norms of the larger society." Our theory of offending assumes that parenting can provide African American children with a solid foundation upon which other strong bonds are developed. Indeed, we discuss this process in our next chapter on racial socialization. However, our theory also posits that there are other reasons than poor parenting for why African Americans may develop weak bonds with conventional institutions. We assert that different forms of racial discrimination cause African Americans to develop weak ties with conventional institutions.

There are a multitude of ways that African Americans can encounter racial discrimination within their schools including, but not limited to, their white peers rejecting them because of their race (e.g., not allowed access to the "in-group"), being called racist epithets (e.g., the "N" word), being told racist jokes, being bullied because of their race, being physically attacked, teachers only calling on white students, teachers belittling black students, teachers assuming that they are "lazy" or prone to violence (i.e., invoking a stereotype threat), incidents of hate crimes targeting African Americans (e.g., a display of a white doll dressed in a Ku Klux Klan robe and a black doll with a noose around its neck), racially biased texts and curricula, racial tracking, discriminatory penalties (e.g., whites get detention while blacks get suspended from school for the same incident), disproportionately placing African American students in special education classes, lowered teacher expectations, less encouragement to take advanced courses, and the school authorities' denial and refusal to acknowledge that there is racism within their schools—that is, that racial stratification exists (Alliman-Brissett and Turner, 2010; Donaldson, 1996; Goldsmith, 2004; Mattison and Aber, 2007; Noble, 2006; Rosenbloom and Way, 2004; Wong, Eccles, and Sameroff, 2003). For example, the research indicates that 46 percent of African American students reported that they were given a lower grade than they deserve because of their race (Rivas-Drake, Hughes, and Way, 2009). And, Gregory and Weinstein (2008) found that African American students behaved more defiantly and less cooperatively when interacting with teachers that they perceived as being untrustworthy.

Scholars have found that pejorative stereotypes of African Americans pervade the classroom. Research indicates that teachers perceive African American middle school students as more defiant, disrespectful, and rule-breaking than other groups (Gregory and Weinstein, 2008). Therefore, not surprisingly, research shows that 51 percent of black students believe they are more likely to be suspended and 51 percent believe that the school is more likely to call the police because of their race (Ruck and Wortley, 2002). These percentages become more glaring when compared with whites. Ruck and Wortley (2002:192) note that "Black students were approximately 32 times more likely than White students to perceive discrimination with respect to the use of police at school and 27 times more likely to perceive that they would be treated worse by the police at school." Of note, in 2004 suspension data from the U.S. Department of Education Office for Civil Rights showed that African Americans were approximately three times more likely to be suspended than other groups and that these differences remained significant after controlling for the student's socioeconomic status (Gregory and Weinstein, 2008).

Importantly, the toxic effects of peer-based discrimination on weakening the ties that African American youths have with their schools should not be underestimated (Chavous, Rivas-Drake, Smalls, Griffin, and Cogburn, 2008). Scholars have found that within the context of schools, peer-based discrimination is particularly salient for how African Americans perceive their own race (i.e., their public regard). The more African American students perceived being racially discriminated against by their peers the more negatively they perceived their race (Rivas-Drake et al., 2009). Ruck and Wortley (2002) add that African American youths are more likely to perceive differential treatment, have less positive attitudes toward students of other groups, and have fewer positive out-group interactions in schools that are racially and ethnically self-segregated. In short, African American students confront a different reality than whites when they open the door to their school. For some African American students, whether they attend integrated or what has been referred to as "apartheid schools" that are populated by all blacks or minorities (Frankenburg, Lee, and Orfield, 2003), it may be a toxic racist environment contaminated with both pervasive negative stereotypes that "put them down" and instances of discrimination because they are African American.

Evidence is accumulating that supports our thesis that perceived racial discrimination undermines the ability of black youths to develop strong bonds with their schools. Wong et al. (2003) analyzed data from a longitudinal study (from seventh grade to the completion of the eighth grade) of an economically diverse sample of African American adolescents living in Maryland. Discrimination within the school by peers was measured with items such as the frequency that African Americans felt they got into fights, were not associated with, and not picked for particular teams or activities because of their race. Measures of teacher-based discrimination included how often students felt that their teachers called on them less, graded them more harshly, disciplined them more harshly, discouraged them from taking a class, and thought they were less smart because of their race. Consistent with our thesis, Wong et al. (2003) found that experiences of racial discrimination at school from one's teachers and peers predicted declines in grades, academic ability, self-concepts, and academic task values (see also Chavous et al., 2008). Also of interest, Wong et al. (2003) found that racial discrimination predicted increases in the proportion of peers who were not interested in school. Notably, these scholars found that perceived racial discrimination was related to delinquent behavior even after controlling for a host of other covariates.

In a related study, Dotterer, McHale, and Crouter (2009) examined whether weak school bonds developed among African American youths who perceived discrimination by their school peers (e.g., "how often have kids at school excluded you from their activities because you are African American?") and teachers (e.g., "how often have you had to work harder in school than white kids to get the same praise or the same grades from your teachers because you are African American?"). Using the first phase of a longitudinal dataset collected from two large eastern images create expectations of others, and they tend to filter out information that is inconsistent with their preconceived opinions of these groups (Sigelman and Tuch, 1997).

Negative stereotypes arise from a number of distinctive social and racial and ethnic experiences and can cut across both racial and ethnic groups (Bobo and Charles, 2009; Hochschild and Weaver, 2007). For example, researchers have routinely documented that African Americans are significantly more likely to be depicted as criminals on news programs (see, e.g., Dixon, 2000, 2007, 2008; Dixon and Linz, 2000, 2006; Entman, 1994; Entman and Rojecki, 2001). Note that it is possible for stereotypes to have a "kernel of truth" associated with them (Niemann, 2001). Official data indicate that 1 in 15 African American and 1 in 36 Hispanic men are incarcerated in comparison with 1 in 106 white men (Pew Center on the States, 2009). Therefore, for example, it could be argued that whites who identify African Americans as being more criminal than members of their own race are not stereotyping but rather are just "letting the data do the talking."

The eminent scholar W.E.B. Du Bois recognized this insidious aspect of stereotypes in his classic *The Philadelphia Negro*: "Being few in number compared with the whites the crime or carelessness of a few of his race is easily imputed to all, and the reputation of the good, industrious and reliable suffer thereby" (Du Bois [1899] 1996:323). Jones (1997:169) adds to Du Bois's dismissal of the "kernel of truth" justification for negative stereotypes, "that even when a stereotype is largely true, it reflects no more than a probability that a member of the group will possess the trait on which the group is being stereotyped." In addition, Quillian and Pager (2001) argue that negative stereotypes of African Americans cause individuals to systematically overestimate the true rate of behavior. For example, they argue that a combination of negative media depictions of African Americans, historical stereotypes, and ethnocentric biases combine to form distorted perceptions in which the association of blackness and criminality is systematically overestimated. In short, there is no legitimate justification for embracing stereotypes, whether they are positive or negative, because they cannot be applied to *every* member of the out-group and they create distorted images that cannot be verified.

Empirical studies unequivocally indicate that pejorative stereotypes of African Americans are a prevailing and enduring component of the American cultural landscape (Devine, 1989; Trawalter, Todd, Baird, and Richeson, 2008; Wood and Chesser, 1994). Bobo and Charles (2009) note that negative racial stereotypes remain the norm in white America with between half and three quarters of whites in the United States still expressing some degree of negative stereotyping of blacks and Latinos, with a smaller share of whites expressing negative stereotypes of Asians (between one tenth and two fifths).

Devine and Elliot (1995:1142), in a follow-up to the classic Princeton trilogy studies, provided 147 students a checklist composed of 93 adjectives and asked them to mark those that "make up the cultural stereotype of Blacks." Note that, based on recent free-response data, they decided to add the concepts of "criminal" and "hostile" to the original checklist of 84 adjectives. Devine and Elliot found that from 1933 to the mid-1990s, a consistent and negative stereotype of African Americans has endured. Devine and Elliot (1995) found that the top nine list of adjectives that

cities, they analyzed three dimensions of school bonds: (1) school self-esteem (e.g., "I usually have been proud of my report card"); (2) school bonding (e.g., "I feel close to people at my school"); and (3) school grades (GPA). Dotterer et al. (2009) found that personal discrimination experiences were a significant and negative predictor of school self-esteem and school bonding. That is, the more African American students reported personal experiences with racial discrimination, the less likely they were to identify with doing well in school and were less attached to their schools. Of note, they did not find a relationship between perceived racial discrimination and lower grades.

Mattison and Aber (2007) surveyed 1,838 high school students including 382 African Americans in two public schools in the Midwest to investigate whether their perceptions of the school's racial climate impacted their achievement and discipline-related problems. Three dimensions of the school's racial climate were assessed: (1) racial fairness (e.g., "At my school, students are disciplined fairly regardless of race" and "Black students are treated fairly at my school"); (2) experiences of racism (e.g., "How often has a teacher treated you badly because of your race?" and "How often has another student treated you badly because of your race?"); and (3) a "Need for Change subscale" (e.g., "The school district should reduce the difference in gifted and talented enrollment between Black and White students" and "The school district should reduce the difference in special education enrollment between Black and White students"). They examined whether these measures of the school's racial climate were related to the student's self-reported GPA and whether they had been suspended or their number of school-based detentions. Mattison and Aber (2007) found that 51 percent of the white students agreed they were treated and disciplined fairly regardless of race compared with 31 percent of the African Americans, black students were two and a half times (8 percent) more likely to report that they experienced racism than whites (3 percent), and about 10 percent of white students agreed schools needed to change compared with 40 percent of African American students. They also report that African American students were eight times more likely to be suspended and received twice as many detentions as whites. Their multivariate analyses revealed that perceptions of a negative racial climate were related to lower grades and more disciplinary actions for both African Americans and whites. Mattison and Aber (2007) conclude that a climate of racism may create disincentives for students to engage in schoolwork, which in turn promotes delinquent behaviors. Thus, "perceptions that the school is racist may set in motion a series of reactions including fighting, insubordination, etc., for which students are disciplined. In this case, misbehavior may be precipitated by perceived racist school structures or racist interactions with students and staff " (Mattison and Aber, 2007:9).

Scholars also have put forth a "resistance theory" that parallels our previous hypothesis that perceived criminal justice injustices are a source of anger and defiance among African Americans. The resistance theory argues that African American students employ "right to respect" coping strategies or exude a tough defiant facade in response to explicit or implicit racism in schools (Spencer, Noll, Stolzfus, and Harpalani, 2001). Gregory and Weinstein (2008), in their study in an urban high school in a mid-size city, found that African American students comprised 30 percent of the school enrollment, but they were 58 percent of the students who teachers referred for disciplinary actions because of "defiance." In contrast, they found that white students were 37 percent of the school enrollment, but only comprised 5 percent of students referred for defiance (see also Gregory, Skiba, and Noguera, 2010; Ruck and Wortley, 2002).

Gregory and Weinstein (2008) argue that African Americans are particularly likely to be defiant when they perceive that teachers are underestimating their academic ability or that they are uncaring because of their race. Indeed, they found that African American students critically discern among teachers that they perceive to be either racists or nonracists. Thus, in support of the resistance theory, these scholars found that "African American students reported uncaring treatment and low academic expectations from teachers with whom they behaved more defiantly and less cooperatively, as rated by themselves and by these teachers. In contrast, the students reported that their nominated teachers treated them with care and high expectations. Moreover, students expressed a willingness to comply with the authority of teachers who had earned trust and legitimacy" (Gregory and Weinstein, 2008:469). In short, these data support our thesis that African Americans are likely to become angry-defiant when they perceive racial injustices, whether they occur in the classroom or on the streets.

We last discuss a study conducted by Unnever, Cullen, Mathers, McClure, and Allison (2009). These scholars reanalyzed the same dataset used by Hirschi (1969), the Richmond Youth Study, to examine whether Hirschi omitted from his analysis the possibility that perceived racial discrimination is a cause of African American youth offending, while controlling for his other bond measures of involvement, commitment, attachment, and beliefs. More specifically, these researchers examined whether personal perceptions of racial discrimination within the context of the school were related to African American offending. They created a measure of perceived school discrimination by summing across three items: (1) whether the black students thought their teachers did not like them, (2) how well they got along with the white students, and (3) whether the black and white students interacted with one another. Unfortunately, Unnever et al. (2009) did not test whether these perceptions of a racially toxic school environment were related to African American students developing weak school bonds. However, they did examine whether these perceptions of a toxic racist school environment predicted black offending. Unnever et al. (2009:396) found that "African American youths who perceived that their school was antagonistic to members of their race were significantly more likely to offend."[1] They concluded that African American youths are more likely to offend if they perceive their school climate to be discriminatory and hostile.

Of interest, Unnever et al. (2009) also examined whether the black youths' perception of racial discrimination in domains outside of school were related to their probability of offending. They investigated whether African American youths in the late 1960s were more likely to offend if they perceived whether blacks were discriminated against in income ("Do you think a person of your race would get paid as much as a person of other racial groups for doing the same kind

of work?"), in housing ("If a family of your racial group rented the same kind of ho[...] of other racial groups, do you think they would have to pay the same amount of [...] employment ("In the city where you live, do you think that Negroes are discrim[...] when people are being hired for jobs?"). Unnever et al. (2009) found that person[...] with racial discrimination ("Have you personally ever been treated badly because[...] and perceptions of a toxic racist school environment were related to African Amer[...] in delinquent behavior, but, none of their vicarious perceptions of racial discrim[...] of their school predicted black offending.

In sum, the totality of the research indicates that perceived racial discrimi[...] places the physical and mental well-being of African Americans at risk, it al[...] males and females to have a greater probability of offending. These results have[...] at different times, have controlled for a wide array of correlates, have been fou[...] ent geographical locales, and when employing and representing different met[...] cross-sectional and longitudinal surveys). In short, the data indicate that racial[...] related to African American offending.

Stereotypes of African Americans

We assert that the effects of racial discrimination on African American off[...] yond the immediate experience of blacks perceiving that they have been dis[...] because of their race (e.g., being denied employment because the person i[...] being given a lower grade in school because they are black). Our theory po[...] reotypes are another form of racism that is related to African American o[...] first provide evidence that pejorative stereotypes of African Americans are[...] outline why these negative depictions are related to black offending.

Prevailing Racial Stereotypes

Scholars argue that an attribute of racialized societies are negative racial an[...] (Beckett and Sasson, 2003; Bobo and Charles, 2009; Bonilla-Silva, 2006[...] and Ray 2009; O'Brien, Crandall, Horstman-Reser, Warner, Alsbrooks, and E[...] (2006:185) states that "stereotypes distort perceptions of out-groups, c[...] between in-group and out-group members, and may help justify nega[...] out-groups." These negative stereotypes flow from a racial ideology that[...] changing dynamics of groups differentially positioned because of their[...] ground (Bobo, 2000). Bonilla-Silva (1997:474) argues that pejorative ste[...] "common sense" becomes and provide the rules for "perceiving and deali[...] racialized society." Scholars refer to stereotypes as "pictures in the head" (I[...] and Hurwitz, 1998; Hurwitz and Peffley, 1997; Peffley, Hurwitz, and Sn[...]

whites checked to describe African Americans were, in order: athletic, rhythmic, low in intelligence, lazy and poor (these were tied), loud, criminal, hostile, and ignorant. In contrast, no whites checked, for example, that African Americans are ambitious, tradition loving, sensitive, or gregarious.

Scholars argue that the "war on drugs" has profoundly impacted the racial stereotyping of African Americans, particularly African American men. That is, they argue that the "war on drugs" has caused most Americans to conflate crime with race and race with crime. Russell-Brown (2009) captures the pervasiveness of this gendered pejorative stereotype of African American men in her provocative label, the *criminalblackman*. Feagin (2001:113) states that the common white stereotype of the dangerous black man is "the staple of white thinking, including the thinking of white leaders and intellectuals speaking or writing about the black 'underclass'" (see also James, 2010). Bjornstrom, Kaufman, Peterson, and Slater (2010) analyzed data from a stratified random sample of television newscasts in 2002–03 and found that the media actively perpetuates these toxic stereotypes. They report that television news over-report crimes committed by African Americans when compared with whites and that blacks are less likely to be portrayed as victims than whites. Furthermore, scholars contend that this more crystallized master stereotype—of the *criminalblackman*—is the basis for the creation of a "New Jim Crow" (Alexander, 2010; Bass, 2001; Noble, 2006; Russell-Brown, 2009). This New Jim Crow is characterized by the mass incarceration and disenfranchisement of millions of African Americans (mostly black men), which is being facilitated by the war on drugs and legitimated by the racial stereotype of the *criminalblackman* (Alexander, 2010). Thus, African Americans are now confronted by the fact that most Americans think of them as being criminals, especially black men.

Research supports the argument that African Americans, particularly African American men, are portrayed as dangerous, violent, super-predators (Barkan and Cohn, 1994; Bobo and Charles, 2009; Chiricos, Welch, and Gertz, 2004; Devine, 1989; Gabbidon, 2010; Gabbidon and Greene, 2009; Jones, 1997; Maykovich, 1972; Trawalter et al., 2008; Walker, Spohn, DeLone, 2007; Welch, 2007). Fishman (2006:199) argues that this stereotype was resurrected from the legacy of slavery as African American men were depicted as "menacing black brutes" that are animalistic, aggressive, and brutal. She also notes that African American women during and immediately after the end of slavery were portrayed as "wanton, hot-blooded, highly sexed, and exotic, as well as very fertile." Feagin (2001:113) adds that this perception of black men runs deep in American culture as "during the first centuries of American development, whites constructed a view of enslaved black men as dangerous 'beasts' a stereotyped view that has rationalized much discrimination over the centuries, including bloody lynchings." Beckett, Nyrop, and Pfingst (2006:130) add that the *criminalblackman* has embedded within it the portrayal of young African American males as "dangerous black crack offenders" (see also Beckett, Nyrop, Pfingst, and Bowen, 2005).

Eberhardt, Goff, Purdie, and Davies (2004:876) add that "not only is the association between blacks and crime strong (i.e., consistent and frequent), it also appears to be automatic (i.e., not subject to intentional control)." They further assert that this automatic stereotype has dire consequences in that the mere presence of an African American man can trigger thoughts among whites that he is violent and criminal.

Based on their research with white students, Eberhardt et al. (2004) found that the stereotype that associates African Americans with crime is bidirectional. That is, among whites, thinking about crime triggers images of African Americans and that thinking about African Americans triggers thoughts about crime. Eberhardt et al. (2004) conclude that the coupling between African Americans and crime is so deeply embedded among whites that blacks are the prototypical embodiment of crime.

This conflating of crime with race and race with crime is further evidenced in a study that asked approximately 400 persons in the Washington, D.C., area: "Would you close your eyes for a second, envision a drug user, and describe that person to me?" The data show that more than 95 percent of the respondents identified the person as an African American. Notably, the pervasiveness of this pejorative stereotype is illustrated by the fact that blacks also indicated that the image in their head of a drug user was an African American (Burston, Jones, and Roberson-Saunders, 1995).

In addition, in an analysis of the General Social Survey (GSS), Unnever and Cullen (2011) found that in 1990, whites considered African Americans 15 times more likely to be violent than members of their own race. They also found that the degree to which whites negatively depict African Americans as prone to violence changes over time. Taken together, these studies clearly demonstrate that a prevailing cultural belief within the United States is that African Americans tend to be "lazy," "poor," and prone to violent crime.

The Impact that Negative Stereotypes Have on African Americans

Scholars argue that these toxic stereotypes permeate the worldview of those who are stigmatized—that is, African Americans. Major and O'Brien (2005:399) state that: "Based on their prior experiences as well as their exposure to the dominant culture, members of stigmatized groups develop shared understandings of the dominant view of their stigmatized status in society [Crocker 1999, Crocker et al. 1998, Steele 1997]. These collective representations include awareness that they are devalued in the eyes of others, knowledge of the dominant cultural stereotypes of their stigmatized identity, and recognition that they could be victims of discrimination [Crocker et al. 1998]. Virtually all members of a culture, including members of stigmatized groups, are aware of cultural stereotypes, even if they do not personally endorse them." Thus, African Americans, even before the age of 10, are aware that other groups perceive them as "less than" and may modify their behavior based on the toxic judgments of others.

The noted artist Gang Starr raps about the insidiousness of the *criminalblackman* pejorative stereotype in his song "Conspiracy" (from the album *Daily Operation*):

> You can't tell me life was meant to be like this
> a black man in a world dominated by whiteness
> Ever since the declaration of independence
> we've been easily brainwashed by just one sentence
> It goes: all men are created equal
> that's why corrupt governments kill innocent people
> With chemical warfare they created crack and AIDS
> got the public thinking these were things that black folks made
> And every time there's violence shown in the media
> usually it's a black thing so where are they leading ya
> To a world full of ignorance, hatred, and prejudice
> TV and the news for years they have fed you this
> foolish notion that blacks are all criminals
> violent, low lifes, and then even animals
> I'm telling the truth so some suckers are fearing me
> but I must do my part to combat the conspiracy

[...]

Summary

Unlike whites, African Americans are immersed in a social milieu that includes stereotypes that "put them down" and encounters with racial discrimination. African Americans can experience these forms of racism across vastly different domains of their lived lives; that is, from having a white friend tell a racist joke, to being racially profiled while shopping or driving, to being unfairly punished in school, or being denied a job because they are an African American. Thus, we argue that most, if not all, African Americans at some point in their lives are forced to deal with pejorative stereotypes, domain-specific stereotype threats, and being personally discriminated against because they are black.

Put simply, we hypothesize that the probability of African American offending increases as blacks become more aware of toxic stereotypes, encounter stereotype threats, and are discriminated against because of their race. Our theory additionally posits that these forms of racism impact offending because they undermine the ability of African Americans to develop strong ties with conventional institutions. The extant literature indicates that stereotype threats and personal experiences of racial discrimination negatively impact the strength of the bonds (attachment, involvement, commitment) that black students have with their schools (Smalls, White, Chavous, and Sellers, 2007; Thomas, Caldwell, Faison, and Jackson, 2009). And, the research is clear; weak social bonds increase the probability of black offending (Carswell, 2007). We additionally argue that these forms of racism can cause African Americans to experience negative emotions—hopelessness-depression and anger-defiance—which, in turn, increase their probability of offending.

We further assert that the strength of the relationship between these forms of racism and offending has been underestimated. As with perceived criminal justice injustices, we argue that researchers have underestimated the true extent to which negative stereotypes, stereotype threats, and personal experiences with racial discrimination negatively impact African Americans. We state that researchers should measure the *degree* to which African Americans experience these forms of racism similarly to how they measure the severity of child abuse. Thus, we recommend that researchers, for example, ask at what age were African Americans exposed to the negative depictions of them and had personal experiences of being mistreated because of their race; who exposed the child to the toxic stereotypes and who discriminated against them because of their race (e.g., was it people in positions of trust and authority?); to what degree was the person socialized into believing negative depictions of them?; how often was the person exposed to pejorative stereotypes and to racial discrimination (e.g., did it happen in daily interactions, did it happen sporadically or chronically?); and, over what length of time was the person exposed to these deleterious racist behaviors (e.g., did it persist across their life span)? Our theory hypothesizes that offending increases with the *degree* to which African Americans experience these racial injustices.

[...]

Notes

1   Research shows that racial tension, as measured by a self-reported item completed by school administrators, increased the level of reported crime in public schools (Maume, Kim-Godwin, and Clements, 2010). Unfortunately, this study did not examine whether the rates of crime increased specifically among African American students.

References

Alexander, M. 2010. *The new Jim Crow: mass incarceration in the age of colorblindness*. New York: The New Press.

Alliman-Brissett, A. E. and S. L. Turner. 2010. "Racism, parent support, and math-based career interests, efficacy, and outcome expectations among African American adolescents." *Journal of Black Psychology* 36:197–225.

Barkan, S. E. and S. F. Cohn. 1994. "Racial prejudice and support for the death penalty by whites." *Journal of Research in Crime and Delinquency* 31:202–209.

Baron, S. W. 2008. "Street youth, unemployment, and crime: Is it that simple? Using general strain theory to untangle the relationship." *Canadian Journal of Criminology and Criminal Justice* 50:399–434.

Bass, S. 2001. "Policing space, policing race: Social control imperatives and police discretionary decisions." *Social Justice* 28:156–176.

Beckett, K., K. Nyrop, and L. Pfingst. 2006. "Race, drugs, and policing: Understanding disparities in drug delivery arrests." *Criminology* 44:105–137.

Beckett, K., K. Nyrop, L. Pfingst, and M. Bowen. 2005. "Drug use, drug possession arrests, and the question of race: Lessons from Seattle." *Social Problems* 52:419–441.

Beckett, K. and T. Sasson. 2003. *The politics of injustice: Crime and punishment in America.* New York: Sage Publications.

Bjornstrom, E. E. S., R. L. Kaufman, R. D. Peterson, and M. D. Slater. 2010. "Race and ethnic representations of lawbreakers and victims in crime news: A national study of television coverage." *Social Problems* 57:269–293.

Blistein, R. 2009. "Racism's hidden toll." *Miller-McCune* 2:48–57.

Bobo, L. D. 2000. "Reclaiming a Du Boisian perspective on racial attitudes." *The ANNALS of the American Academy of Political and Social Science* 568:186–202.

Bobo, L. D. and C. Z. Charles. 2009. "Race in the American mind: From the Moynihan report to the Obama candidacy." *The ANNALS of the American Academy of Political and Social Science* 621:243–259.

Bonilla-Silva, E. 1997. "Rethinking racism: Toward a structural interpretation." *American Sociological Review* 62:465–480.

_____ . 2008. *Racism without racists: Color-blind racism and the persistence of racial inequality in the United States.* Princeton, NJ: Rowman and Littlefield.

Bonilla-Silva, E. and V. Ray. 2009. "When whites love a black leader: Race matters in Obama America." *Journal of African American Studies* 13:176–183.

Brody, G. H., Y. F. Chen, V. M. Murry, X. Ge, R. L. Simons, F. X. Gibbons, M. Gerrard, and C. E. Cutrona. 2006. "Perceived discrimination and the adjustment of African American youths: A five-year longitudinal analysis with contextual moderation effects." *Child Development* 77:1170–1189.

Brondolo, E., N. Brady ver Halen, M. Pencille, D. Beatty, and R. Contrada. 2009. "Coping with racism: A selective review of the literature and a theoretical and methodological critique." *Journal of Behavioral Medicine* 32:64–88.

Burston, B. W., D. Jones, and P. Roberson-Saunders. 1995. "Drug use and African Americans: Myth versus reality." *Journal of Alcohol and Drug Education* 40:19–39.

Carswell, S. B. 2007. *Delinquency among African American youth: Parental attachment, socioeconomic status, and peer relationships.* New York: LFB Scholarly Publishing LLC.

Cernkovich, S. A. and P. C. Giordano. 1992. "School bonding, race, and delinquency." *Criminology* 30:261–287.

Chavous, T. M., D. Rivas-Drake, C. Smalls, T. Griffin, and C. Cogburn. 2008. "Gender matters, too: The influences of school racial discrimination and racial identity on academic engagement outcomes among African American adolescents." *Developmental Psychology* 44:637–654.

Chiricos, T., K. Welch, and M. Gertz. 2004. "Racial typification of crime and support for punitive measures." *Criminology* 42:359–389.

Clark, R., N. B. Anderson, V. R. Clark, and D. R. Williams. 1999. "Racism as a stressor for African Americans: A biopsychosocial model." *American Psychologist* 54:805–816.

Crutchfield, R. D. and S. R. Pitchford. 1997. "Work and crime: The effects of labor stratification." *Social Forces* 76:93–118.

Devine, P. G. 1989. "Stereotypes and prejudice: Their automatic and controlled components." *Journal of Personality and Social Psychology* 56:5–18.

Devine, P. G. and A. J. Elliot. 1995. "Are racial stereotypes really fading? The Princeton trilogy revisited." *Personality and Social Psychology Bulletin* 21:1139–1150.

Dixon, T. L. 2000. "A social cognitive approach to studying racial stereotyping in the mass media." *African American Research Perspectives* 6:60–68.

_____ . 2007. "Black criminals and white officers: The effects of racially misrepresenting law breakers and law defenders on television news." *Media Psychology* 10:270–291.

_____ . 2008. "Network news and racial beliefs: Exploring the connection between national television news exposure and stereotypical perceptions of African Americans." *Journal of Communication* 58:321–337.

Dixon, T. L. and D. Linz. 2000. "Race and the misrepresentation of victimization on local television news." *Communication Research* 27:547–573.

_____ . 2006. "Overrepresentation and underrepresentation of African Americans and Latinos as lawbreakers on television news." *Journal of Communication* 50:131–154.

Donaldson, K. 1996. *Through students' eyes: Combating racism in United States schools.* Greenwood Publishing Group.

Dotterer, A. M., S. M. McHale, and A. C. Crouter. 2009. "Sociocultural factors and school engagement among African American youth: The roles of racial discrimination, racial socialization, and ethnic identity." *Applied Developmental Science* 13:61–73.

Du Bois, W. E. B. 1899b. *The Philadelphia Negro: A social study.* Philadelphia: University of Pennsylvania Press.

Eberhardt, J. L., P. A. Goff, V. J. Purdie, and P. G. Davies. 2004. "Seeing black: Race, crime, and visual processing." *Journal of Personality and Social Psychology* 87:876–893.

Entman, R. M. 1994. "Representation and reality in the portrayal of blacks on network television news." *Journalism Quarterly* 71:509–509.

Entman, R. M. and A. Rojecki. 2001. *The black image in the white mind: Media and race in America.* Chicago: University of Chicago Press.

Farrington, D. P., B. Gallagher, L. Morley, R. J. St. Ledger, and D. J. West. 1986. "Unemployment, school leaving, and crime." *British Journal of Criminology* 26:335–356.

Feagin, J. R. 2001. *Racist America: Roots, current realities, and future reparations.* New York: Routledge.

Fishman, L. T. 2006. "The black bogeyman and white self-righteousness." pp. 197–211 in *Images of color, images of crime*, edited by C.R. Mann, M.S. Zatz, and N. Rodriguez. New York: Oxford University Press.

Frankenburg, E., C. Lee, and G. Orfield. 2003. *A multiracial society with segregated schools: Are we losing the dream?* Cambridge, MA: The Civil Right Project, Harvard University.

Gabbidon, S. L. 2010. *Criminological perspectives on race and crime (2nd edition).* New York: Routledge.

Gabbidon, S. L. and H. T. Greene. 2009. *Race and crime (2nd edition).* Thousand Oaks, CA: Sage.

Gabbidon, S. L. and S. A. Peterson. 2006. "Living while black: A state-level analysis of the influence of select social stressors on the quality of life among black Americans." *Journal of Black Studies* 37:83–102.

Geronimus, A. T., M. Hicken, D. Keene, and J. Bound. 2006. "'Weathering' and age patterns of allostatic load scores among blacks and whites in the United States." *American Journal of Public Health* 96:826–833.

Geronimus, A. T. and J. P. Thompson. 2004. "To denigrate, ignore, or disrupt: Racial inequality in health and the impact of a policy-induced breakdown of African American communities." *Du Bois Review: Social Science Research on Race* 1:247–279.

Giordano, P. C., R. D. Schroeder, and S. A. Cernkovich. 2007. "Emotions and crime over the life course: A neo Meadian perspective on criminal continuity and change." *American Journal of Sociology* 112:1603–1661.

Goldsmith, P. A. 2004. "Schools' role in shaping race relations: Evidence on friendliness and conflict." *Social Problems* 51:587–612.

Gregory, A., R. J. Skiba, and P. A. Noguera. 2010. "The achievement gap and the discipline gap: Two sides of the same coin?" *Educational Researcher* 39:59–68.

Gregory, A. and R. S. Weinstein. 2008. "The discipline gap and African Americans: Defiance or cooperation in the high school classroom." *Journal of School Psychology* 46:455–475.

Harrell, S. 2000. "A multidimensional conceptualization of racism-related stress: Implications for the well-being of people of color." *American Journal of Orthopsychiatry* 70:42–57.

Hirschi, T. 1969. *Causes of delinquency.* Berkeley: University of California Press.

Hochschild, J. L. and V. Weaver. 2007. "The skin color paradox and the American racial order." *Social Forces* 86:643–670.

Hurwitz, J. and M. Peffley. 1997. "Public perceptions of race and crime: The role of racial stereotypes." *American Journal of Political Science* 41:375–401.

James, J. 2010. "Campaigns against 'blackness': Criminality, incivility, and election to executive office." *Critical Sociology* 36:25–44.

Jones, J. M. 1997. *Prejudice and racism.* New York: McGraw-Hill.

Keith, V. M., K. D. Lincoln, R. J. Taylor, and J. S. Jackson. 2010. "Discriminatory experiences and depressive symptoms among African American women: Do skin tone and mastery matter?" *Sex Roles* 62:48–59.

Klonoff, E. A., H. Landrine, and J. B. Ullman. 1999. "Racial discrimination and psychiatric symptoms among blacks." *Cultural Diversity and Ethnic Minority Psychology* 5:329–339.

Lippmann, W. 1922. *Public opinion.* New York: Free Press.

Lynch, M. 2006. "Stereotypes, prejudice, and life-and-death decision-making: Lessons from laypersons in an experimental setting." Pp. 182–210 in *Lynch mobs killing state race and the death penalty in America*, edited by C. J. Ogletree and A. Sarat. New York: New York University Press.

Major, B. and L. T. O'Brien. 2005. "The social psychology of stigma." *Annual Review of Psychology* 56:393–421.

Mattison, E. and M. Aber. 2007. "Closing the achievement gap: The association of racial climate with achievement and behavioral outcomes." *American Journal of Community Psychology* 40:1–12.

Maykovich, M. K. 1972. "Reciprocity in racial stereotypes: White, black, and yellow." *American Journal of Sociology* 77:876–897.

Niemann, Y. F. 2001. "Stereotypes about Chicanas and Chicanos: Implications for counseling." *The Counseling Psychologist* 29:55–90.

Noble, R. L. 2006. *Black rage in the American prison system.* New York: LFB Scholarly Publishing LLC.

O'Brien, L. T., C. S. Crandall, A. Horstman-Reser, R. Warner, A. Alsbrooks, and A. Blodorn. 2010. "But I'm no bigot: How prejudiced white Americans maintain unprejudiced self-images." *Journal of Applied Social Psychology* 40:917–946.

Odom, E. C. and L. Vernon-Feagans. 2010. "Buffers of racial discrimination: Links with depression among rural African American mothers." *Journal of Marriage and Family* 72:346–359.

Payne, A. A. 2008. "A multilevel analysis of the relationships among communal school organization, student bonding, and delinquency." *Journal of Research in Crime and Delinquency* 45:429–455.

Peffley, M. and J. Hurwitz. 1998. "Whites' stereotypes of blacks: Sources and political consequences." pp. 58–99 in *Perception and prejudice: Race and politics in the United States*, edited by J. Hurwitz and M. Peffley. New Haven: Yale University Press.

Peffley, M., J. Hurwitz, and P. M. Sniderman. 1997. "Racial stereotypes and whites' political views of blacks in the context of welfare and crime." *American Journal of Political Science* 41:30–60.

Pew Center on the States. 2009. *One in 100: Behind bars in America 2008*. Washington, D.C.: Pew Charitable Trusts.

Quillian, L. and D. Pager. 2001. "Black neighbors, higher crime? The role of racial stereotypes in evaluations of neighborhood crime." *The American Journal of Sociology* 107:717–767.

Rivas-Drake, D., D. Hughes, and N. Way. 2009. "A preliminary analysis of associations among ethnic-racial socialization, ethnic discrimination, and ethnic identity among urban sixth graders." *Journal of Research on Adolescence* 19:558–584.

Rosenbloom, S. R. and N. Way. 2004. "Experiences of discrimination among African American, Asian American, and Latino adolescents in an urban high school." *Youth and Society* 35:420–451.

Ruck, M. D. and S. Wortley. 2002. "Racial and ethnic minority high school students' perceptions of school disciplinary practices: A look at some Canadian findings." *Journal of Youth and Adolescence* 31:185–195.

Russell-Brown, K. K. 2009. *The color of crime: Racial hoaxes, white fear, black protectionism, police harassment, and other macroaggressions (2nd edition)*. New York: New York University Press.

Schott Foundation for Public Education. 2010. "Yes we can: The Schott 50 state report on public education and black males 2010." *Schott Foundation for Public Education*.

Seaton, E. K. 2010. "The influence of cognitive development and perceived racial discrimination on the psychological well-being of African American youth." *Journal of Youth and Adolescence* 39:694–703.

Seaton, E. and T. Yip. 2009. "School and neighborhood contexts, perceptions of racial discrimination, and psychological well-being among African American adolescents." *Journal of Youth and Adolescence* 38:153–163.

Seaton, E. K., T. Yip, and R. M. Sellers. 2009. "A longitudinal examination of racial identity and racial discrimination among African American adolescents." *Child Development* 80:406–417.

Sellers, S. L., V. Bonham, H. W. Neighbors, and J. W. Amell. 2009. "Effects of racial discrimination and health behaviors on mental and physical health of middle-class African American men." *Health Education and Behavior* 36:31–44.

Sigleman, L. E. E. and S. A. Tuch. 1997. "Metastereotypes: Blacks' perceptions of whites' stereotypes of blacks." *Public Opinion Quarterly* 61:87–101.

Smalls, C., R. White, T. Chavous, and R. Sellers. 2007. "Racial ideological beliefs and racial discrimination experiences as predictors of academic engagement among African American adolescents." *Journal of Black Psychology* 33:299–330.

Spencer, M. B., E. Noll, J. Stoltzfus, and V. Harpalani. 2001. "Identity and school adjustment: Revisiting the 'acting white' assumption." *Educational Psychologist* 36:21–30.

Steele, C. M. 1997. "A threat in the air: How stereotypes shape intellectual identity and performance." *American Psychologist* 52:613–629.

Thomas, O. N., C. H. Caldwell, N. Faison, and J. S. Jackson. 2009. "Promoting academic achievement: The role of racial identity in buffering perceptions of teacher discrimination on academic achievement among African American and Caribbean black adolescents." *Journal of Educational Psychology* 101:420–431.

Trawalter, S., A. R. Todd, A. A. Baird, and J. A. Richeson. 2008. "Attending to threat: Race-based patterns of selective attention." *Journal of Experimental Social Psychology* 44:1322–1327.

Uggen, C. 2000. "Work as a turning point in the life course of criminals: A duration model of age, employment, and recidivism." *American Sociological Review* 65:529–546.

Unnever, J. D. and F. T. Cullen. 2011. "White perceptions of whether African Americans and Hispanics are prone to violence and their desire to punish." Unpublished manuscript.

Unnever, J. D., F. T. Cullen, S. A. Mathers, T. E. McClure, and M. C. Allison. 2009. "Racial discrimination and Hirschi's criminological classic: A chapter in the sociology of knowledge." *Justice Quarterly* 26:377–409.

Walker, S., C. Spohn, and M. DeLone. 2007. *The color of justice: Race, ethnicity, and crime in America (4th edition).* Belmont, CA: Wadsworth.

Welch, K. 2007. "Black criminal stereotypes and racial profiling." *Journal of Contemporary Criminal Justice* 23:276–288.

Williams, D. R., H. W. Neighbors, and J. S. Jackson. 2003. "Racial/ethnic discrimination and health: Findings from community studies." *American Journal of Public Health* 93:200–208.

––. 2008. "Racial/ethnic discrimination and health: Findings from community studies." *American Journal of Public Health* 98:S29–S37.

Wong, C. A., J. S. Eccles, and A. Sameroff. 2003. "The influence of ethnic discrimination and ethnic identification on African American adolescents' school and socioemotional adjustment." *Journal of Personality* 71:1197–1232.

Wood, P. B. and M. Chesser. 1994. "Stereotype adherence in a university population." *Sociological Focus* 27:17–34.

Zahn, M. A., R. Agnew, D. Fishbein, S. Miller, D.-M. Winn, G. Dakoff, C. Kruttschnitt, P. Giordano, D. C. Gottfredson, A. A. Payne, B. C. Feld, and M. Chesney-Lind. 2010. "Causes and correlates of girls' delinquency." *Office of Juvenile Justice and Delinquency Prevention.*

Discussion Questions

1   How did African Americans become part of the racial picture in America?

2   How are the injustices of the criminal justice system offending African Americans?

3   Why does an African American person confront a different reality than a white person when he or she opens the door to school?

4   Negative stereotypes deplete the emotional resources of African Americans, increasing their likelihood of developing negative emotions like hopelessness and depression. Discuss.

5   African Americans experience different forms of racism across vastly different domains of their lives. What are some of these forms of racism, and how do they undermine the ability of African Americans?

CHAPTER 9

Racism Against Asian Americans

Anti-Asian Violence and the Vincent Chin Case

Judy Yung, Gordon H. Chang, Him Mark Lai

In the 1980s, as the United States deindustrialized and sank into a recession in response to rapid changes in the global economy, hate crimes against Asian Americans erupted. It was not a coincidence that the first outbreak occurred in Detroit, Michigan, where the auto industry, unable to compete with foreign imports, had all but collapsed. In 1982 unemployed workers and the mass media were blaming Japanese imports for the depressed economy when Vincent Chin, a twenty-seven-year-old Chinese American, was brutally killed in a barroom brawl by two white auto workers. During the fistfight that preceded the murder, one of the men was heard saying, "It's because of you motherfuckers that we're out of work." They had obviously mistaken Chin for a Japanese as well as unfairly blamed all Asian people for the economic problems of the country.

In 1982, in America, a Chinese American named Vincent Chin was beaten to death with a baseball bat by two men—after being accused by them of causing the unemployment of U.S. autoworkers. His killers were each fined $3,000 and given three years' probation.

When news spread of the lenient sentences given for the crime of brutally taking a life, there were storms of protest.

The Vincent Chin case has come to mean far more to Asian Americans than a failure of the criminal justice system, though this aspect of the case serves as a lesson to all. This case has come to represent the racial hatred, scapegoating and very real discrimination that Asian Americans of all our diverse nationalities have been forced to endure since our forebears set foot on this land. To the extent that what happened to Vincent Chin could happen to any one of us, all Asian Americans are in jeopardy.

The Chin case is also a mandate to those of us who are fortunate enough not to have suffered Vincent's fate. The nationwide response to it symbolizes what can—and must—be achieved by Asian Americans acting together on behalf of our common need to live in our nation free from the threat of racial violence and innuendo. This case has proven that Americans from China, Japan, Korea, the Philippines, Southeast Asia, India and other Asian heritages can make a powerful impact by working together for our mutual interests.

On the night of his slaying, Vincent Chin was 27 years old and his future was promising. He was doing well at work in computer graphics, was well liked, and was looking to buy a new home for his wife and his widowed mother. In fact, Vincent's story typified the experiences of many Asian American immigrants: his father, Chin Wing Hing, came from Guangdong Province to America in search of a new life, which he found in the laundries and restaurants of Detroit. When World War II began, he enlisted, and after serving honorably in the U.S. Army, became eligible for citizenship. As a reward of citizenship, Mr. Chin was permitted to bring his wife, Lily, to this country. There were no children, and a few years later, the couple adopted a five-year-old boy from Guangdong, whom they named Vincent.

Friends and teachers say Vincent was a fun-loving, happy kid. His mother says he could have studied harder, but that he was a good boy, the kind who would help others. When he was nine, he began working in local Chinese restaurants, bussing tables. He had two passions: fishing and reading. "Whenever he had a chance, Vince would try to get to a lake and drop a line—it was his way of relaxing," remembers boyhood friend Gary Koivu, who was with Vincent the night he died.

And Vincent had a sensitive side to his personality—he often wrote poetry to his fiancée, Vikki Wong. She is trying to renew her life and is reluctant to talk publicly about Vincent, but some memories stand out, such as a Valentine's Day poem that Vincent placed in a classified section of a local paper:

> There is no life without you
> There is no joy or laughter
> There is no brightness, no warmth
> All the mornings after.
>
> So stay with me
> And we'll face the tomorrows
> To find if our love
> Can overcome the sorrows.

Though Vincent began college studying architecture, he later changed his mind, thinking that it might not be a secure profession. "Vince said he did not want to work his whole life in laundries and restaurants like his father did," Vikki recalls. So he later studied computer operations at a local trade school, and graduated with honors. He found a job at an engineering firm, combining his drafting and computing skills in computer-aided design work. To help save money for a house, Vincent also worked on weekends as a waiter.

Like many a "red-blooded American male," Vincent enjoyed going out on the town with his buddies. But unlike those other Americans, Vincent had an Asian face. On that warm Saturday night, Vincent and three friends decided to celebrate his upcoming wedding by going to a nude go-go joint that Vincent frequented during his carefree bachelorhood. Though his mother told him he shouldn't go out so close to the wedding date, he laughed and reassured her that "it would be his last night out with the guys." That night, Vincent was the target of a racial attack, and he died four days later as a result of that assault.

The bar that Vincent and his friends—two white and one Asian—went to was a seedy strip joint where women dance by the dollar: one dollar buys a few gyrations right in front of the customer—the more dollars, the more gyrations. Vincent and his friends had gone to have a good time, bringing plenty of dollar bills. But the more time the dancers spent with the free-spending Asian American, the more provoked two other patrons became.

Ronald Ebens, a tall, heavy-set white man, then 43 years old, and his stepson Michael Nitz, a tall, slim 22-year-old, were seated across from Vincent. Dancers from the bar say that Ebens, perhaps resentful that an Asian man should be receiving so much attention while he was not, began calling Vincent racially offensive names, needling Vincent, suggesting that he wasn't a man, talking about what he could do with his mother. One dancer heard Ebens say explicitly, "It's because of you motherfuckers that we're out of work."

A good-natured Vincent uncharacteristically stood up to them as the epithets continued, and a scuffle ensued. Vincent and his friends left the club, followed closely behind by Ebens and Nitz. Outside, in the parking lot, Ebens went straight to the trunk of his car and pulled out a baseball bat. Vincent ran, chased by Ebens and Nitz. When the two larger men were outdistanced by Vincent, they returned to the lot, where Vincent's two white friends and Jimmy Choi were standing—and they homed in on Jimmy, who had been uninvolved in their assaults against Vincent. But Jimmy also had an Asian face, and the two began chasing Jimmy, Ebens still wielding his bat. "I ran for my dear life," shudders Jimmy.

Intent on their purpose, Ebens and Nitz embarked on a search-and-destroy mission. For the next 20 minutes, they drove through streets and alleys searching for Vincent and Jimmy. They hired a third man to "help them get the chinks," as that man, Jimmy Perry, freely admits today. And they found the two Asian Americans waiting outside of a fast-food restaurant for a bus or a car or anything to get them away from their assailants. Ebens, Nitz and Perry crept up behind the two unsuspecting Asians, who noticed their attackers too late. Nitz grabbed Vincent in a bear hug, and his stepfather pummeled Vincent's legs, arms, body—and finally, sent four grand-slam swings into the back of Vincent's skull.

Two off-duty police officers stopped the carnage at gunpoint. "I ordered halt twice; if I hadn't stopped him, he would have gone for another 20 blows," recounts one officer. But for Vincent, it was over. Doctors operated on his battered head all night; surgeons said it looked like someone had beaten an animal. Vincent was placed on life support systems—his brain was already dead. Four days later, on June 23, 1982, his grieving fiancée and his stricken mother consented to turning off the life supports. Instead of attending Vincent's wedding, his friends went to his funeral.

What might have been just another senseless tragedy then turned into a carnival of bungling and sheer incompetence—the product of an insensitive, overburdened system where there is often no justice—just another case. And Vincent Chin was treated as just another case. No one went to the bar to find out what had initiated the murderous hunt. No one even thought to ask if race might have been a factor. A dough-faced detective (from what is reported to be one of the state's most inadequate police departments) says the killing was no big deal and that he is sure there was nothing racial about it—even though he acknowledges he made no effort to find out. Two defense lawyers managed to get the case moved from courtroom to courtroom within Wayne County, and found one judge to set the charges at second-degree murder, prompting another judge to comment on the record, "I am of the opinion that the defendants were undercharged. The elements of first-degree murder are here."

Finally the case went before Judge Charles Kaufman, who overlooked a probation officer's recommendations of incarceration and a psychiatric report warning that Ebens was an "extremely hostile and explosive individual … with a potential for uncontrollable hostility and explosive acting out." While the prosecutors didn't even bother to show up at the plea-bargained manslaughter sentencing, Kaufman ignored the previous courtroom testimony and listened to the killers' lawyers say that Vincent provoked his own death while Ebens and Nitz were innocent bystanders. Judge Kaufman took ten minutes to consider the charges, and sentenced Ronald Ebens and Michael Nitz each to $3,000 in fines and $780 in court costs, payable at $125 per month with no interest, and three years' probation.

That was the total value placed on the life of 27-year-old Vincent Chin, whose only crime was having an Asian face at a time when anti-Japanese and anti-Asian sentiments were rampant.

In rendering his now-infamous sentence, Kaufman offered several rationalizations: "These aren't the kind of men you send to jail … We're talking here about a man who's held down a responsible job for 17 or 18 years, and his son is employed and is a part-time student. You don't make the punishment fit the crime, you make the punishment fit the criminal."

News of the killers' sentences and the judge's opinion drew an immediate response from a shocked and disbelieving Chinese community. A grief-stricken Mrs. Chin, friends and members of the community struggled to understand what had happened and to discover what might be done about the clearly flawed judicial decision. There were emotional meetings of hundreds of Asians and others who had never before come together, suddenly talking about the pain, humiliation and suffering that we had endured silently for generations. We knew that what happened to Vincent Chin endangered all of us, and we knew that we could no longer stand in silence.

March 31, 1983, stands out in the history of Asians in America, for it was the night that individuals and representatives of local and national Asian organizations came together in Michigan and recognized that our fate and indeed our lives depended on our willingness to work in cooperation and in coalition with one another. In the drafty hall of the Detroit Chinese Welfare Council,[1] there was a joining of liberals and conservatives, youths and seniors, scientists, businessmen, Chinese, Japanese, Filipinos and Koreans, Christians and Buddhists, Cantonese- and Mandarin-speakers, American-born and immigrants—all of us put aside the differences that kept us apart and agreed that night to form a new organization to protect our rights as Americans of Asian ancestry, and we named it "American Citizens for Justice."

In the ensuing days, weeks and months, the many volunteers of ACJ donated money, time, effort, and whatever else was needed to discover what caused this miscarriage of justice. We engaged an attorney to look into legal recourse. (Our small force of Asian American attorneys in the Detroit area could not support a sustained *pro bono* effort, unlike some larger communities.) Obtaining court records and reconstructing the events of that tragic evening took much hard work and persistence in a system that seemed all too eager to cover up the mistakes made. The more established civil rights organizations of Detroit recognized our concerns and helped us open doors in an unwieldy bureaucracy. Bit by bit, we were able to reconstruct what happened to Vincent and what happened in the courts.

The more we learned about the case, the more evident it became that a grievous wrong had occurred. ACJ deliberately avoided making accusations of racism against the judge and did not call the killing a racial attack—until statements of additional eyewitnesses, who had never been questioned by police, prosecutors or anyone else from the criminal justice system, forced an inescapable conclusion: that the crime of violating Vincent Chin's civil rights on the basis of his race had taken place, and that it was time for a governmental body to review the evidence that this fledgling civil rights organization had uncovered. In May 1983, an FBI investigation was initiated by the Justice Department; in September, a grand jury probe was announced, and in November, 23 grand jurors returned indictments against Ebens and Nitz for the violation of Vincent Chin's civil rights.

During that long summer of 1983, as the news of what happened in Detroit spread through-out the U.S. and across the globe, Asians began to respond to what many had recognized long ago: the knowledge that the welfare and livelihood of each of us, regardless of national origin, depends on our ability to work together. Even our personal safety is at risk, subject to bigotry and scapegoating for economic or foreign policy problems since we "all look alike." Demonstrations

---

1 Affiliated with the long established Chinese Consolidated Benevolent Association and On Leong Merchants Association, the Detroit Chinese Welfare Council represented the interests of Chinatown to the city and at political functions. Vincent Chin was one of its younger members.

and support activities took place in San Francisco, Oakland, Los Angeles, Denver, Chicago, Toronto, New York, and a huge demonstration was held in Detroit. Mrs. Chin and ACJ were invited to address groups all over the country as new organizations formed in San Francisco, Los Angeles and Chicago. We were able to bring our concerns about anti-Asian sentiments to the nation for the first time, whereas previously Asians were usually featured as the "national threat" or the "national superminority." Mrs. Chin and ACJ representatives appeared on national television— all three news networks, *The Donahue Show*, NBC's *First Camera,* and local TV documentaries in Detroit—and Sacramento ACJ addressed the founding meeting of the Democratic Party's Asian Pacific American Caucus. In Japan, coverage by newspapers and TV prompted Japanese to question visiting American businessmen and government officials who were soliciting Asian business whether Asians are safe in the U.S. and whether Asians can get equal treatment here. The example of cooperative effort set by the Detroit groups was taken up nationally by the Japanese American Citizens League, the Organization of Chinese Americans, and the National Chinese Welfare Association, among others.

While many minority and civil rights groups greeted the Asian American presence in the civil rights arena as a long overdue event, others instead questioned the right of Asians to join the civil rights coalition. ACJ representatives were at times treated to tedious and absurd arguments that Asians are not truly a minority in America, and to the equally absurd question of whether racial slurs make a racial incident. Indeed ACJ was advised by some constitutional lawyers that Asians are not protected under the federal civil rights statutes and that it would be ill advised to consider a civil rights violation. Some legal organizations wrote tortuous essays on the dangers of double jeopardy for the killers—often a specter in civil rights crimes—while other liberal legal groups were either strangely and unusually silent or eager to jump to fellow liberal Kaufman's defense. Conservatives, meanwhile, were quick to jump on the case as a law-and-order issue, but completely ignored its racial aspects. Mostly, though, the response of legal professionals was one of alarming indifference to injustice, which, they say, happens all the time. Partly, it seems, because of their total unwillingness to do anything about it.

There were the usual difficulties encountered when organizations learn to work with one another. Still, support for the efforts of the ACJ and the growing Asian American civil rights network continues. We are living in a depressed economic period that makes it all too easy and convenient to direct frustrations and anger at us. What happened to Vincent Chin was not an aberration or an isolated quirk of fate. The list of assaults and killings of Asians since the Chin case, maintained through an informal network, continues to grow:[2]

---

2   The National Asian Pacific American Legal Consortium, an organization of legal and civil rights organizations formed in 1993 as a result of the Vincent Chin case, is committed to documenting, monitoring, and educating the public about hate violence. Its *Audit of Violence against Asian Pacific Americans* in 2001, the year of the 9/11 terrorist attack, reported 507 incidents of anti-Asian violence.

- A 17-year-old Vietnamese student was stabbed to death in his Davis, Calif., high school after weeks of racial harassment by a group calling itself the "White Student Union."
- A gun was pulled on a Chinese American telecommunications marketing professional working in Texas.
- A Vietnamese man was stabbed to death in Dorchester, Mass., reportedly in a racial incident.
- A Buddhist temple in Greenview, Mass., was blown up by Vietnam War veterans who said they wanted to get even for what happened to them in Vietnam, even though the temple has no Asian members.
- A Vietnamese family was forced from its farm in West Virginia after several cross-burnings.
- The words "Nips Go Home" were spray painted on the store of a Korean family in Davis, Calif.
- The word "Chink" appeared on the cover of *National Review* magazine, a conservative publication. Its editors say they didn't think it would be offensive.
- A 19-year-old pregnant Chinese woman was decapitated by a train when she was pushed in front of it at a New York subway stop by a man whose lawyer says the murderer was "overcome by a fear of Asians."
- A Chinese graduate student, also in Davis, was stabbed to death and police have not ruled out a racial motivation in his killing.
- Every day of the week, countless Asian Americans are insulted, intimidated, threatened, cursed at and told to "go back home" by total strangers, for no reason other than because we look Asian. How many of these insults will turn into senseless racist murders?

The flurry of Asian American activism throughout the country that followed the shocking sentence by Kaufman may seem strange to some observers, but it is a natural result of two centuries of oppression and the final straw for many who've suffered a lifetime of indignities. For many of us, the killing of Vincent Chin and the sentences of probation for his murderers shattered the illusion that Asians are being treated as equals of other Americans. Instead we learned that little has changed: in 1873 a rancher could kill his Chinese servant and be fined $20; in 1982 two men could beat a Chinese American to death and be fined $3,000. No matter how long we stay in this country, and no matter how "accent-free" our children learn to speak English, we are still regarded as foreigners, and as "foreigners" we are suspect as an enemy from overseas.

For us, the price of personal safety in the U.S. is eternal vigilance and involvement. While we, like other Americans, cherish our heritages, we cannot afford the luxury of being silent or isolated from other groups. Our ability to demand the protection of our constitutional rights depends on our willingness to work together and maintain the fragile network that has been woven as a result of the Vincent Chin tragedy. It is to the credit of thousands of Asian Americans who sacrificed their time, money and effort to make sure we did not turn our backs on this life-threatening issue. In doing so, we have written another page in our history. But until the day groups like ACJ can disband because their work is done, we all still have much to do, to try to ensure there will be no more Vincent Chin cases.

Source: *Bridge* 9, no. 2 (1984): 18–23.

A Letter From Lily Chin (1983)

Lily Chin was the moral backbone behind ACJ's national crusade for justice. A Chinese immigrant woman of great courage and fortitude, she never gave up in her quest for justice and the hope that no other mother would ever have to lose a child to hate and prejudice again. Her presence and active participation in the national campaign helped to galvanize broad-base support for the first Asian American civil rights case against hate crime. In 1983, after Judge Charles Kaufman sentenced Ebens and Nitz each to $3,000 in fines and three years' probation for the killing of Vincent Chin, Lily Chin wrote the following letter in Chinese to the Detroit Chinese Welfare Council:

I, King Fong Yu (wife of Bing Heng Chin), grieve my son, Vincent Chin, who was brutally beaten to death by two assailants with a baseball bat. The two killers were apprehended by police and prosecuted in court. During the court proceedings, I, because I am widowed and poor, with no money in my bed, could not retain legal counsel to press the case for my deceased son. As a result, the murderers' attorney had the say. Yesterday, I read in the newspaper, the sentence was only a fine and probation; and the killers were set free. There was also no compensation for the victim's family. This is injustice to the gross extreme. My son's blood had been shed, how unjust can it be? I grieve in my heart and shed tears in blood. Yes, my son cannot be brought back; and I can only wait to die. It is just that my deceased son, Vincent Chin, was a member of your council. I, therefore, plead to you. Please help me. Please let the Chinese American community know, so they can help me raise funds and hire legal counsel to appeal. You must put the killers in prison so my son can rest his soul; and my grief vindicated. This old woman will be forever grateful.

I, King Fong Yu, respectfully submit this letter of appeal.

March 18, 1983

Source: Courtesy of Helen Zia.

In 1984, the U.S. District Court sentenced Ebens to twenty-five years in jail for violating Chin's civil rights and acquitted Nitz. But the victory was short-lived. Ebens's attorney succeeded in appealing the decision on a technicality and getting a retrial in the conservative city of Cincinnati, Ohio, where the jury returned a verdict of not guilty on May 1, 1987. Ebens was acquitted of all charges. Although Vincent Chin's mother, Lily Chin, later won a $1.5 million civil suit against Ebens and Nitz for the loss of Vincent's life, no money was ever paid; nor did Ebens or Nitz ever serve a day in jail for the murder of

Lily Chin speaking at a rally for Vincent Chin, with Jesse Jackson *(left of podium)* and Helen Zia *(right of podium)* in attendance. (Courtesy of Renee Tajima-Pena)

Vincent Chin. Grief-torn and bitter over her son's murder and the miscarriage of justice, Lily Chin moved back to China to live out the remainder of her days. She returned to Detroit after a long illness and died on June 9, 2002, at the age of eighty-two.

Other References

Christine Choy and Renee Tajima, *Who Killed Vincent Chin?* (New York: Filmakers Library, 1989), VHS.

Patricia Wong Hall and Victor M. Hwang, *Anti-Asian Violence in North America: Asian American and Asian Canadian Reflections on Hate, Healing, and Resistance* (Walnut Creek, Calif.: Alta Mira Press, 2001).

Helen Zia, *Asian American Dreams: The Emergence of an American People* (New York: Farrar, Straus & Giroux, 2000).

Discussion Questions

1   What did Japanese Americans suffer during World War II?

2   Why was the Vincent Chin case important to Asian Americans?

3   What were the legal implications of the Vincent Chin case to the courts?

4   Lawyers say Vincent provoked his own death while Ebens and Nitz were innocent. How true is this statement?

5   Was the death of Vincent Chin an isolated case in the Asian American community?

CHAPTER 10

Racism and Multi-Racial Identities

Arenas of Racial Integration

Interracial Relationships, Multi-Racial Families

Kathleen Fitzgerald

Interracial Intimacies: Relationships, Families, And Identities

Gordon's assimilation model identified marital assimilation, also referred to as **amalgamation,** as the most crucial stage of assimilation. The extent to which inter-racial marriages are accepted in a society is an important determinant of a society's level of assimilation. Dominant groups have historically been slow to accept marital assimilation, preferring to maintain their social distance from subordinate groups in interpersonal, intimate relations (Yancey and Lewis 2009). The extent of interracial relationships in any society is a barometer for how important race remains. The data on interracial intimacies show that we are hardly the color-blind society that we profess ourselves to be. Of course, increasing numbers of interracial relationships have resulted in increasing numbers of multiracial families navigating their way through racially segregated worlds, and contributed to more fluidity in racial identities for biracial/multiracial individuals.

History of Antimiscegenation Legislation

Interracial marriages were illegal in thirteen states until 1967, when antimiscegenation laws, which made interracial marriage and sexual relations illegal, were finally overturned in the Supreme Court case *Loving v. The Commonwealth of Virginia*. By the 1930s, thirty-eight states had adopted antimiscegenation laws. Maryland had passed the first antimiscegenation law in 1661, which prohibited whites from marrying African Americans or Native Americans. In the western United States, interracial relationships between whites and Chinese, Japanese, and Filipino Americans were also outlawed, with Nevada passing the first state law in 1861 to ban marriage between whites and Asians. There was an increased fear of miscegenation after emancipation. While these laws made interracial sex illegal, they only applied to consensual sexual relations. Thus, the-well documented practice among white plantation owners of raping slave women was not considered a violation of the law. For over four hundred years, marriage between whites and nonwhites was either illegal or not constitutionally protected in many states (Frankenberg 1993).

Such laws help explain why interracial marriage was incredibly rare prior to 1967. Such laws are examples of **social control**, which are efforts to encourage people to abide by the cultural norms and discourage deviance, or violation of the norm. Laws are an example of **formal social sanctions,** mechanisms designed to prohibit certain deviant behaviors by making them illegal. Social controls that are formalized into laws have the power to punish offenders more seriously than informal sanctions.

Some of the arguments used by whites to support prohibitions on interracial marriage were that God created the races as separate and thus, intended for them to remain so; concern with white racial purity; that interracial marriages diminish the status of the white partner and his or her family; and finally, that mixed-race children will be particularly stigmatized (Romano 2003). Some of these arguments maintained their tenacity well after the 1967 Supreme Court decision, as research finds that as of 1980, white Americans claimed to be willing to live in integrated neighborhoods, go to integrated schools, and even entertain black people in their homes. But at that time, the vast majority of whites disapproved of interracial marriage between blacks and whites (Romano 2003). Whites' approval of interracial marriage has increased since then; this "approval" is conditional. It is often reserved for people other than their own family members (Qian 2005).

Once the Supreme Court declared antimiscegenation laws to be illegal, there were no longer any formal sanctions directed against individuals that chose to engage in interracial relationships. However, while we have seen a dramatic increase in interracial relationships, they still remain remarkably rare. Why is this? Sociologists emphasize the power of **informal social sanctions:** those behaviors directed at people to let them know they are breaking the rules. When strangers glare at an interracial couple in a public space—for instance, at a shopping mall—they are letting their disapproval be known. While a glare from a stranger is hardly as serious as

REFLECT AND CONNECT

What types of informal social sanctions exist to discourage people from engaging in interracial relationships? Why are such informal sanctions effective?

a felony record, such informal social sanctions are actually very effective at maintaining social control: since over fifty years after the last antimiscegenation law was struck down by the high court, still only about 8.4 percent of marriages have been interracial.

Limiting interracial relationships, whether through formal or informal sanctions, is a form of **boundary maintenance;** controlling interracial sex and marriage is an integral part of maintaining distinct racial groups (Childs 2009). In the absence of a taboo on interracial relationships, the racial categories of "black" and "white" would not be able to exist in quite the same way. As researchers point out, "the policing of sexual boundaries ... is precisely what keeps a racial group a racial group ... from the perspective of white supremacism interracial liaisons 'resulted in mixed race progeny who slipped back and forth across the color line and defied social control'" (Jacobson 1998:3). Generally, it has been white Americans that have been the most hostile to interracial families, arguably because their existence is a threat to the racial order and thus, their white privilege (Romano 2003; Spickard 1989; Wallenstein 2002).

People in interracial relationships, as well as those in multiracial families, experience what sociologist Heather Dalmage (2000) identifies as a specific kind of informal social sanction that people who cross the color-line experience, border patrolling. **Border patrolling** refers to actions by both whites and nonwhites that send the message that certain behaviors (be they family formation or dating decisions) are against the rules. Ultimately, border patrollers believe that people should stick with their own kind. Dalmage's research finds that "many whites feel both the right and the obligation to act out against interracial couples" (2000:44). White border patrollers let the deviant individuals know that something must be wrong with them to engage in interracial relationships. Border patrolling helps maintain the myth of racial purity and white privilege.

Whites are not the only people that engage in border patrolling; however, when blacks engage in border patrolling, they do it for different reasons. Blacks express concern over race loyalty. Interracially married blacks are sent the message by black border patrollers that they have lost their identity and culture, they are weak, and that they are no longer "really black" (Dalmage 2000). Black women may feel a sense of rejection when seeing a black man and a white woman together because, due to the prison industrial complex and economic marginalization, there are fewer marriageable black men than there are black women (Wilson 1987). Another source of their rejection is the fact that women are overwhelmingly judged in terms of their physical beauty, and beauty standards in the United States are Eurocentric, favoring whites. Thus, from a black woman's perspective, a black man in a relationship with a white woman emphasizes just how far removed they are from the dominant beauty standards (Dalmage 2000). Certainly the historical sexual exploitation during slavery of black women by white men lingers as a reason black women are often less accepting of interracial relationships.

Sociological research on white experiences in interracial relationships finds that they are no longer able to cling to notions of color-blindness as easily as before they entered an interracial relationship. They are forced to see race in ways they could previously ignore. Sociologist

Ruth Frankenberg identified a phenomena referred to as **rebound racism** to capture the white partner's hurt and pain associated with witnessing racism directed at someone they love. It is a "rebound" in the sense that it does not carry the same sting as it does for the initial target, the partner of color, but watching such hostility and hatred directed at someone you love is painful. This is true for white individuals in interracial relationships as well as for those in multiracial families with biracial children, as discussed later in the chapter.

Attitudes Toward Interracial Relationships

Although formal social control of interracial marriage was altered by the Supreme Court decision in *Loving v. Virginia* in 1967, attitudes toward interracial marriage took much longer to change. Attitudes, particularly toward black-white marriages, have changed enormously since World War II (Romano 2003). In 1958, when Gallup first asked Americans whether they approved of marriage between blacks and whites, only 4 percent approved. By 1983, 50 percent of people surveyed still disapproved of interracial marriage. As of 2007, 77 percent of Americans approve of marriage between blacks and whites and only 17 percent disapprove. As of 2011, approval of black-white marriages was at an all-time high at 86 percent. The most recent Gallup Poll found that 96 percent of blacks and 84 percent of whites approved of interracial marriage between blacks and whites (Jones 2011). Although this is a dramatic shift in attitudes in the postwar era, it would be a mistake to believe there is no longer resistance to and hostility toward interracial relationships.

Evidence of the resistance and hostility toward interracial relationships is found in a study on adolescent dating. In this research, 71 percent of white adolescents with white boyfriends or girlfriends, compared to only 57 percent of those with nonwhite boyfriends or girlfriends, introduced them to their parents. Black adolescents behaved similarly: 63 percent of those with a black boyfriend or girlfriend introduced the friend to their family, whereas only 52 percent of those with nonblack friends did so (Qian 2005). It appears that, for both white and black students, there is some hesitation at bringing home a partner that is of a different race.

If one looks to images of interracial relationships in popular culture, one can sense some of the ongoing resistance. Mainstream box-office films rarely depict black-white intimate interracial relationships, preferring

REFLECT AND CONNECT

Think about the images of interracial couples you have seen on television or in Hollywood films. Do they fit these stereotypical images? Are some interracial couples portrayed more positively than others? Are some interracial couples more invisible than others?

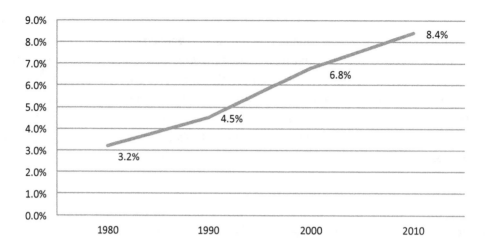

Figure 11.1   Increase in Interracial Marriage Trends, 1980–2010

Source: Pew Research Data, http:// www.pewresearch.org/daily-number/intermarriage-on-the-rise-in-the-u-s.

instead to depict Asian-white relationships (Childs 2009). The film images of interracial couples that do exist fall into one of several themes: intimate interracial relationships do not last, the relationship is based upon lust, curiosity, or deception rather than love, negative consequences inevitably arise from such relationships, and/or these relationships exist as part of a larger deviant lifestyle (Childs 2009). When analyzing black-white interracial couples in Hollywood films, Childs' concludes that there is **implicit censorship** going on, where interracial couples fall outside the realm of acceptable subjects. Implicit censorship refers to "operations of power that rule out in unspoken ways what will remain unspeakable" (Butler 1993:130). Hollywood stereotypes of Asian women in relationships with white men have long portrayed the Asian woman as submissive, hyperfeminine and/or sexual, from such films as *Japanese War Brides* (1952) to *Memoirs of a Geisha* (2005) (Nemoto 2009). Hollywood is sending the message that interracial couples are deviant, with some, particularly black-white couples, so deviant as to be unacceptable.

Interracial Relationships

In the United States, people tend to adhere to the norm of **endogamy,** meaning they become intimately involved with people racially similar to themselves, thus, rates of interracial marriage in the United States are quite low. According to the PEW Research Center, as of 2010, only about 8.4 percent of all marriages are interracial, and this statistic includes all possible interracial mar- riage combinations of Asians, whites, Latinos, blacks, and Native Americans. Interracial marriage rates have more than doubled since 1980 (see Figure 11.1). In 2010, a record 15.1 percent of

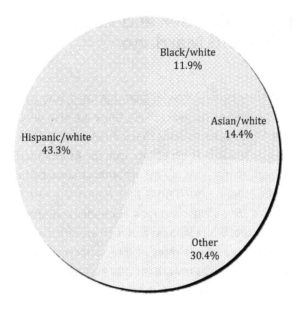

Figure 11.2   Intermarriage Types, New Married Couples in 2010

Note: "Other" includes American Indian, mixed race, or "some other" race. *Source:* www.pewresearch.org.

all new marriages, defined as individuals that married within twelve months of being surveyed, were interracial.

Students often comment on how such statistics make interracial relationships appear rarer than they seem in daily life. There are two ways to consider this: where you live partially determines your likelihood of seeing many interracial relationships in your daily life. Interracial marriage is more common on the West Coast of the United States and the least common in the Midwest, for instance. Interracial dating is more common than interracial marriage; thus, you may see more interracial couples in your life, but many of these people may not end up getting married. Another variable to consider is age, as research finds there is a generation gap on attitudes toward interracial marriage. Traditional-age college students, according to the research, are more open to interracially dating than their parents' generation (Kao and Joyner 2004).

Interracial marriage rates vary along gender and group lines. Hispanic-white marriages are the most common, while black-white marriages are the least common, making up only 11.9 percent of interracial marriages in 2010 (see Figure 11.2). While black-white marriages have increased in the last thirty years, they have increased at a slower rate than interracial unions that do not involve a black spouse (Root 2001b). White-other marriages, which refer to unions between a white and an Asian American or a Native American spouse, have more than doubled since 1980.

The Intersection of Gender and Race in Interracial Dating and Marriage

While there are racial differences in interracial marriage rates, with whites, by far, the least likely to marry interracially, and Asians as the most likely, there are also gender differences in interracial dating and marriage. Some research finds that women tend to interracially marry more than do their male counterparts, and this is especially true for Asian Americans, as Asian American women are much more likely to marry racial/ethnic others than are Asian American men (Yancey and Lewis 2009). However, other research finds that women are less willing to out-marry than are men (Tucker and Kernan 1995). When we look at gender and race together, the picture gets complicated. Research finds that white women and men are the least open to interracial dating, and it follows that they have the lowest rates of interracial marriage. White women and black women show the greatest preferences toward racially exclusive dating patterns, whereas white men and black men are less racially exclusive in their dating preferences (Robnett and Feliciano 2011). Latino males and females show no difference in racial dating preferences, while Asian women are much less likely to prefer to only date other Asians than their male counterparts (Robnett and Feliciano 2011).

However, willingness to date outside of one's own racial group does not mean one is open to dating members of all other racial/ethnic groups equally. Research on racial exclusion preferences in Internet dating profiles finds that, with the exception of white females, the majority of all race/gender groups are willing to date outside of their own race. Asians, Latinos, and blacks are all more open to dating whites than are whites to dating them. White male racial dating preferences noted that 97 percent of them exclude black women, 48 percent exclude Latinas, and 53 percent exclude Asian women (see Figure 11.3). White men are excluded by 75 percent of black women, 33 percent of Latinas, and only 11 percent of Asian women (Robnett and Feliciano 2011) (see Figure 11.4). When stating dating preferences, Latinos, Asians, and blacks are more likely to include whites as possible dates than are whites to include them, thus, social distance between whites and minority groups remains high.

Structural forces such as imperialist policies and wars have influenced the frequency and perceptions of interracial relationships between white men and Asian American women. The US involvement in World War II, Korea, and Vietnam all resulted in a large increase in war brides as well as sexual liaisons between white soldiers and Asian women overseas. Changes in immigration policy, specifically the passage of the 1965 *Immigration Act*, have also contributed to an increase in Asian Americans as potential dating partners. This, however, has not resulted in a preponderance of Asian men seeking non-Asian women as partners, as 58 percent of Asian-white relationships involve an Asian-American woman and a white man. This pattern holds true despite the fact that Asian-American men are typically more educated than white men, a factor that tends to correlate with whether someone is considered marriageable or not (Qian 2005).

Multiracial Families

The increase in interracial dating and marriage has resulted in an increase in multiracial families, with interracial couples joined together as families and often having biracial/multiracial children. Multiracial families occupy a unique place in our racialized society, as they are forced to think about contradictions and complexities surrounding race in ways monoracial families are not. When multiracial families are together in public, it is often assumed by others that they are unrelated (Dalmage 2000). Similarly to white partners in interracial relationships, white parents of biracial/multiracial children also experience rebound racism, as defined previously, when they see their child being discriminated against.

A specific problem multiracial families encounter is border patrolling in the housing market. As Chapter 8 explored, housing markets in the United States are racially segregated. Multiracial families encounter the same discrimination in the housing market that families of color face, such as redlining, particularly if they try to move into white neighborhoods. Thus, multiracial families have often been forced to find housing in black communities. In the 1960s and 1970s, multiracial families experienced discrimination in black communities. There are only a limited number of truly multiracial neighborhoods in the United States and most of those are

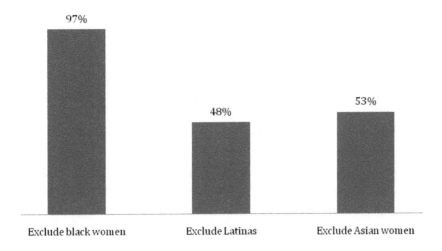

Figure 11.3 White Male Heterosexual Racial Dating Preferences

Source: Robnett, Belinda, and Cynthia Feliciano. 2011. "Patterns of Racial-Ethnic Exclusion by Internet Daters," *Social Forces* 89(3):807–828.

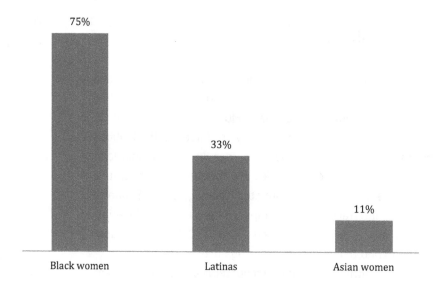

Figure 11.4   White Male Exclusion by Racial/Ethnic Women Dating Preferences

Source: Robnett, Belinda and Cynthia Feliciano. 2011. "Patterns of Racial-Ethnic Exclusion by Internet Daters." *Social Forces* 89(3):807–828.

upper-middle-class communities; Hyde Park near the University of Chicago is a good example (Dalmage 2000).

Biracial/Multiracial Identities

Interracial intimacies may be the most significant barometer of societal assimilation, but looking at the fluid racial identities claimed by biracial/multiracial people allows us to look at how racial integration happens within one's own sense of self. Biracial/multiracial people have always recognized the problematic nature of racial segregation as they never fit neatly into our socially constructed racial categories.

Mixed race individuals have long been portrayed as deviant, mentally unstable, as lacking identity, as longing to be white, and as lonely, being perceived as rejected by both blacks and whites (Fredrickson 1971). This "tragic mulatto" was a popular novel theme in the late 1800s and a recurrent them in film, including *The Birth of a Nation* (1915). Since the 1967 Supreme Court decision in *Loving v. Commonwealth of Virginia*, there has been an increase in interracial marriages and a resulting "biracial baby boom." Even the word **mulatto,** once stigmatized, is having a comeback and more and more biracial individuals are using this term to describe themselves (Saulny 2011; Spencer 2011).

There is nothing new about biracial people, of course. They have existed since the colonial era. In only two areas of the country were mixed-race people, generally referred to as mulattoes, considered a separate racial status: New Orleans and Charleston, South Carolina, because mis-cegenation was a more accepted practice in these regions and free mulattoes acted as a buffer between whites and blacks (Rockquemore and Brunsma 2002). Mulattoes became leaders of free black communities and whites relied on them to help control the large numbers of enslaved blacks (Davis 1991). As explored in Chapter 1, several censuses during the 1800s included such racial categories as mulatto, quadroon, and octoroon. Terms for mixed-race people had disap-peared by the 1930 census, as the **one-drop rule** was in full effect, which meant that a single drop of "black blood" made a person black. The term **rule of hypodescent** refers to the practice of racially mixed persons' being assigned the status of the subordinate group (Davis 1991).

The one-drop rule was sometimes enforced through formal sanctions, such as laws, and at other times, through informal sanctions. In 1982, Susie Guillory Phipps, a Louisiana woman who looked white and considered herself white, had to sue the state of Louisiana to have herself declared white. She lost her lawsuit because she was found to be one thirty-second black, which according to Louisiana law (at the time) made her black despite what she looked like, how she racially identified, or what little she knew of her African ancestry (Dominguez 1986). An example of the lingering influence of the one-drop rule, albeit informally, is President Barack Obama. He identifies himself as black rather than biracial despite his white ancestry. In the United States, as the one-drop rule became ensconced in our culture, the term *mulatto*, became a term like *colored, Negro, black*, and African American in that they all referred to people with any known black ancestry.

People who are biracial/multiracial gained a certain amount of legitimacy with the 2000 census when, for the first time, people were allowed to check more than one racial category. In 2000, approximately 2.4 percent of the population marked more than one race (Saulny 2011). According to the 2010 Census, 9 million people, or about 3 percent of the population, reported more than one race. This change was due to organizing and activism of the **multiracial movement**, which sought to gain public recognition of the multiracial community, to allow people to legally self-identify as biracial/multiracial, and to end the discrimination they faced. The organization initially pushed to have a multiracial category on the census, however, this was rejected and instead respondents were allowed to check more than one racial category.

Although there is nothing new about people who are biracial/multiracial, what is new is that so many are claiming a biracial/multiracial identity rather than being constrained in their racial identity choices to being black, as the one-drop rule proscribed. People that grew up in the pre-Civil Rights era are more likely to identify as black while those born in the post–civil rights era show more fluidity in their racial identity—at different points in their lives identifying as black, biracial, and sometimes even white (Harris and Khanna 2010). Blogger Maria Niles, for instance, describes herself as an "undercover black woman" because she looks white while she identifies as black (Niles 2011). Some individuals that are biracial or multiracial argue that through such self-definition they are rejecting the color lines that have long defined our nation (Saulny 2011).

Figure 11.4   2010 US census race question. Census racial categories change over time. In 2010, Hispanic was not a racial category on the US census, it is now being considered for inclusion as a racial category in the 2020 census. (U.S. Census Bureau, 2010 Census questionnaire)

While this represents a dramatic change in our racial categorization system, it also has been controversial. The NAACP, for instance, was against changing the existing census categories. The census does more than provide the nation with a demographic snapshot of our country. The data gathered is also used to correct inequalities (Williams 2006). It is through the census, for instance, that we know that African Americans, Native Americans, and Latinos are disproportionately impoverished and uninsured. This census data can then be used to argue for federal funds being directed toward these communities for the establishment of community health clinics, for instance.

Many argue that the increasing presence of people's claiming biracial/multiracial identities, does not really challenge our existing racial order because it does not challenge whiteness (Dalmage 2004; Ferber 1998; Spencer 2011). Spencer (2011) argues that we are adding new nonwhite categories, which in no way challenges the racial hierarchy with whites in a position of privilege. While the presence of people claiming biracial/multiracial identities may not disturb the racial hierarchy, the multiracial idea does disrupt notions of race as fixed and biological.

Researchers have also explored another shift in racial/ethnic identity options, that of Native American **reclaimers**, individuals raised as white, with little to no knowledge of their Native American ancestry, who later voluntarily reconnect with their Native heritage (Fitzgerald 2007; Nagel 1996). Their Nativeness becomes a salient aspect of their identity; it informs how they see themselves. Much like the increasing numbers of biracial and multiracial people claiming a nonblack identity, reclaiming a Native American identity does not necessarily upset the racial order, but it does challenge the racial hierarchy because these people are voluntarily rejecting the privileges associated with whiteness.

References

Butler, Judith. 1993. *Bodies That Matter: On the Discursive Limits of Sex*. New York: Routledge.

Childs, Erica Chito. 2009. *Fade to Black and White: Interracial Images in Popular Culture*. Boulder, CO: Rowman and Littlefield.

Dalmage, Heather M. 2000. *Tripping on the Color-Line: Black-White Multiracial Families in a Racially Divided World*. New Brunswick, NJ: Rutgers University Press.

_____ . 2004. *The Politics of Multiracialism: Challenging Racial Thinking*. Albany, NY: State University of New York.

Davis, F. James. 1991. *Who Is Black? One Nation's Definition*. University Park: The Pennsylvania University Press.

Dominguez, Virginia. 1986. *White By Definition: Social Classification in Creole Louisiana*. New Brunswick, NJ: Rutgers University Press.

Ferber, Abby. 1998. *White Man Falling: Race, Gender, and White Supremacy*. Lanham, MD: Rowman and Littlefield.

Fitzgerald, Kathleen J. 2007. *Beyond White Ethnicity: Developing a Sociological Understanding of Native American Identity Reclamation*. Lanham, MD: Lexington Books.

Frankenberg, Ruth. 1993. *White Women, Race Matters: The Social Construction of Whiteness*. Minneapolis: University of Minnesota Press.

Fredrickson, G. M. 1971. *The Black Image in the White Mind: The Debate on Afro-American Character and Destiny, 1817–1914*. New York, NY: Harper and Row.

Harris, Cherise A. and Nikki Khanna. 2010. "Black Is, Black Ain't: Biracials, Middle-Class Blacks, and the Social Construction of Blackness." *Sociological Spectrum* 30(6):639–670.

Jacobson, Matthew Frye. 1998. *Whiteness of a Different Color: European Immigrants and the Alchemy of Race*. Cambridge, MA: Harvard University Press.

Jones, Jeffrey N. 2011. "Record High 86% Approve of Black-White Marriages." *Gallup*, September 12. Retrieved April 14, 2012 (http://www.gallup.com/poll/149390/Record-High-Approve-Black-White-Marriages.aspx).

Kao, Grace and Kara Joyner. 2004. "Do Race and Ethnicity Matter Among Friends? Activities Among Interracial, Interethnic, and Intraethnic Adolescent Friends." *Sociological Quarterly* 45(3):557–573.

Nagel, Joane. 1996. *American Indian Ethnic Renewal: Red Power and the Resurgence of Identity and Culture*. New York and Oxford: Oxford University Press.

Nemoto, Kumiko. 2009. *Racing Romance: Love, Power and Desire among Asian American/White Couples*. New Brunswick, NJ: Rutgers University Press.

Niles, Maria. 2011. "Black History Month: Why I Identify as Black." *Blogher.com*, February 28. Retrieved April 14, 2013 (http://www.blogher.com/black-history-month-why-i-identify-black).

Qian, Zhenchao. 2005. "Breaking the Last Taboo: Interracial Marriage in America." *Contexts* 4(4):33–37.

Robnett, Belinda and Cynthia Feliciano. 2011. "Patterns of Racial-Ethnic Exclusion by Internet Daters." *Social Forces* 89(3):807–828.

Rockquemore, Kerry Ann and David Brunsma. 2002. *Beyond Black: Biracial Identity in America*. Thousand Oaks, CA: Sage Publications.

Romano, Renee C. 2003. *Race Mixing: Black-White Marriage in Postwar America*. Cambridge, MA: Harvard University Press.

Saulny, Susan. 2011. "Race Remixed: Black? White? Asian? More Young Americans Choose All of the Above." *New York Times*, January 29. Retrieved April 5, 2013 (http://www.nytimes.com/2011/01/30/us/30mixed. html?ref=raceremixed&_r=0).

Spencer, Rainier. 2011. *Reproducing Race: The Paradox of Generation Mix*. Boulder, CO: Lynne Reiner Publishers.

Spickard, Paul. 1989. *Mixed Blood: Intermarriage and Ethnic Identity in Twentieth-Century America*. Madison: University of Wisconsin Press.

Tucker, Belinda M., and Claudia Mitchell-Kernan. 1995. "Social Structural and Psychological Correlates of Interethnic Dating." *Journal of Social and Personal Relationships* 12(3):341–61.

Wallenstein, P. 2002. *Tell the Court I Love My Wife: Race, Marriage and the Law–An American History*. New York: Palgrave Macmillan.

Williams, Kim M. 2006. *Mark One or More: Civil Rights in Multiracial America*. Ann Arbor: The University of Michigan Press.

Wilson, William Julius. 1987. *The Truly Disadvantaged: The Inner City, the Underclass, and Public Policy*. Chicago, IL: The University of Chicago Press.

Yancey, George and Richard Lewis, Jr. 2009. *Interracial Families: Current Concepts and Controversies*. New York: Routledge.

Discussion Questions

1 Why was interracial marriage illegal?

2 Why were mixed-race children called Mulattoes?

3 Define the "one-drop rule."

4 Why are mixed-race children claiming biracial or multiracial identities?

5 How much progress has been made on interracial relationships and marriages?

PART III

OTHER FORMS OF OPPRESSION

Introduction

Like racism, other forms of oppression have become a deterrent to many people. These include religion, sex, age, ability, and so on.

Religious discrimination charges have risen since 1997. As the American workforce became increasingly diverse, a growing number of religious belief appeared in the workplace. Christian and Jewish employers were expected to employ Muslims, Hindus, and people of other religions. Consequently, religious accommodations became more complex, and complaints began to arise. Thus, employers were required to provide "reasonable accommodations" based on religious beliefs according to Section 701 of the Civil Rights Act 1964.

The Age Discrimination in Employment Act (ADEA) is an amendment to the Fair Labor Act of 1938. ADEA makes it unlawful to fail or refuse to hire or to discharge any individual with respect to their compensation and privileges based on their age. The prohibition on age discrimination is limited to individuals age forty and above. *Bona fide* occupational qualification (BFOQ) permits employers to use age as a disqualification where age bias is reasonably necessary.

The first law to provide disability was the Vocational Rehabilitation Act (VRA) of 1973. This act was limited to employers who had a job with the Federal Government. Then, in 1990, the Americans with Disabilities Act (ADA) came into existence. Its goal was to prevent employment discrimination against a qualified individual based on a real or perceived disability. This act was amended by President G. W. Bush in 2008 and became known as the Americans with Disabilities Amendment Act (ADAA). The amendment lowered the bar for establishing disability and called for the provision of reasonable accommodation for individuals with disabilities.

Gender-based violence and discrimination against women and girls are rooted in male dominance as part of American history; however, too often the concept of manhood is left out of the conversation. Boys are taught a type of manhood that is based on sexist beliefs like women being less than, property of, and objects to men. Homophobia and heterosexism can be viewed as products of this negative image.

CHAPTER 11

Religious Oppression, Ageism, Sexism and Ableism

Discrimination Based on Religion, Age and Disability

By Robert K. Robinson and Geralyn McClure Franklin

Introduction

This chapter examines the remaining classes receiving protection under Title VII (religion and national origin) as well as those protected under the Age Discrimination in Employment Act and the Americans with Disabilities Act. Because the Vocational Rehabilitation Act of 1973, which applies to holders of federal contracts and subcontracts, contains virtually the same language and requirements as the Americans with Disabilities Act, these two statutes will be discussed together.

Religion

Compared to complaints from other protected classes, Title VII complaints based upon religious discrimination are quite rare. In fact, it was not until 1996 that charges of religious discrimination exceeded 2 percent of the total charges handled by the Equal Employment Opportunity Commission (EEOC).[1] However, religious discrimination charges have risen steadily since 1997, when they accounted for only 2.1 percent of all Title VII charges. In actual number they have increased from 1,709 in 1997 to 4,151 in 2011, a 143 percent increase and 4.2 percent of all charges.[2]

As the American workforce becomes increasingly diverse, a growing number of religious beliefs will appear in the workplace. In addition to Christians and Jews, employers can expect to find employees who are Muslims, Hindus, and Buddhists (just to name a few). Consequently, **religious accommodations** will become more complex, and complaints can be expected to rise.

Exemptions for Religious Entities

Perhaps one of the reasons that religious discrimination charges occur so infrequently is because the religious exemption under the Civil Rights Act of 1964 permits preferential treatment to *bona fide* religious organizations. Often referred to as the Section 702 exemption because of its location in the original Act, the **religious exemption** states that the prohibition on religious discrimination:

> shall not apply ... to a religious corporation, association, educational institution, or society with respect to the employment of individuals of a particular religion to perform work connected with the carrying on by such corporation, association, educational institution, or society of its activities.[3]

In essence, this means religious organizations are permitted to make hiring and discharge decisions based on an applicant's or employee's religious affiliation.

To be eligible for this exemption, the religious corporation, association, education institution, or society activities must show some connection between the position and the religion. If this connection is clearly visible, preferential hiring is permitted; if not, preferential hiring is prohibited (see Figure 12.1).

To illustrate this point, let's examine the case of *Killinger v. Samford University*.[4] In this case, a faculty member was hired to teach courses in religion in the School of Divinity at a Baptist university. After hiring, the faculty member was removed from the Divinity School and relegated to teaching undergraduate classes. The faculty member contended that he was being discriminated against (prohibited from teaching in the Divinity School) because his religious philosophy was incompatible with the fundamentalist theology advanced by the leadership of the Divinity School. The university contended that, as a religious institution, it was covered by Title VII's

---

- Religious associations (i.e., National Council of Reformed Churches, etc.)
- Religious corporations (i.e., Presbyterian Church in America, Southern Baptist Convention, Roman Catholic Church, etc.)
- Religious societies (i.e., Knights of Columbus, Reformed University Fellowship, etc.)
- Religious educational institutions (i.e., University of Notre Dame, Emory University, etc.)

Figure 12.1 Religious Exempted Entities Under § 702

religious exemption. The Eleventh Circuit agreed with the university by concluding: "The Section 702 exemption's purpose and words easily encompass plaintiff's case; the exemption allows religious institutions to employ only persons whose beliefs are consistent with the employer's when the work is connected with carrying out the institution's activities."[5]

Clearly, religious education is at the core of a religious university, especially in its Divinity School. As a Baptist university, Samford was permitted to lawfully discriminate in favor of Baptists when making teaching assignments. The principal criterion of eligibility for a Section 702 exemption is that the organization must clearly be a religious corporation, association, education institution, or society, and it must exhibit some ministerial function. To establish this, the religious institution's primary duties must consist of teaching, spreading the faith, church governance, supervision of religious order, and participation in religious ritual or worship (see Figure 12.2).[6] It is equally important to show that the institution in question is owned in whole or in substantial part by a particular religion. Moreover, if it can be shown that a particular institution is not owned, supported, or managed by a religious entity, no exemption will be permitted.[7] In short, the organization in question would be viewed by the courts as secular, not religious.

Even if the organization in question is owned by a religious institution, it may not necessarily be eligible for the religious exemption. Any organization that claims to be religious but lacks any religious content will be considered a secular organization and not entitled to the Section 702 exemption.[8]

It is important to note that the Section 702 exemption permits religious institutions to discriminate only on the basis of religion, not gender or race.[9] However, the Title VII ban on sex discrimination does not apply in cases where a particular religion has theological prohibitions against ordaining women as ministers or priests, or bestowing positions of church leadership. For example, it is a basic tenet of faith that only men can be ordained as priests in the Roman Catholic Church. Therefore, Title VII cannot be used to require the Catholic Church to ordain women on the

---

- Participation in church governance
- Participation in religious ritual
- Participation in worship
- Spreading the faith
- Supervision of religious order
- Teaching

Source: Little v. Wuerl, 929 F.2d 944, 947–48 (3rd Cir. 1991).

Figure 12.2   Criteria for Establishing a § 702 Exemption

grounds of sex discrimination in employment. However, in other positions not connected to worship (clerical, janitorial, etc.) discrimination based on sex would be prohibited.

Religious Discrimination

Notwithstanding Section 702's religious exemption, which, as we have seen, permits preferential treatment of members of religious faiths, Section 703 makes it unlawful for secular organizations to otherwise discriminate on the basis of religion.

Here, disparate treatment and disparate impact (discussed in Chapters 3 and 4) are applicable. If an employer that is not a religious organization subjects an employee to poor treatment in the workplace because the employer, or its agent, dislikes the employee's religious beliefs, the employer has violated Title VII.[10] As in any disparate treatment situation, the complaining party establishes a *prima facie* case by proving the employer treated him or her differently from other employees because of the individual's religious beliefs.[11] Unless an applicant's religion can be shown to be a *bona fide* occupational qualification (BFOQ), a secular employer may not discriminate on the basis of religion.[12]

Religious Accommodation

Merely ensuring that an employee's religious beliefs have not affected employment decisions is not enough to avoid charges of religious discrimination. Employers may find themselves in violation of Title VII when they fail to make "reasonable accommodation" for an employee's religious practices.[13] Employers must refrain from considering an individual's religious beliefs in making decisions, and they must make accommodations for those beliefs after employment. The additional requirement to provide such accommodation comes from Section 701 of the Civil Rights Act of 1964. This is not to be confused with Section 703, which prevents discrimination on the basis of religion. Specifically, Section 701 states:

> The term "religion" includes all aspects of religious observance and practice, as well as belief, unless an employer demonstrates that he is unable to reasonably accommodate to an employee's or prospective employee's religious observance or practice without undue hardship on the conduct of the employer's business.[14]

Under this concept of religious accommodation, an individual establishes a *prima facie* case of religious discrimination by demonstrating that: (1) the individual has a *bona fide* belief that compliance with an employment requirement would be contrary to his religious beliefs or practice, (2) the individual informed the employer of the conflict, and (3) the individual was disciplined or discharged for failing to comply with the conflicting employment requirement (see Figure 12.3).[15]

Assume that Dave Leroy, a senior machinist, has recently had a religious experience and become a deacon in the First Baptist Church. Due to his recent conversion and position in the

> - The individual has a *bona fide* belief that compliance with an employment requirement would be contrary to his or her religious beliefs or practice.
> - The individual informed the employer of the conflict.
> - The individual was disciplined or discharged for failing to comply with the conflicting employment requirement.
>
> *Source: Cloutier v. COSTCO Wholesale Corp.*, 390 F.3d 126, 133 (1st Cir. 2004).

Figure 12.3 Establishing a *Prima Facie* Case for Religious Accommodation

church, Dave announces that he will no longer be able to work on Sundays. This would be in keeping with his religious obligation to keep the covenant and keep the Sabbath holy.[16] In June, the plant superintendent informs all employees that they will have to work seven-day shifts for the next two weeks in order to meet a client's deadline. Leroy informs the plant superintendent that working on Sunday conflicts with his religious beliefs. The superintendent tells Leroy that if he is not at his workstation on Sunday, he will be fired. When Leroy fails to show up for work that Sunday, his employment is terminated. This series of events would be sufficient to establish Leroy's Title VII claim.

Types of Accommodation

Common methods of achieving religious accommodation include arranging for a voluntary swap of work schedules among employees, instituting flexible scheduling to allow employees to make up time lost to religious observances, or requiring employees to arrive or depart early to meet religious observances. If swaps or flexible schedule patterns cannot accommodate the employee, a transfer to a comparable job within the company may be in order. In some instances it may be that such accommodation could actually benefit an employer. Assume a delivery company offers seven-days-a-week delivery service. Some Jewish and other employees who may have religious objections to working on their Sabbaths would have little concern about working on Sundays, the Christian Sabbath. Seventh Day Adventists, Worldwide Church of God members, and Jehovah's Witnesses also hold religious tenets against working on Saturdays.

Again, because their Sabbath is a day other than Sunday, they could be scheduled to work for Christian employees on that day. Granted, this may make scheduling a little more difficult, but it can solve an accommodation dilemma. In this regard, having a religiously diverse workforce might be used to some employers' advantage.

Undue Hardship Defense

In its rebuttal, the employer must show that it met its obligation to "reasonably" accommodate the employee's religious beliefs and practices, or that the accommodation would impose an undue hardship on the employer.[17] By proving that the employee's desired accommodation would impose an undue hardship, the accommodation becomes "unreasonable." Religious accommodation, unlike the reasonable accommodation required under the Americans with Disabilities Act, does not require employers to bear more *de minimus* costs.[18] Religious accommodation is not accomplished by merely eliminating the conflict between the dress code and an employee's religious practice. This accommodation is only reasonable "provided eliminating the conflict would not impose an undue hardship."[19] What is problematic for employers is that the determination of what is or is not a reasonable religious accommodation is handled on a case-by-case basis.[20] This of course means that often the only means for resolving the reasonableness of an accommodation is through litigation.

An accommodation requiring a business employing 17 employees to hire an additional part-time employee to cover missed work due to another employee's religious observance would, most likely, be considered as imposing an undue hardship. The same requirement for a business employing 250 employees might not. Possible reasons for rejecting the requested accommodation include that it diminishes efficiency in other jobs,[21] infringes on other employees' job rights under company policies or collective bargaining agreements,[22] impairs workplace safety, or places coworkers at a greater risk.[23]

There are some circumstances under which accommodations are more likely to be judged as unduly burdensome. Normally, an accommodation becomes an undue hardship if it results in changing a *bona fide* seniority system. This occurs when, in order to accommodate the employee's religious practices, the employer must deny another employee a shift preference guaranteed by the company's seniority system.

Interestingly, even accommodations involving work schedules can quickly cross the line into undue hardship. Returning to the scenario above involving Dave Leroy, Leroy's employer could prove that accommodating his absence for religious observance would require hiring another machinist; recall that *all* employees were required to work two seven-day weeks, so this would preclude shift changes. The employer could probably establish that accommodating Leroy would cause an undue hardship, since it would involve the expense of hiring an additional employee, either permanently or temporarily.

It should be noted that employers cannot base undue hardship on theoretical fears of loss in efficiency or additional costs, but must present evidence of identifiable losses. Germane to this discussion, an employer erroneously believed that if it allowed an employee to wear a head covering at work during Ramadan, the employer could no longer enforce its uniform policy with respect to other employees. Here the employer failed to demonstrate an actual undue hardship; it merely showed that its employment decision was based on the fear that allowing the accommodation would open "the floodgates to others violating the uniform policy."[24]

The Accommodation Does Not Have to be Acceptable to an Employee

The issue of whether or not the employer's proposed accommodation is reasonable does not hinge on the employee's acceptance or approval. The complaining party cannot reject an accommodation as unreasonable merely on the grounds that it was not one that the employee desired.[25]

Neither can it be rejected because the employer did not provide the employee a choice of alternatives. There is nothing in section 701 of Title VII that requires the employer to offer the employee several accommodations from which he or she may select the one that they find most acceptable.[26] Correspondingly, the employer is not under any compulsion to accept the employee's recommended accommodation, nor is the employer required to demonstrate that the employee's rejected preferred accommodation would create an undue burden.[27] When the employer has reasonably accommodated the employee's religious needs, the statutory obligation has been met.[28]

If an accommodation is requested by an employee or applicant, the employer's only defense is that the requested accommodation would create an undue hardship.[29] Failure to do so will result in a Title VII violation, as will be discussed in the next section.

Dress and Appearance Policies

Employers often assert their right to require employees who come into contact with customers and the general public to adhere to certain grooming, hygiene, and appearance expectations. This is typically done through a clearly delineated dress code or appearance policy. Employers are aware of the importance of employee appearance to the image of their respective businesses and organizations.[30] Many employers believe that it is their prerogative to require their employees to meet minimum grooming standards, especially those employees who project the organization's image to its customers. Marketing theory has long contended that favorable customer impressions affect business outcomes.[31] Those impressions could be particularly shaped by interactions with employees who deal directly with the public (especially "potential" customers). Therefore, it is reasonable to conclude that requiring employees to conform to accepted societal expectations of dress and behavior serves the legitimate business purposes of promoting an orderly workplace and making customers comfortable.

Some federal courts have found these concerns legitimate. The District of Columbia Circuit noted in *Fagan v. National Cash Register Company* that:

> Perhaps no facet of business is more important than a company's place in public estimation. That the image created by its employees dealing with the public when on company assignment affects its relations is so well known that we may take judicial notice of an employer's proper desire to achieve favorable acceptance.[32]

But, what if employees object to dress code regulations? Not surprisingly, employer dress and appearance standards have been challenged as contrary to employees' civil rights under Title VII of the Civil Rights Act of 1964. They are usually challenged on the standpoint that they result in disparate treatment either on the basis of religion or sex. Under religion, some employees are likely to make requests for exceptions or modifications to the employer's appearance rules in order to accommodate the employee's religious obligations.[33] For example, a Muslim female may request to wear a *hijab* as part of her religious practice,[34] or an American Indian may request exception to a hair length policy as a result of his religious practice.[35]

Federal courts have concluded that an undue hardship is established where there are identifiable costs incurred (considered in relation to the size and operating costs of the employer).[36] Whether the proposed accommodation conflicts with another law will also be considered,[37] particularly workplace safety laws. As an example, a Sikh machinist's beard (a requirement of his religious tradition) precludes his ability to wear a respirator in a job which required exposure to toxic gas. Because the beard prevents the respirator from sealing properly, his safety and health are endangered.[38]

In an instance not involving workplace safety, a female employee cashier who had direct contact with customers claimed that her body piercings were religiously significant. The company's appearance policy forbade body piercing for employees whose jobs required direct contact with customers. She was told by management to cover body piercings with flesh colored band aids when working at her cash register. She filed a lawsuit claiming the employer had failed to adequately accommodate her religious beliefs. However, the court concluded that "The temporary covering of plaintiff's facial piercings during work hours impinges on plaintiff's religious scruples no more than the wearing of a blouse which covers the plaintiff's tattoos."[39]

Implications for Employers

Employers are aware of the importance that employee appearance has on the image of their particular businesses, but there is an increasing likelihood of having appearance policies and dress codes challenged as religious discrimination. There is a balancing act that must be performed at this point.

If such policies are to be continued, the employer must be prepared to demonstrate that the appearance expectations should first be justified as serving some legitimate business purpose. These reasons must be articulated and communicated to the employees. In those cases where appearance of an applicant affects a hiring decision, it may even become necessary to empirically validate the selection criterion (appearance) with consumer and market research.[40]

Second, the appearance standard should not impose greater requirements on religious clothing and appearance than on the other individuals in other classes. Are African Americans exempted from the policy that male employees are to be clean-shaven and permitted to wear beards if they have pseudo *folliculitis barbae* (a medical reason), while Muslims are denied the same privilege for religious reasons?[41]

Once implemented, is the policy consistently enforced? Selective or haphazard enforcement invariably leads to complaints, especially if enforcement affects one group more than the other. A policy should be flexible enough to make reasonable accommodations for an employee's *bona fide* religious beliefs. It is recommended that employees seeking an exemption from the policy on religious grounds do so in writing. And if denied, a legitimate business reason should be offered for denying the request and evidence should be retained that the employee understands the reason for the policy (i.e., promoting a safe working environment, maintaining a positive public image, complying with health standards, etc.). Again, consistent enforcement indicates that the proffered reason for denying the request for accommodation is legitimate and is not a pretext to hide a discriminatory animosity toward a particular religious group.[42]

Because of the risk of potential litigation, if an appearance policy is not a component in the performance of the job, perhaps it should be avoided. To illustrate, there is hardly need for an employee appearance standard in an interstate trucking company beyond basic safety considerations. On the other hand, it can be argued that in instances where corporate image is a concern, such as a package delivery company, an employer has the right to expect employees on his or her payroll to project that image. Therefore, appearance and grooming standards should be justified and this justification communicated to all affected employees, especially for those employees responsible for making customer contact. Since appearance expectations may be as important to portraying the company to outside constituencies as polite and professional behavior, employees should be informed that appearance is to be treated as any other performance dimension for evaluation purposes.

Religious Accommodations and Union Dues

One final issue under religious accommodation is the payment of union dues. This issue not only affects unions but might also involve employers who are responsible under their collective bargaining agreements to deduct union dues from the payroll. If an employee's religious faith prohibits joining or paying dues to any organization outside of the church, can they still be required to pay the equivalent of dues to the union that represents them in the bargaining unit?

This situation occurred in *Tooley v. Martin Marietta Corp.*[43] Martin Marietta Corporation and the United Steelworkers of America had negotiated a collective bargaining agreement containing a union shop provision. Under such an arrangement, the company was obligated to discharge any employee who failed to join the union and pay union dues. Three of the employees who were Seventh Day Adventists refused to join the union. They contended that their religion prohibited them from becoming members of or paying a service fee to a union. In an attempt to achieve a compromise, the three workers offered to contribute an amount equivalent to union dues to a mutually agreed-upon charity. The union refused and held the employer to the union shop clause in the collective bargaining agreement, saying the three employees would have to join the union and pay dues or the employer would have to terminate their employment. If the employer failed to do so, it would be in violation of the collective bargaining agreement, and it would be an unfair labor practice under the National Labor Relations Act.[44]

The affected employees argued that both the union and the company were required under Title VII to make reasonable accommodations for their religious beliefs,[45] unless it caused undue hardship. The Steelworkers responded that it did create an undue hardship and was, therefore, not a reasonable accommodation.

This argument focused on the contention that substituting a charitable contribution in lieu of dues created an undue hardship on the union by denying it the funds necessary for the union's operations. The union further argued that the charity accommodation was unreasonable because it was contrary to the National Labor Relations Act's authorization of union shop agreements.

The Court concluded that Title VII was applicable in this case and that both the union and the company were obligated to make a reasonable accommodation. The Court also found that substituting a contribution to a mutually agreed-upon charity was not an undue hardship. Thus, the Court enjoined the union and the company from discharging the plaintiffs for failing to pay union dues so long as they made equivalent contributions to the mutually acceptable charity.

Age Discrimination in Employment

The Age Discrimination in Employment Act (ADEA), like the Equal Pay Act, is not an amendment to the Civil Rights Act of 1964 but an amendment to the Fair Labor Standards Act of 1938.[46] This is an important distinction because the remedies for ADEA violations are not the same as those afforded under Title VII.

The next thing that managers need to know about the ADEA is that it has resulted in one of the fastest-growing equal employment complaints. This is due in large part to the fact that the baby boomer generation is aging and constitutes a significant portion of the workforce. By 2011, age discrimination claims accounted for 23.5 percent of all charges handled by the EEOC.[47]

Additionally, there are variations as to which employers are required to comply with the ADEA's antidiscrimination provisions. Under the ADEA, the term "employer" means a person who is engaged in an industry affecting commerce and has twenty or more employees for each working day in each of twenty or more calendar weeks in the current or preceding calendar year.[48] Compare this to Title VII's application to employers with *fifteen or more* employees.[49]

The ADEA of 1967 makes it unlawful to: "fail or refuse to hire or to discharge any individual or otherwise discriminate against any individual with respect to his compensation, terms, conditions, or privileges of employment, because of such individual's age." Further, it is unlawful for an employer to even segregate or classify employees on the basis of age.[50] However, the prohibitions on age discrimination are limited to individuals who are at least forty years of age.[51] Initially, this protection on the basis of age covered only individuals who were between forty and sixty-five years old.[52] The upper limit was extended to seventy years by a 1978 amendment.[53] As of a 1986

- Education
- Experience
- Output
- Productivity

Figure 12.4 Legitimate Nondiscriminatory Factors under the ADEA

amendment, ADEA discrimination on the basis of age encompasses all employees and applicants who are over forty; there is no upper age limit.[54]

The ADEA's ban on age discrimination means that should an employer refuse to hire an applicant for a job based solely on the premise that the employer thinks the individual is too old for the job, that employer violates the ADEA. If an employee is not promoted because the employer feels that she is too old to perform the work at the next level, the ADEA is violated. If, during a downsizing, an employer decides to lay off all employees over fifty years old, the ADEA is violated.

Like Title VII, the ADEA mandates that employment decisions must be based on factors other than the employee's age. And, like Title VII, the ADEA is not automatically violated every time an over-forty employee is not promoted or is terminated. If the employment decision is based on legitimate reasons other than age, no unlawful discrimination has occurred (see Figure 12.4).

However, if the employee's age *was* a consideration in the employment decision, the whole process is tainted, since the ADEA requires employers to evaluate employees on their merits, not their age.[55]

Establishing a *Prima Facie* Case of Age Discrimination

To establish a *prima facie* case of unlawful discrimination under the ADEA, it must be proved that:

1   The complaining party was in an age group protected by the ADEA.

2   He or she was discharged or demoted (or refused employment).

3   At the time of the discharge or demotion, the complaining party was performing his or her job at a level that met his or her employer's legitimate expectations.

4   Following the complaining party's discharge, he or she was replaced by someone of comparable qualifications who is significantly younger.[56]

The fourth proof, replacement by someone who is "significantly younger," is a relatively recent innovation. Prior to 1996, it was assumed the ADEA would be violated only when the over-forty employee (the protected class under the ADEA) was replaced by someone under forty years old. However, with the Supreme Court's decision in *O'Connor v. Consolidated Coin Caterers, Corp.*,[57] the

ADEA may be violated if an older employee is replaced by an over-forty employee who is significantly younger. In the *O'Connor* case, a fifty-six-year-old employee with twelve years of service in the company was discharged and replaced with a forty-year-old employee. The employer contended that since the forty-year-old employee was also a member of the same protected class (forty years old and older), the ADEA was not violated. The Supreme Court concluded, however, that "[t]he fact that one person in the protected class has lost out to another person in the protected class is thus irrelevant, so long as he has lost out because of his age."[58] The purpose of the ADEA is quite clear: an employee's (or applicant's) age cannot be used in making any employment decision.

No Mixed Motive Under Age Discrimination

It should be noted at this juncture that, unlike Title VII, there is no mixed-motive discrimination under the ADEA. In its 2009 decision, *Gross v. FBL Financial Services, Inc.,*[59] the Supreme Court ruled that ADEA does not provide that a complaining party can establish an age discrimination claim by showing that age was simply a motivating factor (mixed motive). The complaining party must prove by a preponderance of the evidence that age was the reason that the employer decided to take the employment action in question. The ADEA does not require the burden of persuasion to shift to the employer to show that it would have taken the action regardless of age, even when a complaining party has produced some evidence that age was one motivating factor in that decision.[60]

The Employer's Rebuttal

An employer confronting an alleged ADEA violation must demonstrate convincingly that the employment decision is based on a legitimate reason, which means the employer has the burden of convincing the court that its decision was *not* based on the individual's age. If the contested matter involves promotion, the employer must demonstrate that the younger candidate was more qualified. In all cases, there must be a clear connection between the decision criteria and the job in question. This becomes particularly troublesome for the employer because the ADEA permits jury trials for all violations.[61] Remember, under Title VII, trials by a jury are also allowed, but only when a complaining party seeks compensatory or punitive damages.[62] Under the ADEA, jury trials may be requested for any violation.

For the HR staff, this means guaranteeing that education requirements, performance expectations, seniority requirements, and other skill and knowledge requirements have been clearly identified for the position in question. It is equally important to communicate these position requirements to all potential applicants before the selection process even begins. All position announcements should clearly and concisely state all of the required qualifications a successful candidate must possess. This precaution is intended to reduce unrealistic expectations among potential applicants who do not possess the necessary requirements. As always, position requirements and qualifications must be directly related to successful job performance. Consequently, it is imperative that proper job analysis has been conducted on the job in question and the criteria have been validated (see Chapter 14). As with other equal employment opportunity (EEO) matters, the presence of nonessential job requirements unnecessarily exposes an employer to litigation and undermines the organization's rebuttal in court.

In instances where the employer can prove the position was given to the more qualified candidate, the ADEA is not violated. This is a legitimate nondiscriminatory reason because the individual's qualifications determined the employment outcome, not the individual's age.

Age as a BFOQ

Some *bona fide* occupational qualifications (BFOQs) permit employers to use age as a disqualifier, but as with most BFOQs, they are very rare. In *Western Airlines v. Criswell*,[63] the Supreme Court examined an employment practice that imposed a mandatory retirement age of sixty on all flight crew members (pilots, copilots, and flight engineers). The airline's argument for the mandatory retirement was that after the age of sixty, medical research indicated that physical and mental capabilities are prone to "sudden or subtle incapacitation."[64] To strengthen its arguments, the airline cited Federal Aviation Administration regulations that prohibited any individual who had reached the age of sixty from serving as a pilot or copilot on any commercial flight.

The airline adopted this policy and merely added flight engineers. The employer contended that its mandatory retirement of flight crews was a BFOQ reasonably necessary to the safe operation of the airline. Remember, as with all BFOQs, it must be proved that the age-biased BFOQ is "reasonably necessary" for normal business operation and that the "reasonable necessity" is narrowly defined.[65]

The complaining parties provided evidence that the process of psychological and physiological deterioration caused by aging varies greatly with each individual.[66] Not surprisingly, there is evidence showing that some older workers can perform at levels equal to or even better than younger coworkers. The complaining parties argued that mandatory retirement ignores individual differences. The airline, they further argued, should determine mandatory retirements on a case-by-case basis rather than on an arbitrary age ceiling. After all, the ADEA compels employers to evaluate their employees who are forty years or older on their merits and not their age.[67] The flight engineers and several pilots who wanted to become flight engineers also pointed out that in emergency situations, the flight engineer's duties are less critical to passenger safety than the pilot's. The complaining parties then argued that Western Airlines' BFOQ defense for flight engineers was insufficient to justify its legitimate concern for passenger safety.[68]

In its ruling, the Supreme Court concluded the BFOQ exception was meant to be an *extremely* narrow exception to any general prohibition of age discrimination under the ADEA.[69] In essence, the airline had failed to show that all, or substantially all, of its flight engineers over sixty were unable to safely perform their duties. The mandatory retirement age for flight engineers (not pilots or copilots) thus violated the ADEA.

The Complaining Party's Rebuttal

If the employer offers a seemingly legitimate BFOQ, the complaining party may still win the case, provided that he or she can prove the employer's legitimate business reasons are a pretext. If the HR staff has done its job properly, this likelihood is greatly reduced. Again, good job analysis and documentation are critical.

Adea and Disparate Impact

As previously mentioned in Chapter 4, there was a time when the only claim under the ADEA permitted in some circuits was disparate treatment.[70] However, this changed in 2005 when the Supreme Court ruled in *Smith v. City of Jackson* that individuals can establish an actionable case of age discrimination by showing that certain facially neutral practices have the effect of excluding older employees/applicants (those forty years or older) at a disproportionately higher number than under-forty applicants.[71] The major difference between a disparate impact case under the ADEA and one under Title VII is the employer's rebuttal. Under Title VII the employer must usually show that the practice causing the adverse impact is a business necessity/job-related. This entails validation.

However, there is no employer requirement to demonstrate business necessity under the ADEA as there is under Title VII. In cases involving disparate impact because of age, the employer has only to demonstrate that the practice creating the adverse impact is not predicated on age[72]—in effect, this is a legitimate nondiscriminatory reason defense. The method of establishing the *prima facie* case under the ADEA law is the same as it is under Title VII.

Remedies for ADEA Violations

The ADEA is not an amendment to the Civil Rights Act of 1964; therefore the ADEA remedies available to a complaining party who proves age discrimination are limited to reinstatement, back pay, front pay, promotion, and/or attorneys' fees.[73] In the event that willful age discrimination has occurred, the ADEA provides for liquidated damages as well.[74]

No Protection for Those Under Forty

In its 2005 decision, *General Dynamics Land Systems, Inc. v. Cline,*[75] the Supreme Court was confronted with a case in which younger employees, those under forty years of age, claimed that the ADEA protected them from "reverse age discrimination."[76] The Court concluded that the language of the ADEA clearly establishes those who are qualified and forty years or older to be the protected class, and went on to say, "the statute [ADEA] does not mean to stop an employer from favoring an older employee over a younger one."[77] The ADEA makes it unlawful to discriminate against an individual because he or she is forty years or older; it has no such prohibition for those who are younger than forty.

Protecting Workers With Disabilities

The first law to provide federal protection for applicants and workers with disabilities was the Vocational Rehabilitation Act of 1973 (VRA).[78] This is a fairly narrow statute in that it applies only to those employers who: (1) hold a federal contract or subcontract in excess of $2,500, (2) are a depository of federal funds, and (3) receive federal grants or aid assistance.[79] Employers who did not meet these conditions had no obligations concerning employees with disabilities until the Americans with Disabilities Act of 1990 (ADA) was enacted. The VRA provided the foundation from which the ADA would arise.

When the VRA was first enacted, its definition of a *qualified handicapped* person[80] was the same as that of a *qualified individual with a disability* under the ADA.[81] Additionally, the definitions for *reasonable accommodation, undue hardship, physical or mental impairment, major life activities,* and *handicap/disability* in the two acts are virtually identical. To know the provisions of one of these statutes is to understand the provisions of the other. To alleviate this redundancy, the Vocational Rehabilitation Act Amendment of 1992[82] changed the term *handicapped person* to *individual with a disability* and the term *handicapped* to *disability.* Now, the two laws are almost indistinguishable, and because of these marked similarities, our discussion will focus on the ADA. The major difference between the two acts is that the VRA requires employers who hold federal contracts or subcontracts in excess of $10,000 to take affirmative action in hiring qualified individuals with a disability.[83] Beyond this affirmative action requirement, the VRA and the ADA are identical in their employment discrimination provisions.

Americans with Disabilities Act

The ADA was passed by Congress and signed into law by President George H.W. Bush on July 26, 1990. The major objectives of the law are to prevent employment discrimination against a qualified individual on the basis of a real or perceived disability (Title I), prohibit discrimination against individuals with disabilities in public transportation (Title II), and provide for public accommodation and access for persons with a disability (Title III). It is Title I's prohibition against discrimination in the terms and conditions of employment because of an individual's disability that is of particular concern to us. Perhaps the most important thing to remember is that Title I protects only *qualified individuals* with a disability from employment discrimination. It does not protect unqualified individuals with a disability any more than the other EEO laws protect unqualified individuals. It is, therefore, critical for HR professionals to understand when an individual is qualified and when he or she is not. In examining this issue, the HR professional must understand who is required to comply with the Act, who is disabled, and who is qualified.

Covered Entities

The ADA applies to all private sector employers with fifteen or more employees. It applies to all employment agencies regardless of whether they are public or private. Labor unions with fifteen or more members must comply with the ADA, as must all state and local governments. Even joint labor/management committees on apprenticeship are required to follow the provisions of the ADA's Title I. You may have already noticed that the same employers who are covered under Title VII of the Civil Rights Act of 1964 must also comply with Title I of the ADA.

Under the ADA, no covered entity shall discriminate against a qualified individual with a disability because of such individual's disability with regard to job application procedures; the hiring, advancement, or discharge of employees; employee compensation; job training; and other terms, conditions, and privileges of employment.[84]

Although the ADA is very similar to Title VII and the ADEA, there is one significant difference. Under Title VII, the protected classes are fairly easy to identify. Gender is easy to establish: the complaining party is either male or female. Race and ethnicity also can be readily established. Age under the ADEA, likewise, can easily be verified through a number of legal documents (i.e., birth certificates, medical records, etc.). All of these classifications possess an "all or nothing" nature. You are either female or you are not. You are either Hispanic or you are not. You are either over forty years of age or you are not. Disability, however, occurs in degrees. An individual may fall anywhere on the scale from marginally disabled to completely disabled. The extent to which an individual is disabled often determines whether or not he or she is *qualified* to perform a particular job in question and the length to which employers must go to accommodate the individual. The ADA adds further confusion through its definition of *disability*.

Who Is Disabled?

When assessing whether an individual candidate or employee is protected under the ADA, a two-part standard must be met. In achieving this end, two questions must be answered: is the applicant disabled, and is the individual qualified? From the ADA's inception, some critics have contended that it casts an overly broad net on this matter.[85] Under the ADA (and VRA), the term **disability** means a physical or mental impairment that substantially limits one or more of the major life activities of an individual, a record of such impairment, or regarding an individual as having such an impairment. This means that those who currently are disabled are protected under the ADA. Additionally, those who were disabled but have since recovered or have been rehabilitated are covered. Surprisingly, applicants or employees who are not now, nor have they ever been, afflicted with a mental or physical disability covered under the ADA may still be protected if the employer *thought* they had a disability and discriminated against them because of the imagined disability. As strange as this may sound, an employer can violate the ADA by erroneously assuming that a nondisabled individual is disabled.

This situation occurred in the opening scenario. The director of the MHRH rejected the applicant because he *assumed* she could not perform some of the essential job functions (i.e., patient evacuation). It was merely his *perception* that she would not be able to evacuate her patients in a timely manner and that she was a workers' compensation risk. He could offer no basis in fact for this presumption.

1	Caring for one's self	12	Bending
2	Performing manual tasks	13	Speaking
3	Seeing	14	Breathing
4	Hearing	15	Learning
5	Eating	16	Reading
6	Sleeping	17	Concentrating
7	Walking	18	Thinking
8	Standing	19	Communicating
9	Sitting	20	Interacting with Others
10	Reaching	21	Working
11	Lifting		

Figure 12.5   Major Life Activities Under EEOC Regulations

Source: U.S. EEOC, *Regulations to Implement the Equal Employment Opportunity Provisions of the Americans with Disabilities Act*, 29 C.F.R. § 1630.2(i).

Bladder	Immune system
Bowel	Neurological
Brain	Normal cell growth
Cardiovascular	Reproductive
Circulatory	Respiratory
Digestive	Skin
Endocrine	Special sense organs
Genito-urinary	Speech organs
Hemic and lymphatic	

Figure 12.6   Body Systems Whose Dysfunction Constitutes Physical Impairment Under the ADA

Source: Americans with Disabilities Amendment Act of 2008, 29 C.F.R. § 1630.3(h).

An employer runs the risk of triggering an ADA claim any time an employment decision is based on an individual's perceived disability. In one case, an employer refused to hire an applicant for the position of electrician because a drug test indicated his blood sugar was high and the employer assumed he was diabetic.

The employer's action was based on the assumption that the applicant had an impairment that would substantially restrict his ability to perform the essential functions of the job. However, this was a false assumption, and the applicant, who was not disabled as defined under the ADA, was able to perform all the essential functions of an electrician. Because the employer perceived the applicant to be disabled and based the decision not to hire him on that perception, the employer violated the ADA.[86]

The meaning of *disability* under the ADA entails having a physical or mental impairment that substantially limits one or more of the *major life activities*. Unless we know what these major life activities are, this definition is not going to be very helpful. The EEOC, the agency responsible for enforcing the ADA, defines **major life activities** as caring for oneself, performing manual tasks, and so forth (see Figure 12.5).[87] As for *physical impairment*, this can be any physiological condition, disfigurement, or loss of one of seventeen body systems (see Figure 12.6).

Old Standards	New Standards
Breathing	Bending
Caring for one's self Hearing	Breathing
Learning	Caring for oneself Communicating Concentrating
Performing manual tasks Seeing	Eating
Speaking	Hearing
Walking	Learning
Working	Lifting
	Performing manual tasks Reading
	Seeing
	Sleeping
	Speaking
	Standing
	Thinking
	Walking
	Working

Figure 12.7   Major Life Functions as Expanded under the ADAA

Source: The Americans with Disabilities Amendment Act of 2008, 42 U.S.C. § 12102(2)(A) (2012).

Mental impairment encompasses any mental or psychological disorder that results in mental retardation, organic brain syndrome, emotional illness, mental illness, or specific learning disabilities. These are very broad areas and encompass an extremely wide range of conditions.

The Americans with Disabilities Amendment Act of 2008

The Americans with Disabilities Amendment Act (ADAA) was signed into law by President George W. Bush on September 25, 2008, and became effective on January 1, 2009. The ADAA expanded the number and scope of *limitations on major life activities* that could constitute a disability. Previously, there had been only nine limitations on major life activities, there are now eighteen (see Figure 12.7).[88] It should be further noted that the EEOC has added interacting with others, reaching, and sitting, to the list of limitations in their regulations (see Figure 12.5 above).

Additionally, the ADAA lowers the bar for establishing a disability, as well as eliminating the consideration of mitigating measures in making disability determinations. For example, an employee who suffered from epilepsy that was in remission due to medication was previously not considered to be disabled, because the medication mitigated the condition.[89] Under the new amendments, mitigated conditions like epilepsy, diabetes, and high blood pressure would now constitute disabilities under the ADAA. This is to say that they could be used to establish the first part of the two-part standard previously mentioned, "Is the applicant disabled?" However, the ADAA does note that wearing ordinary glasses or contact lens would mitigate an individual's disability. An individual with diabetes, even though it is controlled by insulin, would meet the requirements as an individual with a disability, while an individual with 20/80 vision, corrected to 20/20 with glasses, would not.[90]

Qualified Individual with a Disability

If you have at least a general idea of what qualifies as a disability, then it is easier to determine that any person who has a physical or mental impairment based on these criteria would be an "individual with a disability." In employment situations, the ADA does not protect "individuals with a disability." It only protects "*qualified* individuals with a disability."[91] The next step is to ascertain when a candidate with a disability is qualified.

A **qualified individual with a disability** is one who can perform the essential functions of the job in question with reasonable accommodation; therefore the principal concern is whether or not an individual with a disability can perform the essential functions of a particular job with or without reasonable accommodation.[92]

The essential functions, according to the EEOC, can be ascertained by examining three criteria.[93] First, a function is essential if the position in question exists for the purpose of performing that function. For example, driving a truck is the purpose of the job position of long-distance truck driver. Therefore, this is the essential function of that job. The next issue deals with the number of other employees available to perform the function or among whom the performance of the function can be distributed. If a task associated with the job can be assigned to another employee without disrupting the primary purpose of the job in question, that task would not be essential. Suppose one of the duties of a long-distance truck driver included changing the motor oil every 3,000 miles. Since this task could easily be assigned to company maintenance person-nel, it would not be an essential function. However, driving the truck safely from destination to destination could not be assigned to another employee—it would be an essential function. The final factor considered by the EEOC involves the degree or skill required to perform the function. Returning to our previous example, changing oil requires little skill and expertise compared to actually driving, maneuvering, and backing up a tractor trailer. The more skill required to perform a task, the more difficult it is to assign to an employee in a different job category. Additionally, requisite expertise makes the task more essential to the job in question.

All of this means that basic job analysis for each position in an organization is absolutely critical. It further means that job analysis, and the resulting job descriptions and job specifica-tions, must be continually monitored and reviewed to ensure they provide *current* and *accurate* information about each specific job. If the essential tasks, duties, and responsibilities associated with any given job are flawed, it is unlikely that reasonable accommodation can be ascertained. This is why job analysis is so critical when dealing with ADA accommodations (see Chapter 14).

Having clearly established what the essential functions of the job are, the HR professional can then concentrate on the individual's qualifications. If the candidate can presently perform the essential functions without any assistance from the employer, that candidate is a qualified individual with a disability. To deny such an individual employment based on a physical disabil-ity (when he or she has previously proved able to perform the essential job tasks) would be an obvious violation of Title I of the ADA.

Had the director of the MHRH in the opening scenario tested the applicant's ability to evacuate patients (an essential job function), there might have been a different outcome. She could have been tested by participating in a fire drill involving real patients. If the applicant could not adequately evacuate her patients within a prescribed time frame (determined by job analysis and local fire codes), she would be unqualified for the position in question. Since the ADA protects only "qualified" individuals with a disability (either real or perceived), the applicant would lack cause to file under the ADA.

Interestingly, not all candidates can demonstrate work performance so clearly. Some candi-dates may require reasonable accommodation.

Reasonable Accommodation

Reasonable accommodation refers to modifications that would permit the individual with a disability to perform the essential functions of the job in question, provided these modifications do not create an undue hardship for the employer. The first thing a manager or HR professional should do when any individual requests reasonable accommodation under the ADA is to clarify the individual's degree of impairment. The actual physical or mental impairment must "substan-tially limit" a major life activity. Since the enactment of the ADAA in 2008, any determination as to whether an individual is "substantially limited" in performing a major life activity must consider the individual's impairment as compared to most people in the general population.[94] This a very low bar, and many impairments, such as diabetes, are still considered to be disabilities even when ameliorated with medication. However, not every impairment will constitute a disability within the meaning of the Act.[95] For example, if a person with astigmatism (the inability of the eyes to focus properly) can function perfectly normally as long as she wears corrective lens (contact lens or eyeglasses), she would not be considered to have a disability under the ADA.[96] While she is wearing her glasses, her major life activities are not "substantially limited." On the other hand, an employee who was confined to a wheelchair, even though he is capable of mobility, would not be capable of the same mobility of a person without disabilities. He would meet the ADA's requirement for "disability" because he would be "substantially limited" in his ability to walk. The one employee's corrective measures (eyeglasses) overcame her limitations in performing daily activities in light of the general population; hence, she would not have met the ADA's definition of being "disabled."[97]

In the case of a person who is paraplegic, he is limited in his ability to go about his daily activities despite his corrective measure, the wheelchair. His mobility is improved by the wheelchair, but it is still short of that of a nonparaplegic.

Managers and HR professionals must always remember that assessment of whether or not an individual is disabled under the ADA must be done on an individualized basis. Also, remember that the final determination of whether an individual has a disability is not necessarily based on a diagnosis of the individual's impairment, but on whether if the impairment is corrected, it still substantially limits a major life activity.[98]

Once it is determined an applicant or employee is considered disabled under the ADA, the decision maker may now move to the next question: Can the individual perform the essential job functions with or without reasonable accommodation? Again, if the individual can perform the essential job functions without any accommodation, he or she is qualified. If not, what is the appropriate reasonable accommodation that would permit performance of these functions?

In determining reasonable accommodation, the employer might ask the individual for reasonable documentation about the disability and functional limitations. But employers should be careful. The ADA prohibits the employer from requesting medical information that is not pertinent to the accommodation.[99] This usually precludes employers from requesting complete medical records on the individual in question, because such records would include a good deal of information not related to the accommodation.[100] The EEOC recommends that when requesting medical information, employers should specify what types of information they need regarding the disability and the functional limitations it imposes. Remember, once this information is obtained, the employer is responsible for keeping it confidential.

Making accommodations under the ADA is far more complex and complicated than religious accommodation under Title VII. The EEOC has developed three categories of "reasonable accommodation" under the ADA. Under the EEOC's guidance, when attempting to accommodate an applicant or employee, an employer should consider modifying the job application process, modifying the work environment, or modifying the benefits and privileges of employment.[101]

Modifying the Job Application Process

Modifying the job application process entails avoiding anything in the selection process that could be construed as discriminating against applicants because of disability. First and foremost, an employer cannot ask an applicant if he or she has a disability. In fact, the EEOC contends that an employer may not even ask an applicant if he or she needs reasonable accommodation before a conditional job offer is made.[102] The only exception to this is under circumstances in which the applicant's disability is apparent, or the applicant has voluntarily disclosed information about his or her disability. In most instances, the employer is permitted to inquire if reasonable accommodation is necessary only after an offer of employment has been made.

Employers may also be required to modify tests or testing methods to accommodate applicants. A deaf applicant might require a sign language interpreter for an interview. An applicant with attention deficit disorder may require someone to read a written examination.

If the accommodation requested by the applicant causes the employer an *undue hardship*, the applicant would not be a *qualified individual with a disability*. The accommodation would not be reasonable, and the employer would not be compelled to hire the applicant. For example, a person who is paraplegic applies for the position of truck driver at a small delivery company. But technology is not available that would permit the applicant to perform the essential functions of the job. Therefore the accommodation needed would indeed cause undue hardship.

Modifying the Work Environment

In the second category of accommodation—physical modifications to the work environment—a number of actions may be taken. First, the employer's existing workplace can be made more accessible. This includes reconfiguring work areas to make them wheelchair accessible.

Physical modifications may require manuals and work procedures to be provided in Braille. Making other physical modifications to work areas might be as simple as lowering a worktable so it can be reached by an employee in a wheelchair. But it could also be as elaborate as acquiring a state-of-the-art TTY keyboard telephone system to allow a deaf and mute employee to make and receive telephone calls.[103]

Another work environment accommodation is *job restructuring*. This involves identifying the essential job functions (see Chapter 14) and eliminating or reassigning nonessential job functions that the disabled employee cannot perform. A paraplegic secretary confined to a wheelchair has the job description in Figure 12.8. Noting that it accounts for only 2 percent of her job, assume that she is expected to stock printer paper in the supply room. Although the door is sufficiently wide to allow her easy entry and exit from the supply room, boxes of copy paper weigh 25 pounds each and must be stored on shelves that are as high as 6 feet from the floor. The employer could lower the shelves (and double the size of the storage area), or this one aspect of the job could be assigned to another employee. Since the stocking duties are a marginal portion of the secretary's duties, assigning these tasks to another employee would be the more reasonable action to take.

JOB DESCRIPTION

Job Title: Word-Processing Secretary
Department: Administrative Services
Position of Immediate Supervisor: Director of Administrative Services

I. GENERAL SUMMARY OF RESPONSIBILITIES

Types, edits, and distributes various correspondence to clients and internal staff. Transmits and proofs various essential status reports for day-to-day operations.

II. SPECIFIC DUTIES AND RESPONSIBILITIES

1 Types daily correspondence and reports (50%)
2 Proofs and prints out final copies for distribution (10%)
3 Receives handwritten copies and places them in priority files (2%)
4 Types special projects, such as proposals, quotations, system analysis, and customer and client surveys (20%)
5 Transmits documents through the use of electronic mail (10%)
6 Logs updates, volume, and turnaround time records of completed work (2%)
7 Receives and places priority on rush requests and special projects (2%)
8 Serves as a backup for the receptionist (2%)
9 Stocks the office supply closet (2%)
10 Performs other duties as directed

III. JOB SPECIFICATIONS

1 High school diploma or GED, 1–2 years of college helpful
2 Knowledge of Microsoft Word, Corel WordPerfect, Microsoft Excel, and Corel Quattro Pro
3 Must have a good eye for neatness and attention to detail.
4 Must lift 25-pound containers to a shelf of 72″
5 Ability to work well with others in developing proposals and projects

---

Figure 12.8 Job Description for a Word-Processing Secretary

Source: Modified from E.H. Burack and N.J. Mathys, *Human Resource Planning: A Pragmatic Approach to Manpower Staffing and Development* (2d ed.). Lake Forest, IL: Brace-Park Publishing, 1987.

Often, permitting an employee to work in a *flexible or part-time schedule* would be sufficient accommodation. This is particularly effective for those employees who have become disabled since hiring.

Suppose an employee requests that her workday be reduced to six hours per day to allow her to attend physical therapy sessions in the afternoon. Usually, the employer would be required to adjust the employee's schedule, if it does not significantly disrupt the employer's operations (cause undue hardship).

Modifying the Benefits and Privileges of Employment

When job restructuring, workplace modification, and flexible scheduling will not accommodate the employee with a disability, the employer may want to consider reassignment.

It is important to note that the employer is not required to create a position for the employee. The employer is only required to consider reassignment to a vacant position for which the employee is qualified. In addition, the employer is not required to promote the employee to a higher position. Under most circumstances, the employee must be reassigned to a vacant job that is equivalent in terms of pay, status, benefits, and other relevant factors as the job the employee is leaving.[104]

The final accommodation available to employers is use of accrued paid leave and/or unpaid leave. Situations that could require leave as an accommodation include medical therapy, recuperation time, training for prosthetic devices, repair time for wheelchair-accessible vans, training for sign language, acquiring a seeing-eye dog, or avoiding temporary workplace conditions that adversely affect the disabled person.[105] Normally, the employer will allow the employee to exhaust any accrued paid leave and then permit a certain amount of unpaid leave.

Suppose an employee is scheduled to receive a new prosthetic leg. The installation, therapy, and training on the artificial limb are projected to take two weeks (ten workdays). The employee has accrued four days of paid leave. The employer could reasonably expect to permit the employee to use the four days of paid leave and then six days of unpaid leave.

The use of employee leave has become complicated with the enactment of the Family and Medical Leave Act (FMLA) of 1993, which mandates that covered employees are entitled to twelve weeks of unpaid leave in the event of specified emergency situations and are allowed to return to their jobs (the FMLA is addressed in greater detail in Chapter 10). Employers now must

- Cost of the accommodation
- Size (number of employees)
- Number and type of facilities
- Composition and structure of workforce
- Essential job functions

Figure 12.9 Considerations When Establishing Undue Hardship Under the ADA

decide which law is more applicable to a given situation, the ADA or the FMLA. There may be some instances in which both could apply.

Undue Hardship

Any accommodation demanded of the employer is reasonable only as long as it does not create an undue hardship on the employer. Unfortunately for managers and HR professionals, this is determined too often on a case-by-case basis.[106]

In determining **undue hardship**, the ADA requires that five factors be considered (see Figure 12.9).[107] First, the overall cost of the accommodation must be compared to the overall financial resources of the facility, number of persons employed by the facility, and its projected effect on the operating expenses of the facility. Second, the overall financial resources, number of employees, and number and location of all the facilities owned by the employer are considered with regard to the cost of the accommodation. Third, the accommodation must be considered in light of the type of operation in which the employer is engaged—this includes considering the organizational structure, the functions of the workforce, the geographic separateness of facilities, and the degree of administrative or fiscal interdependence between the facility and other operations of the employer. Fourth, the impact that the accommodation will have on the operation of the facility in question must be considered. All of these considerations are extremely broad and make developing viable HR policies difficult. Finally, provided proper job analysis was performed on the job in question, the employer is *not* required to change the *essential job functions*.

To illustrate the impact of these considerations, let's assume that an employee of a small grocery store has been diagnosed with non-Hodgkin's lymphoma. The grocery store currently assigns four clerks and one assistant manager per shift; three of the clerks restock the shelves. The employer has determined that there are just enough clerks per shift to efficiently serve its customers, keep shelves restocked, maintain cleanliness, and reduce shoplifting. In order to receive chemotherapy and adjust to its debilitating effects, the employee requests three weeks' leave, a reduced work schedule, and fewer duties. The employer insists that accommodation will require hiring another employee and redistributing work responsibilities on the shift during which the disabled employee works.

Based on the small size, lack of fiscal resources, functions of the workforce, and impact on daily operations at the grocery store, the requested accommodations might be judged to create an undue hardship. However, the same circumstances in a large regional chain of grocery stores might not create an undue hardship and, therefore, an accommodation would be reasonable.

In one instance, a hearing impaired applicant was given $200,000 in compensatory damages and back pay for the company's failing to make a "reasonable accommodation." The individual in question had been denied employment as "loader/scanner" at a distribution center because he was unable to hear the beep that would notify him that a product's bar code had been read

In making pre-employment inquiries, employers may not ask:

- Whether the candidate has (or ever had) a disability, how he/she became disabled or about the nature or severity of a disability;
- To provide medical documentation regarding his/her disability;
- Coworker's, family member, doctor, or another person about the candidate's disability;
- About genetic information;
- About prior workers' compensation history;
- Whether he/she is currently taking or has taken any prescription drugs or medications, nor can they monitor the taking of such drugs or medications if the candidate is accepted for employment; and,
- Questions about impairments that are likely to elicit information about a disability (e.g., What impairments do you have?).

In making pre-employment inquiries employers may ask:

- About an applicant's ability to perform specific job functions. For example, an employer may state the physical requirements of a job (such as the ability to lift a certain amount of weight or the ability to climb ladders), and ask if an applicant can satisfy these requirements;
- About an applicant's non-medical qualifications and skills, such as the applicant's education, work history, and required certifications and licenses;
- Applicants to describe or demonstrate how they would perform job tasks.

Figure 12.10   Pre-Employment Medical Inquiries Under the ADA

Source: U.S. EEOC, *EEOC Enforcement Guidance on Disability-Related Inquiries and Medical Examinations of Employees under the Americans with Disabilities Act* (ADA). http://www.eeoc.gov/policy/docs/guidance-inquiries.html (accessed November 4, 2013).

by the scanner. The EEOC contended that the individual should have been provided adaptive equipment or given a position in another part of the facility.[108]

Pre-Employment Medical Inquiries

The ADA has greatly restricted the use of pre-employment medical examinations and inquiries (see Figure 12.10). It has also created a very fine line between permissible inquiries and prohibited ones during interviews. For example, it is unlawful to ask applicants if they have a disability or to inquire into the nature or severity of any perceivable disability.[109] However, it is permissible to ask applicants if they can perform job-related functions.[110] At the same time, pre-employment medical examinations are unlawful, but under certain circumstances, an employer may require an applicant to take a medical examination *after* a job offer is made and *before* the applicant begins working.[111] One of the certain circumstances previously mentioned would be cases in which *all* new hires, regardless of disability, are required to take a post-hiring medical examination.

In *EEOC v. Wal-Mart Stores, Inc.,* the nation's largest retailing firm agreed to pay a settlement of $6.8 million arising out of charges that its employment practices discriminated against applicants with disabilities.[112] The EEOC alleged that the company's "Matrix of Essential Job Functions" asked applicants about medical conditions and disabilities prior to a job offer. Because this was considered to be a pre-employment medical inquiry, the company was, in essence, engaging in an unlawful practice in violation of the ADA.

In a later case, the EEOC alleged that Wal-Mart discriminated against an applicant with cerebral palsy when it failed to give him a job as a cashier. Unlike the previous situation, Wal-Mart had evaluated the individual's work-related ability and lack of retailing work experience before concluding that he could not perform the essential tasks.[113] This time, the company prevailed.

Direct Threat to Others/Threat to Self

In the event that post-offer medical examinations indicate the medical condition of the individual would pose a threat to his or her health or that of others, the employer is not required to hire or retain the individual.[114] For example, assume that a post-offer medical examination reveals that an individual has a respiratory condition that would become significantly worse if the employee were exposed to certain chemical agents and the essential functions of the job require such exposure. Hiring the employee would result in either the employee's exacerbating the disability or, perhaps, even death, thus the employer could legitimately refuse to hire the individual in question.

According to EEOC regulations governing enforcement of the ADA, **direct threat** means a significant risk of substantial harm to the health or safety of the individual or others that cannot be eliminated or reduced by reasonable accommodation.[115]

For example, a bulldozer operator on a pipeline project complains that several times in the previous three weeks he has become dizzy for a time and has blacked out while operating his dozer. The employer may require the operator to have a medical examination in order to determine whether or not these symptoms prevent him from safely performing his job. In all cases, it is the employer's obligation to establish that he or she had a reasonable belief, based on objective evidence (observations, medical examinations, etc.) that the employee would pose a direct threat to others as a result of his or her medical condition.[116]

Determining direct threat, either to self or others, is not to be taken lightly. The EEOC requires that the following four factors must first be considered by the employer:

1   the duration of the risk;

2   the nature and severity of the potential harm;

3   the likelihood that the potential harm will occur; and

4   the imminence of the potential harm.[117]

Confidentiality of Medical Information

The other restriction is that once the medical information has been collected, the employer is responsible for keeping it confidential. Generally, it is unlawful for an employer to even ask a job applicant if he or she is an individual with a disability, or about the nature or severity of such disability.[118] Often, this responsibility is delegated to the HR department, which in most organizations is responsible for maintaining employee medical records. In the case of employee medical records, the key words have now become "extremely limited access."[119] The only circumstances under which these files can be accessed by anyone are clearly detailed by the ADA and limited to only three.[120] First, management personnel may be informed of medical conditions requiring work restrictions or other reasonable accommodations. Second, company first aid and safety personnel may be informed if the employee's disability might require emergency treatment. Finally, the medical records may be made available to government officials investigating ADA compliance. Other than those instances, the medical records should be kept safeguarded. Most disclosures of employee medical records are likely to result in ADA violations.

Drug Testing Rehabilitation and the ADA

The term "qualified individual with a disability" also includes any individual who is participating in a supervised drug rehabilitation program and no longer using illegal drugs, has completed a supervised drug rehabilitation program and is no longer using illegal drugs, or is erroneously regarded as engaging in using illegal drugs and is no longer engaging in such use.[121] Note that in each instance the phrase "is no longer engaging in the use of illegal drugs" is essential to remaining a qualified individual with a disability. The ADA does not protect current substance abusers. In fact, the Act specifically authorizes covered employers to prohibit the use of drugs and alcohol in the workplace, requires that employees not be under the influence of drugs and/or alcohol during work hours, and holds drug and alcohol users to the same employment and performance standards as other employees.[122]

The ADA clearly states that employers have the right to require their employees to conform to the requirements established under the Drug-Free Workplace Act.[123] Although the ADA has placed severe restrictions on the use of medical examinations by employers, "tests to determine the illegal use of drugs shall not be considered a medical examination."[124] This exemption permits employers to conduct pre-employment drug screening and drug testing following an employment offer.

Notes

1 This scenario is based on the findings of fact in *Cook v. Rhode Island,* 10 F.3d 17 (1st Cir. 1993).

2 *Cook,* 10 F.3d at 34, n. 13.

3 U.S. Equal Employment Opportunity Commission, *Charge Statistics FY 1997 Through FY 2011,* http://www.eeoc.gov/eeoc/statistics/enforcement/charges.cfm (accessed December 4, 2012).

4   Ibid.

5   42 U.S.C. § 2000e-1(a).

6   113 F.3d 196 (11th Cir. 1997).

7   *Killinger v. Samford University,* 113 F.3d at 200.

8   *Little v. Wuerl,* 929 F.2d 944, 947–48 (3rd Cir. 1991).

9   *EEOC v. Kamehameha School,* 990 F.2d 458 (9th Cir. 1993).

10 *Fike v. United Methodist Children's Home of Virginia, Inc.,* 547 F.Supp. 286 (E.D. Vir. 1982).

11 *EEOC v. Mississippi College,* 626 F.2d 477 (5th Cir. 1980).

12 *Shapolia v. Los Alamos National Laboratory,* 773 F.Supp. 304, 305 (D. N.M. 1991); aff'd without comment, 13 F.3d 406 (10th Cir. 1993).

13 *Breech v. Alabama Power Company,* 962 F.Supp. 1447, 1456 (S.D. Ala. 1997).

14 *Kern v. Dynalectron Corp.,* 577 F.Supp. 1196 (N.D. Tex. 1983).

15 29 C.F.R. § 1605 (2011).

16 42 U.S.C. § 2000e (j) (2011).

17 *Beadle v. City of Tampa,* 42 F.3d 633, 636 n.4 (11th Cir. 1995); *Bhatia v. Chevron U.S.A., Inc.,* 734 F.2d 1382, 1383 (9th Cir. 1984).

18 Exodus 20:8; Deuteronomy 5:12.

19 *Chalmer v. Tulon Company of Richmond,* 101 F.3d 1012, 1019 (4th Cir. 1996).

20 *TWA v. Hardison,* 432 U.S. 63, 84 (1977); *Endres v. Indiana State Police,* 334 F.d 618, 623 (7th Cir. 2003).

21 *EEOC v. Ilona of Hungary, Inc.,* 108 F.3d 1569 (7th Cir. 1997).

22 *Smith v. Pyro Mining Co.,* 827 F.2d 1081, 1085 (6th Cir. 1987).

23 *Protos v. Volkswagen of Am., Inc.,* 797 F.2d 129, 134–35 (3d Cir. 1986); *Webb v. City of Philadelphia,* 562 F.3d 256 (3d Cir. 2009).

24 *Virts v. Consolidated Freightways Corp. of Delaware,* 285 F.3d 508 (6th Cir. 2002).

25 *Balint v. Carson City,* 180 F.3d 1047, 1054 (9th Cir. 1999).

26 *EEOC v. Alamo Rent-A-Car, LLC,* 432 F. Supp.2d 1006 (D. Ariz. 2006).

27 *Lee v. ABF Freight System, Inc.,* 22 F. 3d 1019 (10th Cir. 1994).

28 *Wilshin v. Allstate Insurance Co.,* 212 F. Supp. 2d 1369, 1373 (M.D. Ga. 2002).

29 *Ansonia Board of Education v. Phillbrook,* 479 U.S. 60, 68 (1986).

30 Ibid.

31 *EEOC v. Firestone Fibers & Textiles Co.,* 515 F.3d 307, 312–13 (4th Cir. 2008).

32 P. Sheehan, "Dressed to Impress," *Lodging Hospitality* 59 (2003): 48, 50.

33 T. Adcock, "Casualties of Casual Dress Code," *New York Law Journal ONLINE,* (2002). http://www. law. com; S. Cline, "Office Attire Swinging Back to Professional from Casual," *Colorado Springs Business Journal,* March 11, 2005; P. Sheehan, "Dressed to Impress," *Lodging Hospitality* 59 (2003): 48, 50.

34 481 F.2d 1115, 1124–25 (D.C. Cir. 1973).

35 *Booth v. Maryland,* 327 F.3d 377, 382–383 (4th Cir. 2003); *Brown v. Johnson,* 116 Fed. Appx. 342, 343 (3d Cir. 2004); *Cloutier v. Costco Wholesale Corp.,* 390 F.3d 126 (1st Cir. 2004).

36 *Holmes v. Marion Community Office of Family and Children,* 349 F.3d 914 (7th Cir. 2003).

37 *Hussein v. Waldorf Astoria Hotel,* 31 Fed. Appx. 740 (2d Cir. 2002); *Vargas v. Sears & Roebuck Co.,* 1998 U.S. Dist. LEXIS 21148 (E.D. Mich. 1998).

38 29 C.F.R. § 1605.2(e)(1).

39 *Sutton v. Providence St. Joseph Medical Center,* 192 F.3d 826 (9th Cir. 1999).

40 *Bhatia v. Chevron USA, Inc.,* 734 F.2d 1382 (9th Cir. 1984).

41 *Cloutier v. Costco Wholesale Corp.,* 390 F.3d 126 (1st Cir. 2005).

42 G. Panaro, "Is Hiring on the Basis of Appearance Illegal?" *Fair Employment Practices Guidelines* 581 (October 2003), http://www.bankersonline.com/operations/gp_appearance.html (accessed December 6, 2012).

43 *Fraternal Order of Police v. City of Newark,* 170 F.3d 359 (3d Cir. 1999).

44 *EEOC v. United Parcel Service, Inc.,* 587 F.3d 136 (2nd Cir. 2009).

45 648 F.2d 1239 (9th Cir. 1981).

46 29 C.F.R. § 158(a)(5) (2011).

47 *Wilson v. National Labor Relations Board,* 920 F.2d 1282, 1287 (6th Cir. 1990).

48 Pub. L. 90–202, 81 Stat. 602 (Dec. 15, 1967).

49 U.S. Equal Employment Opportunity Commission, "Enforcement Statistics and Litigation," http://www.eeoc.gov/eeoc/statistics/enforcement/adea.cfm and http://www.eeoc.gov/eeoc/statistics/enforcement/all.cfm (accessed December 6, 2012).

50 29 U.S.C. § 630 (2011).

51 42 U.S.C. § 2000e (b).

52 29 U.S.C. § 621.

53 29 U.S.C. § 623.

54 Pub. L. 90–202, § 2 (1967).

55 Pub. L. 95–256, § 3a (1978).

56 Pub. L. 99–592, § 2(c)(1) (1986).

57 *Western Air Lines, Inc. v. Criswell*, 472 U.S. 400, 422 (1985).

58 *O'Connor v. Consolidated Coin Caterers Corp.*, 517 U.S. 308 (1996).

59 517 U.S. 308.

60 *O'Connor v. Consolidated Coin Caterers Corp.*, 517 U.S. at 312.

61 *Gross v. FBL Financial Services, Inc.*, 557 U.S. 167 (2009).

62 Ibid. 178.

63 29 U.S.C. § 626(c)(2).

64 42 U.S.C. § 1981a(c).

65 472 U.S. 400 (1985).

66 *Western Airlines v. Criswell*, 472 U.S. at 404.

67 *Dothard v. Rawlinson*, 433 U.S. 321, 334 (1977).

68 *Criswell*, 472 U.S. at 409.

69 Ibid. at 422.

70 Ibid. at 408.

71 Ibid. at 412.

72 A.N. Bitter, "*Smith v. City of Jackson*: Solving an Old-Age Problem," *The Catholic University Law Review* (56): 647–682.

73 *Smith v. City of Jackson,* 544 U.S. 228, 236 (2005).

74 Ibid. at 239.

75 *Cancellier v. Federated Department Stores,* 672 F. 2d 1312 (9th Cir.), cert, denied 459 U.S. 859 (1982).

76 *Skalka v. Fernald Environmental Restoration Management Corp.,* 178 F.3d 414 (6th Cir. 1999).

77 540 U.S. 581 (2004).

78 *Cline,* 540 U.S. at 585.

79 Ibid. at 600.

80 29 U.S.C. § 791 *et. seq.* (2011).

81 29 U.S.C. § 794.

82 Pub. L. 93–112, §. 7 (1973).

83 42 U.S.C. § 12 111(8) (2011).

84 Pub. L. 102–569, 106 Stat. 4346 (Oct. 29, 1992).

85 29 U.S.C. § 793.

86 42 U.S.C. § 12 112(a).

87 G.S. Becker, "How the Disabilities Act Will Cripple Business," *BusinessWeek,* September 14, 1992, p. 14.

88 *EEOC v. Chrysler Corp.,* 917 F.Supp. 1164 (E.D. Mich. 1996).

89 29 C.F.R. § 1630.2(l).

90 42 U.S.C. 12102(4)

91 42 U.S.C. 12102(4)(E)(i).

92 U.S. Equal Employment Opportunity Commission, *Notice Concerning the Americans with Disabilities Act (ADA) Amendments Act of 2008* (March 25, 2011). http://www.eeoc.gov/laws/statutes/adaaa_notice.cfm (accessed January 2, 2013).

93 42 U.S.C. § 12112.

94 42 U.S.C. § 12111(8).

95 U.S. Equal Employment Opportunity Commission, *The Americans with Disabilities Act: Your Responsibilities as an Employer* (Washington, DC: Government Printing Office, 2005), pp. 3–4.

96 29 C.F.R. § 1630.2(j).

97 Ibid. at 483.

98 U.S. Office of Federal Contract Compliance Programs, *The ADA Amendments Act of 2008: Frequently Asked Questions,* http://www.dol.gov/ofccp/regs/compliance/faqs/ADAfaqs.htm#Q4 (accessed February 11, 2013).

99 Ibid.

100 *Bragdon v. Abbott,* 524 U.S. 624 (1998).

101 U.S. Equal Employment Opportunity Commission, *Enforcement Guidance: Reasonable Accommodation and Undue Hardship under the Americans with Disabilities Act* (October 17, 2002), http://www.eeoc.gov/policy/docs/accommodation.html (accessed January 2, 2013).

102 Ibid.

103 Ibid.

104 Ibid.

105 *Davis v. Frank,* 711 F. Supp. 447 (N.D. Ill. 1989).

106 29 C.F.R. part 1630, appendix 1630.2(o) (2007).

107 U.S. Employment Standards Administration, *Compliance Guide to the Family and Medical Leave Act* (2008), www.dol.gov/dol/esa/public/regs/compliance/whd/1421.htm (accessed January 23, 2008).

108 *Stone v. City of Mount Vernon,* 118 F. 3d 92, 101 (2nd Cir. 1996).

109 42 U.S.C. § 12111(10)(B) (2007).

110 U.S. Equal Employment Opportunity Commission, *Annual Report Fiscal Year 2002* (Washington, DC: U.S. Government Printing Office, 2003).

111 42 U.S.C. § 12112(d)(2)(A).

112 U.S. Equal Employment Opportunity Commission, *Notice Concerning the Americans with Disabilities Act (ADA) Amendments Act of 2008* (March 25, 2011), http://www.eeoc.gov/laws/statutes/adaaa_notice.cfm (accessed January 2, 2013).

113 42 U.S.C. § 12112(d)(2)(B).

114 U.S. Equal Employment Opportunity Commission, *Annual Report Fiscal Year 2002.*

115 *EEOC v. Wal-Mart Stores, Inc.,* 2005 U.S. Dist. Lexis 40868 (W.D. Mo. 2005).

116 *Chevron U.S.A., Inc. v. Eschazabal,* 536 U.S. 73, 86–86 (2002).

117 29 C.F.R. §§ 1630.2(r).

118 U.S. Equal Employment Opportunity Commission, *Enforcement Guidance: Disability-Related Inquiries and Medical Examinations of Employees under the Americans with Disabilities Act (ADA),* http://www.eeoc.gov/policy/docs/guidance-inquiries.html (accessed January 2, 2013).

119 29 C.F.R. §§ 1630.2(r).

120 42 U.S.C. § 12112(d)(2)(A).

121 42 U.S.C. § 12112(d)(2)(B).

122 42 U.S.C. § 12112(d)(3)(B).

123 42 U.S.C. § § 12114(a) & (b).

124 42 U.S.C. § 12114(c).

125 42 U.S.C. § 12114 (c)(3).

126 42 U.S.C. § 12114(d).

127 Some materials for this case were drawn from *Chevron U.S.A. v. Echazabal,* 536 U.S, 73 (2002).

128 Some materials for this case were drawn from *EEOC v. Oak Rite Manufacturing,* 2001 U.S. Dist. LEXIS 15621 (S.D. Ind. 2001).

129 Some materials for this case were drawn from U.S. Equal Employment Opportunity Commission, *Enforcement Guidance: Reasonable Accommodation and Undue Hardship under the Americans with Disabilities Act,* http://www.eeoc.gov/policy/docs/accommodation.html (accessed January 2, 2013).

Discussion Questions

1   How do reasonable accommodations help support the religious beliefs of an individual working for an institution with no religious affiliation?

2   What role does an undue hardship defense play in a reasonable accommodation for religious beliefs?

3   Why can't an employer use age in making any employment decision?

4   What did the Americans with Disabilities Amendment Act in 2008 change when compared to the original ADA?

5   To what extent can "reasonable accommodation" be provided around disabilities?

Rethinking Manhood

An Interview with Ted Bunch

Anonymous

For Ted Bunch, gender-based violence and discrimination against women and girls are rooted in a history of male domination that has deeply influenced the definition of manhood in our culture. Bunch is the co-founder of A CALL TO MEN, a violence prevention organization that provides training and education for men, boys, and communities. Bunch has lectured in countries such as Israel, South Africa, Ghana, and Brazil, among others, and was appointed by UN Secretary General Ban Ki-moon as a Committee Member to UNiTE, an international network of male leaders working to end violence against women. In an interview with the *Journal,* Bunch discussed the concept of manhood and how social norms and culture have impacted the current notion of masculinity.[1]

> *Journal of International Affairs: Your organization, A CALL TO MEN*
> *seeks to promote a "more healthy, loving, and respectful definition*
> *of manhood." How does this definition manifest in real life?*

Ted Bunch: Our mission is to create a world where all men and boys are loving and respectful, and all women and girls are valued and safe. The definition is based on the deconstruction of the traditional image of manhood, keeping the wonderful things about being a man and letting go of the ideas and beliefs that are harmful to women, children, and men. It is not only about the individual men who perpetuate the violence, it is also about the collective socialization of men. All men in our society are taught on some level that women have less value than men, that women are the property of men, and that women are objects for men. We pass this collective socialization down to our boys.

We are primarily a prevention organization, focusing on preventing violence against women specifically. We were born out of the Battered Women's Movement, and we celebrated ten years in 2012. Tony Porter, the other co-founder and partner of the organization, and I started working together almost twenty years ago on the issue. We both worked with men who were domestic violence offenders. As we worked with them, it became clear that these men who are abusive—physically, verbally, and emotionally—know how to be respectful and non-abusive. They show this capability all the time with their bosses on the job, and with police who come to their houses to arrest them for violence. Actually, men who perpetrate violence against women demonstrate great control and even conflict-resolution skills when there is a negative consequence if they do not do so. Therefore, men's violence against women is rooted in the collective socialization of men, and the foundation of our collective socialization is born out of sexism and male domination. Men's violence against women is very controllable, and it is actually a learned behavior that can be unlearned. The belief that women have less value than men is widespread. You can see it right now with youth football. If you go to a practice where a seven-year-old kid is playing football, the coach will often say something like, "You got to throw harder than that, son, you throw like a girl." Girls throw just fine, but we start teaching our boys very early that a boy should not want to be a girl or do anything like a girl. That is also where gender-based violence such as bullying comes in. Most of the kids who are bullied are those who are furthest away from the traditional image of manhood. We have been taught that these images and characteristics include: being tough, not crying, being physically strong, dominating, and showing no fear—all of those types of things. So one issue is to believe women have less value than men.

The other issue is that we are taught that women are the property of men, and you can see that every day. If a man anywhere in America was hitting a woman, and you walked up to him and said "Stop it," the first thing he would say is "Mind your own business." This is because men have been taught that women are the property of men. The third issue is that men are taught that women are objects. We teach our boys very early to objectify women, and to believe that they are here to serve us and to bring us pleasure. That is why you see men, even teenage boys, saying things to girls on the street. Our boys learn a type of manhood that is based on these wrong beliefs from adult men and learn our cultural and social norms, which have entitlements and privileges given to men by men, and reinforced by men. This is not an indictment on men or manhood at all. Actually, it is an invitation for men to become part of the solution. Most men are great guys, but we have been taught or socialized to mind our business and to be silent, especially as it relates to how other men impact women. While the overwhelming majority of violence against women is from men, the overwhelming majority of men are not violent. But, we are silent about the abuse other men perpetrate, and that is as much of a problem as the violence itself.

Where we find patriarchy, we find sexism. Where we find sexism, we find women who are not valued, and we find violence against women.

Journal: Does this definition transcend the diversity of cultures in the world? Or will a healthy definition of masculinity look different everywhere you go?

Bunch: The definition would look the same in the sense that it would have at its core that men are loving and express their full range of emotions, and that women are valued, respected, and honored. That is at the core of the definition of manhood that A CALL TO MEN. We are talking about valuing who a woman is, respecting her, not objectifying her, not treating her as property, and seeing her as equal to men. We are talking about a definition that lifts women up, where men do not put other men down by calling them names that are related to women or a woman's body parts, and in which such names would no longer be considered insults. Homophobia and heterosexism are big pieces of this traditional image of manhood, and major components that make up the "man box". Homophobia is the glue or duct tape that keeps the man box together. When we look at other cultures—and I have been all over the world—the situations are similar.

I remember speaking to a group of men in South Africa about the issues of value, property, and objectification. I said to them, "OK, so you are teaching your son how to play soccer, and the coach says, 'You gotta kick harder than that, son, you kick like a' ..." and I left the sentence open for them to finish, and all of them said, "girl!" So, where we find patriarchy, we find sexism. Where we find sexism, we find women who are not valued, and we find violence against women. Just as, if we were to intervene in any culture, we really have to find out what sexism looks like within this culture, and those are the points of entry that we need to address. The question is, how can we value women and girls more in our culture? That may require men to give something up. But, we usually do not realize what we gain as we give up this perceived entitlement and power. The power is really not ours; it is just what our society has structured for men, based on privileges given to men, passed down to men, and reinforced by men. As we give that up, we gain our humanity, a better sense of who we are, and the respect from family members and loved ones, particularly women. They respect us because of our humanity, not because of fear.

Journal: Your goal is also to shift social norms that define manhood and have created an environment that supports, tolerates, and often encourages men's violence against women. Can you give us an example of such social norms?

Bunch: Violence and discrimination toward women exists in our daily lives.

Let us just look at the statistics, for instance. When we look at domestic violence, somewhere between one out of three and one out of four women—the statistics vary—are the victim of men's violence, which we call domestic violence. There are more women affected by domestic violence every day than there are those affected by breast cancer or heart disease. Rape and sexual assault demonstrate similar patterns. Most women who are raped or sexually assaulted are between the ages of sixteen and twenty-four, and about one out of four women or girls has been sexually assaulted. Three women are killed by their male intimate partners through domestic violence every day. These are staggering statistics, but we have not put in a lot of effort to solve the problem. There are laws and legislation on the issue, but there has not been an outcry about it, mainly because men remain silent. Since women do not have the power, resources, or voice that men do in our culture or our country, we men need to raise our voices so that men can also affirm the experiences of women. If men listened to women and respected their voices and experiences, we would not even be having this conversation.

> *Journal: In thinking about regions of the world where occurrences of rape are high, such as in South Africa, India, Guatemala, etc., to what degree is a particular expression of masculinity at fault, and to what degree is the problem structural (courts, law enforcement, etc.)?*

Bunch: What is structural in all those places, as well as in the United States, is sexism. Sexism is really the foundation of the problem, and violence and abuse are the manifestation of sexism. How that plays out in different cultures and in their expression of masculinity varies, but it is no doubt operating and present. As a result, some men express their sexism through violence and abuse. Others may express it in ways that are non-physical but that are still discriminatory, unfair, and gender-based. These beliefs are then passed on by men to each other and to their boys. The beliefs argue that men are supposed to be in charge, to dominate, to have control and power, and to know what to do. In addition to that, people are supposed to listen to men, especially women. Therefore I think what is universal is sexism. And sexism exists because patriarchy exists.

Therefore I think what is universal is sexism. And sexism exists because patriarchy exists.

Manhood, domination, power, and control are often at the expense of someone else. That is one of the tenets of contemporary masculinity.

Journal: So you would agree that rule of law and enforcement also plays a role. It sounds like the way that women are viewed in society is fundamental to that.

Bunch: Yes. Law enforcement plays a huge role, but we cannot legislate the belief systems through laws. Law enforcement can provide accountability for domestic violence offenders, as anyone committing a crime needs to be held accountable. However, if you look at women who are violent towards men, the sentencing is generally much greater than for men who are violent towards women. If you look at those lethal crime cases in which men have murdered their wives or girlfriends, the sentencing on average is less than when a woman murders her husband or boyfriend. This shows that institutional sexism is present and obviously a problem.

Journal: Sexual assault is an important problem in the United States military. Your organization trained soldiers at the United States Military Academy at West Point and the United States Naval Academy at Annapolis. What are the causes of this high level of rape in the military?

Bunch: The military has a very male-dominated culture, and in most male-dominated cultures, women are abused. In the military, you see a higher proportion of abuse. During wartime, there is more stress and fear than during peace. When men are fearful, stressed, or angry, they often take that out on women. The military is just a reflection of our society, and the problem is magnified due to its male-dominated culture. In any male-dominated culture, women really suffer greater consequences, and the military is a good example of that. The problem is compounded by the issue of rank. In a corporate setting in civilian life, if your superior is involved in sexual harassment, the victim has equal employment opportunity laws for support, and a process for grievance redressal that is governed by employment law. You may not have the same recourse in a military setting. If it is a higher-ranking officer, you are reporting to them in a different way than if it is just a job. The training we provide to the military is mostly around response teams for sexual assault or domestic violence. However, their job is to be the victim's advocate. The military, like the larger society, needs to address the issue of sexism in order to create a safe environment for women.

Journal: People have also pointed out that many rape victims in the military are men. Do you think masculinity should still be the focus in solving that problem?

Bunch: Yes, that is very true. I am glad that you brought that up, because there is a much higher rate of rape of men in the military than anywhere else, except for prison. Rape in the military, just like in prison, is about domination, power, control, or humiliation. It is about dominating, or humiliating the victim. We really have to look at masculinity and ask why it has to be at the expense of someone else. Manhood, domination, power, and control are often at the expense of someone else. That is one of the tenets of contemporary masculinity—that as men we are supposed to be in control and have power over others. This, like bullying, can be tied to gender-based violence, because men who are raped in the military are usually not hyper-masculine in the traditional sense. They are not the toughest guys in the ranks. It is usually the guys who are physically weaker. These cases all get down to power, control, and masculinity. Men are not generally taught to negotiate through words or express feelings. We are taught to negotiate through physical force and aggression. That is the current form of masculinity.

Journal: What new insights or unique contributions do you think your approach—namely a man working with men and boys to improve the lives of women—has brought to feminism?

Bunch: I think our perspective is unique in the sense that we are raising, lifting up, and amplifying love and a fullness of masculinity and manhood by encouraging men to express emotions—such as sadness, fear, or asking for help, emotions that are considered negative. We believe that we are not supposed to be vulnerable, to show any weakness, or to need help. I am a humanist; feminism is part of that. I think our message summarizes what women have been talking about for a very long time. Therefore, our message is very much influenced by the experiences of women, and we provide hope and care for men as well. To me, feminism is really about caring for one other, loving one other, and not seeking to dominate. I do not think that is just feminism. It is really about humanity. It has not been safe for men to embrace their fullness, because when they do, other men are taught to laugh at them, dismiss them, or put them down. Many people are even taught that kindness is weakness. Certainly feminism has laid the groundwork, and we are standing on the shoulders of women who have been in the forefront for years doing this work. But our message is about manhood.

Journal: What are some key lessons that you have learned since you started this project?

Bunch: My experience is that when men know better, they do better. Promoting a healthy, loving, and respectful manhood is the cure for domestic violence and sexual assault. Men are also thirsty for a better way, and the liberation of men is directly tied to the liberation of women.

Journal: Would you like to add anything?

Bunch: I would just like to say that as we work with men, our message is clear: women do not need to be saved or rescued. Women are fully capable people. Instead, men need to not be violent, and safety takes care of itself.

Notes

1 This interview is a condensed and edited version of the exchange between the *Journal* and Ted Bunch.

Discussion Questions

1 What does "rethinking manhood" mean for all in society?

2 How are men socialized into sexism and male dominance?

3 Homophobia and heterosexism are big pieces of the traditional image of manhood. How true is this statement?

4 Is sexism a foundational problem?

5   "Society has structured men based on privileges given by men, passed down by men and reinforced by men." How true is this statement?

PART IV

SOCIAL CHANGE AND ANTI-RACISM

Introduction

Moving beyond racism and guilt, and working toward social change is the collective effort of all. The first step toward eradicating racism is to work with those who benefit the most from racist structures and play the biggest part in maintaining them. To achieve this, we must first understand how it began, how it impacts all, and find new ways of being together. Consequently, without racial justice there can be no other forms of justice. There is therefore the need to create institutional structures to fully engage in practical efforts to make society a just and open space: a level playing field as some define it.

CHAPTER 12

Social Change and Anti-Racism

Moving from Guilt to Action

Antiracist Organizing and the Concept of "Whiteness" for Activism and the Academy

William Aal

As an antiracist organizer and trainer over the last twenty years, I have grasped at any tools that might make my work easier and more effective. Many of us who work at the grassroots level against racism do so because we see it as the fundamental problem underlying and linking other forms of oppression and social injustice in the United States. None of us were born antiracist organizers; we became such as we saw devastating effects that racism has on people of color, on the humanity of white people, and on the moral and spiritual fabric of society. Like others grappling with the pervasive and seemingly intractable problem of racism in this country, I have studied history, Marxism and other forms of political economy, social psychology, sociology—anything that might help one to understand how our society got organized the way it is and what it will take to change it.

I became an "expert" at being racist from having been born and raised "white" in a country that is structured along racist lines. At the same time, because I am a beneficiary of this system, the impact of racism is almost entirely invisible to me. In order to get real insight into the dynamics, it has been necessary for me to read history and analysis by people of color to get the view from "outside." In order to survive each day, whether there is a white person in the room or not, they have to deal with the consequences of a world ordered by white skin privilege. They are the experts on whiteness and its impact on themselves, "white" people, and the United States as a whole.

In the work that I and other trainers and organizers do, it is invaluable to define the concept of white identity as privilege. Many people self-identified as white experience themselves as beyond history and without community. Their culture is one of consumption—of ideas, art, and spirituality, as well as of material objects. When trying to encourage "white" people to help eliminate racism, it is helpful to encourage them to remember that by fighting racism we act to restore our own humanity and culture as well. We welcome the academic study of whiteness as a way to reclaim history, yet many of us are uneasy with this trend as well. This essay grew out of a concern that "whiteness" as an academic subject of study can easily slip from being the examination of an important social/political category to becoming just another career path. People often start out with a commitment to serve, but the process of professionalization takes them away from the community. This is a pitfall that is systemic to U.S. work culture. I see the same dynamic in the dichotomy between diversity training and anti-oppression organizing. As a "diversity trainer," it is also easy to end up making a career of working in the corporate sector and becoming disassociated from the oppressed communities. In fact, there is a whole generation of people coming through various university programs in multicultural work or "cross-cultural" training or similar fields who are looking for work as trainers or organizers and yet have had very little experience as activists.

I felt very ambivalent about writing for an academic book when first approached. I didn't want my work to become more fodder for the academic paper mill. On other the hand, I have wanted to make a contribution to the antiracist movement in this country by challenging academics to produce materials useful to the struggle for justice and to actively engage—because we could really use a hand!

One lesson I have learned over the years is that in order to eradicate racism activists and organizers need to start working with those who benefit from racist structures and who play the biggest part in maintaining them. So it makes sense for me to use this opportunity to address academics who are overwhelmingly white and are certainly among those who benefit from and maintain the status quo. Therefore, they can play an important part in bringing about change.

There are intellectual projects that could take all of us further. What we need in the movement is a better understanding of how "whiteness" as a set of overlapping identities, structures, and power relations keeps the United States divided along the lines of race, class, and gender. We need to know more about how we got into the predicament in which most of the "white" people in the United States either are unaware of the impacts that their daily lives have on "others," both inside the United States and around the world, or don't care. We need to reclaim our history through an antiracist lens, especially remembering and learning from those of our ancestors who have stood for justice.[1] And we also need to contribute to the process of creating new ways of being together across lines of difference in classrooms, conferences, and the community.

The stories we tell need to be deep, to promote critical thinking, and be both accessible and relevant for people outside the academy. I long for someone to engage with the thinking of Antonio Gramsci, Stuart Hall, bell hooks, Cornel West, Edward Said, Roberto Unger, and others in ways that relate these cultural and intellectual struggles with everyday life. The work of these intellectuals makes an enormous contribution toward revealing the fact that the structures of injustice are not natural phenomena ("the way the world has and will always be") but were created by humans in specific historical contexts and therefore *can be changed*. By helping us understand the formative contexts of daily life and the institutional arrangements that maintain oppression, engaged academics could help foster new ways of thinking about our social/ political problems.

Stories from a Few Antiracist Whites

To clarify my own thinking, I decided to talk with a few other trainer/activists around the United States about what the idea of whiteness means to them and what they would want from the study of whiteness. I talked with three people who have been doing antiracist work for many years. Two of them have Ph.D.'s and work in academic settings, though they both have taken decidedly nontraditional paths. Each of us is committed to a form of social justice that includes looking at the intersecting axes of class, gender, and race. We take it as a given that without racial justice, there can be no gender justice and vice versa. At the same time, each of us understands that racism is at the center of much of what it means to be white in America. We understand that our worldview, our sense of what is ours without asking and our knowledge of what we are not supposed to talk about, is structured by our white identities. I asked them three or four questions about their motivations for doing the work, their vision for the future, what they thought about "white studies," and what they would want from such an endeavor. When I mentioned the ambivalence I myself felt about the field, they acknowledged similar feelings. We all have learned a lot from academics and at the same time have been outraged by some of the dynamics described later in this article. These conversations challenge academics to turn some of their own tools of critical analysis on their own work: to examine how they make choices about what to focus on, whose interests the research they are doing serves, and to whom they are accountable.

Mark Scanlon Green is an academic who has also done a lot of antiracist organizing and brings a gender analysis to his thinking about race. His Ph.D. dissertation was on the subject of white males and diversity work. He now works in a private academic setting, working principally with students of color. Mark took up antiracist work, coming out of a complex personal/family history, his identity as a gay man, and a political commitment to change from the age of fourteen. "My choice to focus on white men is personal and political," he says.

> As a white man who has become actively involved in the diversity movement, I have wondered how it is that I have chosen to challenge the system that assigns me higher status and more power than it does to people of color and white women. If all the unearned privilege I have is a boon to my personal and professional development, why would I, or for that matter, any other man in his right mind, choose to work to eliminate its influence? ... I have also realized, however, that over the years, many of my political

"fellow travelers" were every bit as racist, sexist, and heterosexist as the larger society they claimed they wanted to change. And since racism is at the heart of the American experience, without dealing with it, we can't move forwards with a progressive social agenda. If the Rosetta Stone is found that decodes the process by which some white men, who are at the pinnacle of social status and power, actively engage themselves in changing the system, significant social change becomes possible.

Eventually he ended up feeling attacked from several fronts in the "diversity" arena. He says, "It is much harder for a white man to be out front as a trainer." White people didn't accept his leadership, and people of color didn't trust a white person doing "diversity training." Mark gave up active organizing with white people since he couldn't see social change occurring from doing "diversity work." He doesn't see himself as an activist anymore. He has chosen as his life work to be supportive of people of color getting access to higher education and puts the majority of his academic commitment in that direction, mentoring students from nontraditional backgrounds. He is committed to "academic excellence" not only to help students get access but also to insist that they grab that access, make it theirs in whatever way makes sense to them, and to shine in their competence.

His vision of a world that has dealt with racism is one based on equal access to resources—educational, economic, and political. It has to do with principles of justice as opposed to "equality." He wants academics looking at whiteness to be focused on eliminating the barriers to access within the academy that white people keep putting in front of people of color. The challenge is to make space for people of color on a truly equal footing; liberalism, individualism, and tokenism need to be combated.

Sharon Howell, raised poor, was the first in her family to go to college. She is now an academic as well. A lifelong antiracist, she has been a member and a leader of a non-Marxist revolutionary organization that was dedicated to creating a revolution with people of color in the lead. She works at a large midwestern university and is a leader in her community as an antiracist and antihomophobic organizer. She currently leads the major grassroots effort to rebuild Detroit. Along with Margo Adair, she is a founding member of Tools for Change, a consulting group that conducts workshops around antiracism and economic justice in work settings and for political groups.

Sharon would rather do anything else than have to deal with racism. There are more interesting things to do in the world, she says, like reconstruct Detroit so that it is a city that sustains all its people. But, according to her, racism gets in the way of that project. Detroit was destroyed because of racism. And now the majority of people left in the city are people who can't afford to leave, so—white, black, Arab, Asian, or Latino—they have common ground to stand on. Much of Detroit looks like a war zone. Whole blocks of houses have been bulldozed to the ground because absentee landlords abandoned their properties as economic values went down. There is little blue-collar work left in Detroit proper and its surrounding suburban areas, as the big auto makers have moved toward automation and outsourcing overseas and to other, nonunionized parts of the city. So the racial question has now more clearly than ever become one of class. The folks at the bottom have to deal with each other in order to survive. Yet race still is a "wedge issue" that is used to divide people.

So, for Sharon, it is necessary to deal with racism at all levels, interpersonally, within organizational structures and in "civil" society. Interpersonal racism, the kind that keeps white people and people of color from being able to trust each other because of white people's conscious or unconscious identification with the white power structure, needs to be dealt with to build long-lasting relations of solidarity. A former member of the National Organization for an American Revolution (NOAR), a revolutionary organization dedicated to the revolutionary leadership of African Americans and other people of color, she and her writing partner and political comrade Margo Adair started doing organizational consulting with groups committed to progressive social change in the mid-1980s. They, like Mark, realized that the relationships of oppression that exist in the dominant society are reproduced within those groups. Their analysis of organizational culture as an outgrowth of European American (white) middle-class patriarchal culture led them to look at how patterns of power govern access to resources and structure relations in groups committed to ecological or social justice.

They developed the concept of internalized privilege to help explain why people in positions of power usually don't see how their actions impact others and move through the world with a sense of entitlement. They also put forward the idea of "wonderbreading" which is what assimilation does. In order to make it into the category of "white" and receive its privileges, people were forced to give up their loyalty to their own traditions, language, community, and principles. In this framework, "white" is solely an identity of privilege. Value is no longer placed on community, place, or history but, instead, on access to power and commodities. Business decisions are based on purely economic rationality, without taking into account these other dimensions. Communities are reduced to individuals and families to reproductive units. Culture becomes devoid of richness. Understanding these dynamics reveals what white people have to gain by ridding society of racism. Sharon sees it as important to help people of European descent see how their identification with white privilege keeps them from moving toward racial justice and how their guilt over that compounds the problem even more.

Her vision of a society based on principles of justice has led to work on Detroit Summer, a multigenerational project dedicated to rebuilding the most devastated parts of Detroit. Each summer, youth from Detroit and all around the country work with neighborhood people cleaning up parks, reconstructing homes, and re-creating a vital community. Leadership development and the study of Detroit's history and culture are integral parts of the project. Sharon sees this work as part of her life commitment. Her request to other academics is that they engage in projects of social justice that will inform their writings about social movements and help deepen their commitment to eliminate racism.

Marian Meck Root grew up in "Middle America," in the mainstream Lutheran church. At an early age, she realized the spiritual void left by people's refusal to deal with racism. She is a theologian in a major East Coast city and is part of a feminist theological center that keeps antiracism at the heart of its work.

She and her co-workers are grappling with the spiritual void left by racism, asking the question "How did this happen that we as a (white) people and as individuals are so spiritually afraid and weak?" She believes that when white people begin to address this question, they will begin to unearth some clues about ending racism. It is a project that can't be undertaken individually but, rather, communally. It is one according to her that can't be approached merely from the rational, linear patriarchal side. "It requires going against ... the dominant culture especially of the academy which projects its own fears onto the feminine."

In her exploration of the concept of whiteness she defines white "to mean those of us who have had enough European ancestry to benefit from having white skin and who have been raised to assume that our culture is generic or universal and to act out of a sense of racial and/or cultural superiority even when we deny or cannot see ourselves doing that." She talks about spirituality as in some sense acknowledging mystery and giving up the illusion of control. Pointing out that white folks are very attached to control and domination, she draws the conclusion that we have a hard time with mystery and hence spirituality. For Marian, Europeans haven't always been this way; it is a historical development of recent vintage. It helps explain our yearnings for spirituality and some of our racist appropriation of other people's spiritual traditions.

While acknowledging the yearning, she notes that spirituality has much to do with ancestors and that white Americans have distanced themselves, literally, from theirs. "We don't know ourselves because we don't know where we come from." Looking back on thousands of years of European history, she sees a progressive disintegration of tribal life, that is, life connected to the land and to ancestors. Without romanticizing tribal existence, she states that there was a felt relationship between the spiritual and the material, between intuition and rational ways of knowing. She calls for a reconnection of mind and body and spirit as well as for a reintegration of our communities. In order carry out this project, we as white people have to forgive our ancestors and ourselves, and we have to hope for forgiveness by people of color without having the right to expect it.

What Marian wants from "whiteness studies" is a critique of Western rational thinking and individualism. This critique would help overcome the dualist splits between mind and body, individual and community, spirit and idea. The critique would embody a way forward to a healing transformation.

As for myself, I am an owner of a small house painting business and work with environmental and economic justice organizations. I am a former member of NOAR, along with Sharon, and am also an associate of Tools for Change. I work on coalition-building with people of color around issues of ecological and economic justice.

I came to an antiracist sensibility when I was ten or eleven. I grew up in a lower-middle-class, single-parent, Jewish family in upstate New York. We lived in a mixed ethnic neighborhood. I saw how much easier our lives were as a "white" family than those of my "black" friends and their families in similar economic circumstances. In the 1950s and early 1960s, we were able to see our cash-poor life as merely a temporary setback on the way to a fully middle-class life. Help from her parents alleviated my mother's temporary unemployment, and she knew that with her college education she would eventually be able to get a better job in the expanding civil service economy. My African American neighbors would have to wait a generation for members of their family to get access to education before being able to obtain that kind of work—and even then economic life would be precarious at best. Experiencing that difference had a profound impact on how I interpreted the success stories that my upper-middle-class Jewish and white Christian friends were given by their families. It made it impossible for me to accept the myths of individual progress or the metaphors of assimilation or the "melting pot" that were the basis of white American cultural hegemony.

As the Vietnam War unfolded, I began to see the links between racism at home and U.S. imperialism around the world. It became clear to me that the reasons racism and its related manifestations of sexism and homophobia were still present in the United States was because "white" people, and "white" men especially, were not willing to give up the position and power that they (we) gained by our white skin privilege. Of course, at the time I didn't have an analysis, only a feeling that something was wrong.

When I first became involved in the movement for racial justice in the 1960s, the social project seemed clear: to eliminate racism as an underlying ordering of public space and to create opportunities for women and men of color to enter into business, academic, and religious spheres on an "equal basis." We started with a basic understanding that racism is rooted in unfounded negative attitudes about people of color (prejudice) tied with the power to oppress them (institutional bias). All that was needed was to "change people's attitudes" and to make sure that policies in educational institutions, restaurants, residences, and banks provided equal access to resources.

In college in the early 1970s, I was exhilarated by the development of the various identity movements, as they allowed people who had been locked out of society to express their humanity to the society at large and begin to claim power for themselves. At the same time, as I watched the tendency of people in those movements to claim their piece of the American pie, I became confused. For me it was the very existence of that pie that required the United States to maintain the race, class, and gender divides, that kept some people rich while the majority remained poor. I also saw something like the pain that "wonderbreading" engendered for my parents' generation affect some African American friends of mine when they started going to college. They lost intimate contact with their childhood friends and sometimes with their families, as they chose to "make it" in academia or the business world. In short, I began to see the limitations of the concept of "equality" since in fact "equality" really meant "play by the rules of the game and don't question the status quo." It didn't allow for the transformation of the social context to include all the experiences and values that are embodied by those who have been locked out. In short, people were being welcomed to join a society whose rules were set by the oppressors.

Since identity politics by itself didn't call for the total transformation of society, only for either a piece of the pie or for carving out autonomous spaces for blacks, Latinos, women, gays, lesbians, or other disadvantaged people, it began to feel in the 1980s that we would have a fractured society that wasn't necessarily a more just one. With my membership in NOAR, I was able to see the power of being in an organization dedicated to the leadership of African American people for the whole country. I was challenged to be a leader in this context and to think collaboratively with people very different from myself. What NOAR was unable to incorporate into its practice was a deep understanding of the subjective side of reality, social power, and cultural differences. Despite our political unity, which included an understanding of racism as the underlying contradiction of the United States, we were still unable to deal with racism and internalized it within our own ranks.

I joined Tools for Change because, as a group, we grapple with these kinds of issues and help organizations deal effectively with them. Central to our work is a focus on the subjective side of politics, which includes the particularities of culture differences, the importance of the sacred, and the dynamics of both formal and informal power. We try to encourage people and organizations to become visionary. Without vision, we find ourselves re-creating the same patterns of life. In this context, I am attempting to develop an organizational development model of "opening the imagination to change," which incorporates vision, addresses issues of power, and encourages critical thinking. In this way I hope to be able to help organizations deal with race and class hierarchies by rethinking their mission and re-visioning the way they do their work. I would like to challenge academics to do the same. It would be an exciting program that turned its critical gaze inward to try to create a real space for people of color.

My own vision for racial justice involves a society that goes beyond celebrating difference, actually embodying cultural differences and gender and gender orientation differences—in short embracing all of its contradictions and highlighting them. People would no longer have to assimilate to make it; equal access would be a given.

Whiteness and Activism

Whiteness as a conceptual framework in a political context first emerged out of a need to confront some of the limitations of antiracist organizing. At the same time, whiteness has been part of the U.S. sensibility since the country's founding. Many groups and strata of "white" people have been conscious of their whiteness and protective of their privileges. The whole process of "assimilation" was one of immigrants coming to the United States and struggling to become "white" in order to access the legitimacy and resources associated with that status. But by the late 1950s white skin privilege was no longer morally unquestioned in public discourse, and by the mid-1960s its legal status was challenged. By the mid-1970s, at least within the movements for social justice, it wasn't supposed to exist. Yet racism has kept its hold on the fabric of our society and in the structures of even those organizations committed to social justice. The rhetoric of antiracism present in these organizations often has actually acted as a buffer against challenges to racism. People have a self-image of being antiracist, yet the middle-class norms that preclude them from admitting mistakes or showing ignorance make it nearly impossible for them to address these issues. When antiracism is addressed, conversations become focused on intentions rather than the impact.

After years of antiracist organizing, we have learned that white people can't ask people of color to do "our" work for us. Many organizers reluctantly came to the conclusion that the issue was white people's inability or lack of will to examine our own privilege. We were reluctant because we didn't want to deal with other white people—we distrusted them, as we distrusted ourselves. Many of us had come to hate our own whiteness as we learned of the legacy of racism. Not trusting other white folks, we felt better being in the company of people of color. We did not want to come to grips with our own history. Some of us felt that we didn't even have a culture. But, in order to eradicate racism, we realized that we had to start working with those who benefit from racist structures and who play the largest part in maintaining them.

Those of us who do antiracist organizing and training have found that white people have developed a lot of avoidance and defense strategies. I see every day how much investment white folks have in holding onto their power. Recently, this was brought home to me again. After a major success in grassroots organizing against the World Trade Organization meeting in late 1999 in Seattle, where a huge coalition of labor, environmental, human rights activists, and community people took to the streets, a lot of money started flowing to continue the organizing. Many of the groups that organized around this event took part in evaluations of the work. Jointly we critiqued our movement around the lack of diversity. Just after the evaluation, one part of the coalition, a mostly white student group was offered money for organizing at the University of Washington campus, which is also mostly white. They never even consulted with a partner youth of color group that had been organizing very effectively on this issue over a longer period. When challenged, the white group said they had never even thought about it. They had merely seen it as an opportunity to do the work. They would have done outreach to youth of color, but they never thought to share resources with or to take leadership from an already existing group. To date, I am not aware of steps taken to approach the youth of color group.

We have seen how white people, especially those who are better educated, are very good at using antiracist language to allow themselves to feel good about themselves without actually having to change. What we have had to develop are some ways to help white people understand what a high price they pay for their privileged position—so that ultimately they can see that the reason to work for justice is also to free themselves.

We have found in our antiracist work that the first hurdle to get around is a paralysis of guilt and defensiveness. Most white people know very well their skin color is tied to social privileges—so they feel guilty and at the same time don't feel personally invested in change. They don't understand very well the historical nature of our racist social structure, and so they find it very hard to imagine real change and what that might look like. Noel Ignatiev's *How the Irish Became White* is an example of academic work that can help "regular white folks" understand whiteness in the context of their own history. It helps them begin to see their own place in all of this. Although it is often very painful, using the concept of whiteness has been helpful in workshops as a tool for breaking through many patterns that hold back white people from organizing together to eliminate racism.

One of the first things I do in antiracist workshops is to ask people about their family backgrounds, to help them get in touch with their own history. From there, we can begin to ask questions like "What strengths do you draw from your family history?" and "What did you and/or your family have to give up to be white?" For people to really become invested in change, they need to get a sense of the violence they do to themselves and others in order to live in this kind of society. They need to get in contact with the grief from which they spend so much time and energy dissociating. When white people understand how much energy they expend to create the kind of amnesia that is a necessary part of whiteness, they can begin to see whiteness as a crippling condition that makes it very hard to imagine what a racially just society could be about. At this point, the transformation for justice is as much for "us" as for some distant and impersonal "them."

At the same time, in order to understand the depth and subtleties of the way racism works in the United States, people need to understand history and be able to make critical analyses of the power dynamics they encounter. By looking at the way that class and race intersect, participants can begin to see the way in which these dynamics hold each other in place. They are introduced to the concepts of position (what social strata you come from), stand (whom you are accountable to), bias (whose interests do your attitudes serve), and impact (who benefits and who loses from your actions). Understanding the difference between impact and intention can help people sort out very thorny situations and can help us move from guilt into action. In these workshops, I appeal to the heart and the imagination and the head. Our own history and our own grief—that is the heart. Understanding the historical nature of whiteness—that is what helps us imagine alternatives. Developing a critical analysis of the power structure and what can be done to change it—that is the head.

White Studies in the Academy

Many academics have become engaged in the study of whiteness as a part of their political work to fight racism in the academy as well as outside, and they courageously pursue their work in the face of great opposition from more established disciplines. Yet the realities of the academic environment soon become painfully evident. There is little support for new faculty, especially in the social sciences and humanities. There is an attack on Ethnic and Women's Studies and related disciplines, and academic institutions as a whole are less and less open to new types of knowledge.

Marian Root, in her piece "The Heart Cannot Express Its Goodness," invokes James Baldwin's statement that the price of whiteness and membership in the privileged ranks is the loss of community. Both Root and Sharon Howell note that this loss of community forces us to be "self-reliant or perish." Capitalism relies on individualism and competition. The university as a middle-class institution both reinforces and reproduces these values. It is organized by and rewards middle-class values like individualism and competitiveness. Collective work is generally not rewarded or even recognized—yet fighting racism has to be more than anything a collective project. Of course, those who can afford individualism are exactly those who have power. Individualism is taught in most U.S. schools from first grade on; it is embedded in the grading system and entrance requirements for undergraduate and graduate programs. Try to imagine a collective Ph.D.!

I do appreciate that this book is an exception to the rule, due to its having a collective editorial board. And, as I have said before, there are many who enter academia out of a sense of responsibility to communities of color. Unfortunately, there are structural forces at work that make it difficult for such academics to stay connected with those communities.

I have a picture in mind. It is not a photograph of academic reality but, rather, a painting, a view from an outsider's eyes. Academics are forced by the requirements of academic life to search for "new" intellectual terrain to explore and stake out.[2] Identity studies seem to follow a life cycle: as time goes on, important political projects begin to attract people who are looking to find a new niche in which to build their careers. At first, the terrain seems "virginal" and untouched (pick your favorite gender-laden term). So the explorer moves around the new territory, poking into people's history, sociology, psychology, and biology, overturning loose stones and pulling up plants. The explorer seeks to unveil knowledge, and the one who is there first creates a claim on large areas of the terrain. The knowledge belongs to the explorer who "discovers" it. Of course, in culture and social studies, the terrain involves human beings; the "new" knowledge is about their lives, their cultures, and their dreams. The academic in general has no sense of accountability to those who are the "subjects" or "objects" of investigation.

As new investigators arrive, they scour around for new and unusual parts of the territory, perhaps a unique species or perhaps a hidden corner. They compete for control over the territory by writing in a manner that uses the most abstract prose. Papers are written in a language so difficult to access that most of us lose patience. After an appropriate tour de force, perhaps the author gains access to scarce academic resources, a temporary teaching post; perhaps if he or she is lucky, the fabled tenure-track position. The people or group studied has not benefited from any of this process, although later they might get thanked in the credits. Sometimes they find their privacy violated and see sacred aspects of their culture now displayed in books and articles, to be read by anonymous strangers who know little, if anything, about the context in which those mysteries were created. Then there is the worst-case scenario: they find that they no longer have control of an aspect of their lives that previously they had had. Instead, they find an insidious slippage into dependency has been initiated by the whole process. This critique is not new. For example, the field of anthropology has long challenged researchers and applied anthropologists to do relevant and accountable work.[3] Obviously, this particular trajectory has nothing to do with a struggle for social justice or with those of us who try to organize against racism.

Part of the explanation has to do with how academics do their work. The prevailing view of academic work comes from the dominant ideology of empirical science: first discover a phe-nomenon, then analyze it, and then use it to support your argument (in this case for change). From my experience, this model of advocacy is ineffective either as a way to effect change within organizations or as a way to bring people into movements. No critique by itself has ever sustained transformation over time on either a personal or a group level. Creating a new society requires vision, passion, and commitment. Scholarship that engages reason, the imagination, and the heart and that empowers the community can help that process. Vine Deloria Jr., bell hooks, Stuart Hall, and Howard Zinn are role models for those who wish to follow this path.

Useful scholarship would help us connect ourselves to the historical and social complexes that we refer to when we speak of whiteness. But doing scholarship in the service of antiracism also means that scholars need to pay attention to the language in which they communicate their thoughts and their findings. Unlike academics, antiracist organizers cannot afford to distance themselves from the community, nor can we afford to slip into a language that alienates and excludes. There is no antiracist organizing without connection to the community. So that is one thing academics who are truly interested in whiteness in terms of antiracist work might try to think about: are they writing for tenure committees alone, or are they writing for all of us?

I look forward to an academy that values community, collaboration, and justice as much as rigor, creativity, and novelty. I have been inspired by the words of Roberto Unger in his *Politics*:

> In this work, true satisfaction can be found only in an activity that enables people to fight back, individually or collectively against the established settings of our lives—to resist these settings or even to re-make them. Those who have been converted to this idea of a transformative vocation cannot easily return to the notion of work as an honorable calling within a fixed scheme of social roles and hierarchies, nor can they remain content within a purely instrumental view of labor as a source of material benefits with which to support themselves and their families.[4]

What would a transformative vocation be? What kinds of life and career choices would need to be made? And what kind of institutional structures could we create that would allow activists the time and resources to reflect on their work and academics to engage fully in the practical effort to make society a just and open space? This is a challenge for activists and scholars alike.

Notes

1 Mab Segrest's *Memoirs of a Race Traitor* (Boston: South End Press, 1994), Lillian Smith's *Killers of the Dream* (New York: Norton, 1978), and Linda Stout's *Bridging the Class Divide and Other Lessons for Grassroots Organizing* (Boston: Beacon, 1996) are all written by southern "white" women committed to racial justice. Each in her own way examines the experience of racism in the South and gauges the effects of racism and sexism on her own life and society. All talk about the possibility and impact of standing in resistance to white supremacy. See also Noel Ignatiev, *How the Irish Became White* (New York: Routledge, 1995), and Howard Zinn, *A People's History of the United States* (New York: Harper and Row, 1980).

2 The Portuguese word *explorador* has two meanings: to explore and to exploit. Sometimes I wonder whether the English word should carry both connotations.

3 See Dell H. Hymes, ed., *Reinventing Anthropology* (Ann Arbor: University of Michigan Press, 1999).

4 Roberto Mangabeira Unger, *Politics, a Work in Constructive Social Theory, Volume 1* (Cambridge: Cambridge University Press, 1987), 13.

Discussion Questions

1 What is the concept of whiteness all about?

2 Who benefits the most from racism, and how do they benefit?

3 Why do we need to look at history to eradicate all forms of oppression?

4 What does it mean to "move beyond guilt"?

5 How can society become a just and open space?

CONCLUSION

America was built on a tangled history. It is such history that makes it a unique nation among nations. Trying to sanitize or bleach any part of history makes it irrelevant. From the annulation of the Indians, to the slavery of the African and the annexation of Mexico are all part of this tangled identity that makes America great. Examining human relationships in terms of oppression creates a foreseeable path into the future. Nothing can be done to repair the wrongs of the past. No matter how much time goes by, the past still lingers on. And America's past will spook anyone who looks back. The past must be dealt with for what it was, the past. History should be taught for what it was not diluting its past or downplaying any groups or identity. This gives room for change into the future. The present is a gift to understand the challenges of the past so that the same mistakes are not made. America needs to look forward and create a nation where race and other forms of oppression become irrelevant to the wellbeing of the future. For this to happen, a new chapter must begin in a new generation of Americans. Social justice and anti-oppressive consciousness must be advanced to serve the new generation. It may not satisfy everyone. But nothing will no matter how politically correct such notions become.